FORTYTUDE

FORTYTUDE

*Making the Next Decades the
Best Years of Your Life—
through the 40s, 50s, and Beyond*

. . . .

SARAH BROKAW

with MEIMEI FOX

voice

HYPERION • NEW YORK

Copyright © 2011 Sarah Brokaw

All rights reserved. No part of this book may be used or reproduced in any manner whatsoever without the written permission of the Publisher. Printed in the United States of America. For information address Hyperion, 114 Fifth Avenue, New York, New York, 10011.

The Library of Congress has catalogued the hardcover edition of this book as follows:

Brokaw, Sarah.
  Fortytude : making the next decades the best years of your life—through the 40s, 50s, and beyond / Sarah Brokaw.
—1st ed.
    p. cm.
  ISBN 978-1-4013-4119-0
 1. Middle-aged women—Psychology. 2. Aging—Psychology.
3. Self-realization in women. 4. Self-esteem in women. I. Title.
  HQ1059.4.B75 2011
  155.3'33—dc22

2010016993

Paperback ISBN: 978-1-4013-4182-4

Hyperion books are available for special promotions and premiums. For details contact the HarperCollins Special Markets Department in the New York office at 212-207-7528, fax 212-207-7222, or email spsales@harpercollins.com.

Book design by Susan Walsh

FIRST PAPERBACK EDITION

10 9 8 7 6 5 4 3 2 1

THIS LABEL APPLIES TO TEXT STOCK

We try to produce the most beautiful books possible, and we are also extremely concerned about the impact of our manufacturing process on the forests of the world and the environment as a whole. Accordingly, we've made sure that all of the paper we use has been certified as coming from forests that are managed, to ensure the protection of the people and wildlife dependent upon them.

Dedicated to Grandma Jean, a brown-eyed,

left-handed, five-foot-two-inch, buxom, small but mighty woman

(who has been my role model for as long as I can remember)

CONTENTS

. . . .

FORTY CANDLES

· · · ·

IT STARTS WHEN WE'RE 35.

For many women within five years of their fortieth birthday, their biggest worry isn't their relationship (or lack of one), their boss, their kids, their financial situation, or even their health.

It's the calendar.

We can't deny the fact that we age. No matter how hard we try to remain youthful, we are getting older. Aging is simply part of the natural and beautiful cycle of life, as sure as the seasons changing. Yet few events, it seems, are as unnerving to women as thinking about that fortieth candle on the birthday cake.

I first began to observe this phenomenon several years ago among the 30- to 50-year-old clientele who frequented my Manhattan therapy practice. They had a single common obsession: "I don't want to turn 40." The "big four-oh" was the dreaded number, even for my youngest visitors. From ages 29 to 39, each woman anticipated this milestone with fear, acting as if her life would end the moment she passed into her fifth decade. In fact, a good number of my clients had so much anxiety about this critical age that it was the sole reason they'd begun to see me. I was in my late 30s, and I found myself sharing their concerns in more than the usual "empathetic therapist" way. Often at night, I stayed awake riddled with worries about what lay ahead in my personal and professional life.

It got me wondering: Why was it that so many women—including myself—had such a powerful aversion to reaching 40? I began examining the psychological research, as well as popular writing on the subject. Someone must have explored the anxiety that the fifth decade triggers for women and have offered guidance, I thought. But no one had. And that is why, in my thirty-eighth year, I decided to write this book.

As we say good-bye to our youth, we lose our carefree sense of being immortal and having all the time in the world to figure out our lives. Many of us experience fear of the future. This book's purpose is to help us remove our hands from our eyes and face our fears—and moreover, to transcend them. The truth is that our 40s can be a decade of loss, but those years also hold the potential to be a time of tremendous gain.

In the course of researching and writing this book, I facilitated discussion groups across America—from New York, New York, to Seattle, Washington; Oxford, Mississippi, to Provo, Utah; San Francisco, California, to Bozeman, Montana; Dallas, Texas, to Chicago, Illinois; Greenwich, Connecticut, to Orange County, California; and Memphis, Tennessee, to Washington, D.C. In addition, I conducted individual interviews with women from all different walks of life: single mothers struggling to make ends meet and high-powered executives; recovering crack addicts and Ivy Leaguers; surfers, social workers, and stay-at-home moms; women in their late 30s longing to have children and 50-plus-year-olds who already have cleared many of the hurdles we'll discuss; breast cancer survivors, victims of abuse, and women who have lost both their parents.

As part of this process, I asked the women to examine a long list of positive values that I had compiled. We then had conversations about which of these values most served to sustain and enhance women's lives as they entered their fifth decades. It soon became clear that the women—regardless of age, race, sexual orientation, or socioeconomic status—all were powerfully drawn to five of what I call the Core Values: grace, connectedness, accomplishment, adventure, and spirituality.

In the following chapters, I'll explore these five Core Values in depth and share the stories of the remarkable women who most embody them. These are women who have chosen to greet life's challenges with fortitude instead of fear. They have overcome adversity, danced through life's unpredictable turns, and found confidence, joy, and peace along the way. They are my inspiration, and I hope they will be yours, too. Let's take what they've learned and use it to help us not only embrace the loss of youth and transcend our anxieties but also celebrate the beginning of the rest of our lives.

FORTYTUDE

THE MIDLIFE
SPARKLING MOMENT

· · · ·

WHETHER IT'S NATURE or nurture or a combination of both that's to blame, we begin at age 35, with a sinking feeling in our stomachs, to recognize our own mortality. Our youthful beauty starts to fade as wrinkles become undeniable facts that we face every time we look in the mirror. We must confront our diminished sexual desirability in the eyes of society. If we're on the career path, we notice competition from younger women in the workplace. If we haven't yet had all the children we want, we come head-to-head with fertility issues. We start getting mammograms, and often we lose a friend, relative, or colleague to breast cancer. Many of us watch our parents fall ill or pass away. It's real: we're getting older, we're fragile, and one day we, too, will die.

Many women approaching 40 and beyond are struggling to define themselves as independent people as well as daughters, sisters, friends, wives, and mothers. An unsatisfying career or lack of spiritual fulfillment can further complicate the issue, causing us to ask: "Is this all there is?"

Unfortunately, the majority of messages that we receive from pop culture, the media, and even our friends and parents portray 40 as if it's nearing the end—the end of the good times, at least. The clock is ticking. In ten years, you'll be 50, and then the fun is *really* over. My clients often say they feel that society tells them, "You're supposed to have it all figured out by now." If you haven't—if you're still searching for answers in your personal or professional life, or both—you feel like a failure.

Many women see 40 as the end of their attractiveness, their sexuality, their youthfulness, and sometimes even their creativity. Most of these fears are based on nothing more than societal myths (perhaps residues of a male-dominated culture eager to keep women down, just at the moment when they begin to flourish). We do not lose any of these qualities with age—on the contrary, as we grow older, we can feel more radiant, confident, capable, and powerful than ever. But there are very real biological pressures that increase significantly as we pass this watermark birthday: breast cancer rates skyrocket, our parents get older and pass away, and our chances of naturally conceiving a healthy child start to decline sharply at age 35.

So much negativity is attached to aging that we often come to believe our identities are tied to our ages. But this is simply not true; we are not our ages. It is possible to hold a positive view of your individual, creative path from age 40 onward because, in fact, the fifth decade is nowhere near the end of your life. In my psychotherapy practice, I explore with my clients a new excitement about having made it thus far and about going further. We identify the challenges that we face as we come to terms with our ages, and we create our identities on our own terms. What does it mean to be your most authentic self, to do what you want to do, and to enjoy your life in the way you really desire?

Turning 40 does not have to be a problem. For many women, this milestone can be a time of self-reflection, which is a truly powerful experience. It may be a time to sit with the ever-nagging question, "Am I where I'm supposed to be?" and come to peace with what is. Or it might be a time to realize that there are steps you haven't taken, roads as yet unexplored, and to make a strong commitment to moving forward in the coming years. While certain challenges inevitably coincide with embarking on your fifth decade, it can be a beautiful and invigorating time in your life.

Furthermore—and this is not a white lie I'm telling to make you feel better—many frequently overlooked benefits come with age. For example, a long-term study conducted at the University of Wisconsin–Madison's Institute on Aging revealed that people in their late 40s and 50s reported significantly higher levels of well-being than did those in their 30s and early 40s. Women in particular learn to focus more on the positive and less on the negative as they grow older. And even our brains don't deteriorate as much as we've been led to believe. White matter, the insulated nerve fibers that allow our neurons to communicate with the greatest efficiency, continues to *increase* until we die and actually reaches its peak from ages 45 to 55 or 60.

Sparkling Moments

When clients talk to me about what's going on in their lives, they almost always refer to the root of the matter as a "problem," which immediately causes them stress. I suggest that instead of labeling current events and challenges as "problems," they consider calling them "sparkling moments."

If you have a "problem," you're inclined to believe that something is wrong with you. You feel a constant, nagging need to fix it. If you can't, you figure something is even *more* wrong with you. Problems also elicit fear. You might find yourself obsessing in the middle of the night, "What happens if I don't solve this problem right away?"

Having a "sparkling moment," by contrast, doesn't imply that you're dysfunctional or that you must leap into action to rectify the situation. When you view your challenges as opportunities to change, experiment, push yourself, grow, and learn new skills, then you have sparkling moments. Sparkling moments can bring more than a little relief—they can even add a degree of excitement to your life. When you no longer feel the pressure to fix something that's wrong or suffer from the negative energy that problems inspire, you gain the mental space to make informed and empowered decisions.

Many mental health experts believe that we experience "identity crises" at various stages in life. I prefer to reframe these turning points, too, as "sparkling moments." And I believe that our confusion around age 40 has partly to do with the contradictory messages we receive from society at this critical juncture.

For example, most people have a sparkling moment after they graduate from college. They can no longer rely on their course syllabi to figure out their daily, weekly, and monthly goals. They have to begin to pursue work, community, and friendships, instead of relying on the nurturing college environment. They ask themselves, "What do I do now? Go to graduate school? Join the workforce? Go for the money? Enter social service work that may not pay as much but may be more satisfying? Get married right away?"

The message that society conveys to people when they reach this point in their 20s is generally positive. Given the current economic crisis, recent college graduates might feel pressure to find a job, but they also know that they have plenty of time to figure out their lives. It's still socially acceptable for them to be struggling to make ends meet, and they have the freedom to explore options. They might try a temp job or move to a new city. Society encourages them to view this period as an opportunity for self-discovery. "Challenge yourself to grow, to learn new things, and to determine what fulfillment and authenticity mean to you," it seems to say. "Experience different relationships, jobs, lifestyles, and cultures."

Thus 20-somethings begin exploring. They allow themselves to try on different identities until they find the one that fits. Society grants them permission to figure these things out without making lasting commitments, because they are so young.

However, the message we receive as we approach the midlife sparkling moment has a more negative, critical tone: "You're turning 40 and you're not married? You don't have children? You don't own a house? You've traveled around the world but you don't have money in the bank? You haven't reached a pinnacle in your career? You've stayed at home with your kids and don't have a career at all? You still don't know what you want to be when you grow up? You're nearing 40 and you don't have your life all together? *What's wrong with you?*"

As a result, many of us find ourselves asking if we've blown it completely and it's simply too late to recover. Of those of us who do have the family, the job, or both, many feel as if there is something in ourselves—a goal or an aspiration—that we neglected along the way.

Yet at midlife, we often lack the encouragement to continue to explore—to obtain another degree, to start a business, to climb Mount Everest, or even to have a baby. When you're in your 20s, finding your way is cool. When you're in your 40s, the coolness has evaporated like Arctic glaciers under an ozone-depleted sky.

The voices in our heads tell us that we "should" be a series of conflicting things. We *should* continue to explore our options, but we *should* also be committed to marriage and family. We *should* be living our own dreams, while at the same time, we *should* be meeting our parents' expectations. We *should* be effortlessly beautiful, and we *should* cease defining ourselves in terms of our attractiveness and sexuality. We *should* be devoted to a career, and we *should* be sublimating our own needs to those of our spouses, children, and elderly parents.

Women struggle with this double bind: be who you want to be but, at the same time, conform to traditional expectations. We often feel confused about what our lives *could* be, if we are doing the right thing, and whether we will ever find our own versions of the "white picket fence" without sacrificing our hearts' desires. These crazy-making, seemingly impossible-to-resolve contradictions may arise in our mid-30s, but they can continue to frustrate us throughout our fifth decades.

The issues surrounding turning 40 are different for every woman. One might be married with children but feeling unsatisfied because she has not returned to the workforce. Another might have worked hard throughout her career but lack the financial security she had expected. In other words, we may have sailed toward our fortieth birthdays from every conceivable direction, but now we find ourselves in the same boat.

Regardless of where we're coming from or what distant shores we hope to visit in the coming decades, making the most of this midlife sparkling moment is essential. This milestone offers us a chance to reflect upon our values and assess the choices we have made. Taking the time to evaluate all aspects of our lives—friends and family, health and wellness, career and financial situation—will allow us to find greater peace and fulfillment. We can either choose to be content with where we are right now—in spite of the conflicting messages society keeps feeding us—or decide to focus on self-improvement, to reprioritize, and to start heading in a new direction. Thus turning 40 can be a trigger for fear and frustration, or it can prove a wonderful opportunity to examine our lives and, where appropriate, correct our course.

My Own Story

Recently, I had a sparkling moment when I realized that my life didn't necessarily match up with my parents' values or their way of life. Their traditional values—work hard, come home and eat dinner with the family, do your chores, go to bed, and do the same thing again the next day—didn't reflect my goals and desires.

My father, the NBC news anchor Tom Brokaw, had such admiration and reverence for the World War II generation that he coined the term "Greatest Generation." He wrote a book about those Americans who fought in World War II or remained on the home front taking care of the country's needs, and those who built the United States back up following the war. To this day, my dad maintains a hardworking, self-sacrificing approach to life based on his traditional set of values.

My father and mother (who have been blissfully married for forty-seven years) passed these values along to their daughters, for which I am extremely grateful. My parents were products of the Greatest Generation and so they reflected those values, but they also gave us lots of room to grow on our own. They financed international travel and study abroad so we could have many more choices than they had at our age. They encouraged us through word and by example to see life as an unending adventure. Yet it did not dawn on me until recently that I was questioning the choices I had made thus far in life because they had not led me to the traditional milestones of womanhood: engagement, marriage, and children.

I experienced this moment of clarity when an investment banker client of mine told me a story about her own parents. She had complained to her father that she was exhausted by the strain of her work. He had replied, "There were so many people in my generation who didn't have just one job, they had two. And you would never hear them complain." It sounded exactly like something my own father would say. As we discussed ways in which this client could free herself from parental expectations, and why she should feel entitled to her own experience, I realized that I ought to be following my own advice.

I have known for a long time that I didn't have it in me to follow the traditional path—nor did I desire to do so. I always have felt that being authentic and obeying my heart mattered most. I have found it profoundly scary at times not to follow the path my parents forged or acquire what society portrays as the "right things"—husband, children, house. But I generally believe that I'm doing the right thing for me. So why do I, like the client I just mentioned, allow myself to feel undermined by the very values I choose *not* to ascribe to? Why do I sink into a place of self-doubt, feeling somehow like a failure because I haven't traveled the traditional road?

Many of us hear our parents' criticisms, disapproval, and condescension in our heads from time to time—and I'm no exception. That is why when I'm working with a client who is expressing fear over any particular issue, I ask, "Whose voices are you hearing?" So often, our parents' belief systems continue to influence the choices we make. When I work with women on these kinds of decisions, we discuss how they can break free from the parental voices still "calling the shots" and instead discover who they are and who they will be as they go forward in life.

What amazed me during my own "aha moment" was that I somehow had fallen into the very trap that I so often help my clients get out of. While I had lived the life I wanted up to that point, I was still letting my parents' traditional values be judge and jury. I was unconsciously measuring myself according to their standards. I was listening to their voices rather than to my own.

When I graduated from college, I didn't know what I wanted to do with my life. So I took my Duke University degree to Guam, where, at the equivalent of a Club Med for Japanese couples, I slid my five-foot-two body into an ill-fitting, faux satin, pink strapless dress that was designed for a five-foot-ten woman, lip-synched to "Santa Baby" during the evening, and then rose early the following morning to teach snorkeling in an outdoor aquarium. How ridiculous is that? I am sure they were incredibly proud of me at the Duke career counseling center!

After lip-synching and breathing through a tube lost their novelty, I moved to Tokyo, where I worked as the only American in the Patagonia retail store and honed my drinking skills to great effect. While that experience certainly didn't help me lose the "freshman fifteen" I had packed on at Duke, it did offer many benefits. I learned Japanese and immersed myself in the culture of Japan, adjusting to unfamiliar customs such as not eating in public, taking off shoes before going inside, and bowing to introduce myself rather than shaking hands. I lived in a tiny Japanese neighborhood with no other expatriates around, so I had no place to seek refuge. This setting forced me to grow up fast. It also was the first time in my life when my last name didn't raise eyebrows or provoke questions, which was a relief.

From Tokyo I moved to San Francisco, where I committed myself to figuring out my next step. People were still telling me that I had my whole life ahead of me, that I could do whatever I wanted, that I was young and the world was full of possibilities. But at 26, I felt it was time to get serious. I decided to attend graduate school at New York University. I graduated from the School of Social Work two years later, worked in a hospital for another two years, and then opened my own psychotherapy practice at age 30. I wasn't married with children, but I had my career.

Shortly after I began my practice, the tragic events of 9/11 occurred. Consequently, I began working with deeply traumatized individuals who had been in the buildings but were able to escape, and also with people who had observed what happened. I began two support groups and saw almost three hundred people within three months after the attack. Working with the survivors of 9/11 made me appreciate fully how important the mental health profession is. Any lingering concerns about therapy being a luxury for the wealthy rather than a service of real value to the world vanished. It quickly became apparent how desperately people needed help. I was honored to be able to step up and utilize my skills for the benefit of the community.

Fast forward to a year and a half ago. I was nearing 40. According to society's dictates, I was supposed to be feeling as if time were running out. And I did start to panic. "Why should I feel this way?" I wondered. "I'm successful, but I'm not married and don't have kids. While 40 is not *old*, I no longer hear people telling me that I have my whole life ahead of me. Most women I see my age have the house-family-husband package—I don't. What, then, is my identity? What are my values? How can I get excited about who I am, where I am, and who and where I want to be while my clock is ticking?" I looked around and saw other capable women struggling with the same questions.

Then I had my epiphany with the client who brought up her father's judgment, and I realized that I was still stuck measuring myself according to my parents' values. When I looked back at my sometimes misguided life path, I discovered that actually I have been on a wonderful adventure. There were many times when I didn't know what I truly needed, and there were times when, out of fear, I relied on other people's opinions and advice to make decisions. But all in all, I have had many incredible, eye-opening experiences as an adult. As soon as I was able to evaluate my life without hearing my parents' voices, I was able to focus on what I have achieved thus far. I was able to see even my "failures" as growth opportunities that shaped me into the person I am today. Shifting my focus in this way has helped me approach "the big four-oh" with fortytude.

What Is Fortytude?

As the years go by, how do we reconcile society's opposing points of view about what it means to be a "successful" 40-year-old woman? And how do we make the most of this critical life juncture to ensure that we get to be who we most want to be in our 40s, 50s, and beyond?

It takes courage to look within, but this is what we must do. By examining ourselves closely and coming to a deeper understanding of what matters most to us as unique individuals, we can separate the societal messages from our own hearts' calling, let go of ideas of what *should* be, and instead embrace what *is*. You can take a stand and say proudly: "This is who I am." Or, if you're at a point where you're reinventing your life, you can say: "This is who I want to be—and I'm going to go for it!" This process takes a kind of strength that I call "fortytude."

For the past several years, I have asked myself these questions: "Why do some women feel comfortable turning 40, while others become overwhelmed by the life challenges inherent in entering the fifth decade? Why are some women who are not in relationships or raising children happy to be by themselves, while others feel lonely and 'less than enough' because they don't have a family? Why are some women frustrated by what they haven't yet accomplished in their careers relative to their colleagues, whereas others are inclined to celebrate what they have achieved? Why do some women become obsessed with and jealous of younger women, while others become generous and inspiring mentors?"

The purpose of this book is to identify what differentiates fulfilled, vital women from women paralyzed by fear at crossing the threshold into their fifth decades. In other words, what qualities do women with fortytude typically possess? By "successful," I don't necessarily mean being financially or vocationally successful, or even having the perfect family, although many women achieve both. Instead, they are successful in terms of their approach to life. They have made the transition into their late 30s and early 40s with a sense of freedom and optimism, a heartfelt openness to life's unpredictability, and a level of comfort with themselves and their bodies.

Fortytude means not just getting over a hurdle—be it a serious health challenge, the end of a marriage, or a financial struggle—but also finding happiness and joy in the calm periods that follow. It also means adopting a take-the-bull-by-the-horns approach to life if you're not happy with where you are, or if life deals you a particularly painful blow. For example, I know of several women in their mid- to late 40s who had cancer but have been cancer-free for at least six years, and who are truly enjoying themselves. Yes, they have had their very difficult moments, which many of us can't even begin to comprehend. But, as one of the women beautifully summarized, "Cancer has forced me to look at my two options and make a choice. Option one: lead my life as if it were one huge adventure. Option two: treat it like a nightmare from which I will never wake up. I chose option one."

This seems like the obvious choice for all of us. Why, then, does it often prove so difficult? And what can we do to ensure that we, like this fiercely optimistic cancer survivor, consistently say "yes!" to life? What can we do to develop that kind of fortytude?

The Five Core Values

While there is no magical notion or potion that can make the complex transition to our 40s easy, the five Core Values can help us to thrive, to lessen our fear of uncertainty, and to become curious rather than judgmental about where we are and what we have. Cultivating these values can enrich life in our fifth decades and beyond, to a point where it is not just bearable but exciting, joyous, and fulfilling.

Without a doubt, the landmark that is the fortieth birthday casts a long shadow over women's lives, as it engages us in internal conversations about fertility, physical appearance, relationships, financial and career expectations, physical health, parenting, and taking care of our own aging parents. But to the degree that women possess these five Core Values, they have been able to navigate the perilous journey from age 35 on with a dramatically higher level of comfort, satisfaction, and joy.

I now see my role as helping my clients not only to create a new conversation about who they are and the influences that have shaped their inner being but also to discover their connection to these five Core Values. I'm not claiming to have found a cookie-cutter solution for every vexing conundrum, nor am I of the belief that one good hour in therapy can solve all your problems. What I do know is that consciously engaging in these values allows women to cope with whatever (and whoever!) shows up in our lives.

The five Core Values are

- Grace
- Connectedness
- Accomplishment
- Adventure
- Spirituality

When a woman embraces all of these values, she has a mental and emotional framework that empowers her to be her most authentic—and actualized—self. These five Core Values constitute the special strength that it takes to approach one's fifth decade with a healthy blend of courage, realism, and hope.

PART I

GRACE

. . . .

When we make peace with life events, even when things don't go the way we want, we exhibit grace. When we manage stressful situations with humor, we exhibit grace. When we are accepting of others, we exhibit grace. Grace is not about physical beauty or having a ballerina's poise. It is composed of generosity, forgiveness, and equanimity in the face of trying times.

Behaving with grace can prove challenging when we feel vulnerable. These are the moments when we must dig deep, appreciating what we do have, reaching out to our loved ones for help, and trusting in our higher selves to get us through. We have a degree of control over many of the issues that I'll discuss in this book—friendships, careers, family, sense of adventure, and spirituality, to name a few. But other issues, including inevitable changes to our physical appearance, the loss of fertility, or cancer, we can't control.

To help cultivate grace under pressure, I often employ a metaphor that seems to resonate with most women. Imagine you're on your way to an important appointment. All of a sudden, you hit a horrible traffic jam. There's a big accident ahead, and as you come to a halt, you realize that you're going to be stuck there for some time. You have two choices: tightly grip the wheel, feel your blood pressure rise, have a fit about missing your appointment, and curse the driver who caused the accident; or take a deep breath, accept the current reality, and reschedule your appointment. You might make a phone call to an old friend or listen to relaxing music.

Life is that highway. There will always be the metaphorical traffic jams, accidents, thunderstorms, and other drivers filled with road rage interfering with our plans and creating imbalance in our world. Unpredictability is the one constant. So it's not whether we'll encounter challenges in life but rather how we handle them that matters. Believe me, I don't preach "Don't worry, be happy!" or some other pat slogan. But I do invite you to recognize that there are options for how you manage unexpected events. Fearing change means putting yourself on the defensive—raging against the traffic jam, even though rage does you absolutely no good. Choosing to respond with grace, by contrast, allows you to sit back, adjust your expectations, and appreciate this unanticipated gift of time alone.

One

BEAUTY BATTLES

. . . .

PERHAPS THE MOST pervasive challenge to a woman's sense of grace as she approaches her fortieth birthday has to do with changes to her physical appearance. Not one of us can avoid the stubborn arrival of outward signs of aging.

When we consider our modern culture of youth and glamour, we quickly understand why women feel so much anxiety about our looks as we grow older. Flip through any fashion magazine. In advertisements, we are bombarded by images of adolescent and 20-something women who are held forth as the standards of "beautiful" (airbrushed, digitally stretched out, and heavily made up as they are), with the obvious implication that older (and natural) women aren't worthy of our attention.

It's true that this trend is slowly changing. Hollywood has been embracing women in their 40s, 50s, and even 60s on the silver screen—think of Sandra Bullock, Holly Hunter, Glenn Close—and we now see older women in some ad campaigns. But still, when it comes to beauty, it is clear that our society values younger women more highly.

During the course of our spiritual and emotional maturation, we come to recognize that placing too much value on appearance can be unhealthy, and that our ultimate worth comes from somewhere deeper than our skin. We journey inward, seeking to identify ourselves with our true natures rather than judging ourselves and other people based on appearances. We also realize that beauty has more to do with who we are—our commitment to making the world a better place, our sacrifices on behalf of our family and friends—than how we look.

Yet in spite of this movement from external to internal beauty, from "looking hot" to embodying grace, it is difficult for many women to adjust to and embrace their changing appearance as they age. Of course, the battle to be beautiful begins, for most women, long before the fortieth birthday. Most of us tried a diet, or at a minimum worried about our weight, while we were still in junior high school. We may (or may not) have gained healthier self-images in our 20s and 30s. Many of us wage lifelong wars against weight, forever comparing our own bodies to the size two figures of models and celebrities, and forever struggling to lose those unwanted extra pounds.

As they approach 40, women who have had children can't help but notice the wear and tear pregnancy put on their bodies, including stretch marks and sagging breasts. We all face an ever-increasing number of wrinkles, and, often, we feel that we are unavoidably beginning to look like our mothers.

Why are the outward signs of aging so terrifying to us? First, they serve as inescapable reminders of our mortality. But there's another level to our panic about our fading beauty. Many women who have been married for a while are concerned that their husbands, who were drawn to them in their 20s because of their fantastic legs or ivory skin, will no longer be attracted by the late 30s or 40s versions of themselves. They worry that their husbands will begin to look outside the marriage to be turned on . . . maybe to 22-year-olds with the ivory skin and fantastic legs that they once possessed. Single women express a similar concern: men won't be interested in dating them once they turn 40, because they will be considered over the threshold age of "beautiful" in our culture.

No matter how grounded we are in our sense of self, our careers, our families, our friendships, and our other passions, most of us worry about how we look. It matters to us that we are perceived as attractive. This is normal and natural—we are, after all, social beings. We want to remain beautiful as we age—not only for our mates, our friends, and even our co-workers but also for ourselves. We want to be the best versions of ourselves that we can be. The question is not *whether* we'll face this challenge of changes to our physical appearance but rather *how* we will choose to respond to it.

• • • •

Lori Larsen, a 41-year-old nurse from Madison, Wisconsin, exhibited fortytude by taking on her weight, after being motivated by her sister's death to make a change. Previously, Lori's high body mass index (BMI) had posed a serious threat to her health and served as a major impediment to sharing a happy life with her family.

Forever the "fat girl," Lori was teased in school and jealous of her naturally tall, beautiful younger sister, Kristin, who was her father's favorite. Lori wore glasses and had to dress in plus sizes, while skinny Kristin had long legs and glowing, olive-toned skin.

Lori compensated for being overweight by working hard to be the best at everything else in her life—the perfect daughter, the perfect student, and so on. She graduated second in her high school class and went on to college and a nursing program. Lacking in confidence because of her weight, she always tried to be cheerful, no matter how she felt. Lori had few romantic involvements and doubted that she would ever find love.

And then it happened for her. While working her way through school, Lori served as a caretaker for a 50-year-old man who had been incapacitated by a stroke. They became close, and the man said he'd like to set Lori up with his son. Lori said, "No way! Boys don't like me." Then one day while she was working, in walked Mark. His father had arranged it so that Mark and Lori would be at the house at the same time. The two hit it off, and two years later they were married. They've stayed together for the eighteen years since, during which time they've had three children.

At age 35, Lori felt satisfied with her family life but bored with her job as a nurse in the ob-gyn ward of a hospital and miserable about her ever-increasing weight. Then her younger sister, Kristin, committed suicide. Lori was shocked. Lori had always thought *she* was the one with the low self-esteem, given how beautiful her sister was. She hadn't even known that Kristin suffered from depression.

Needless to say, Lori was devastated by her sister's death. In honor of Kristin, Lori resolved to live her own life more fully, starting by taking control of her weight. She wanted to be engaged in her children's lives in the way that her slimmer, more athletic younger sister had been. Kristin would take Lori's daughter, Brooke, hiking, running around the nearby college campus, and to museums, while Lori hid at home, embarrassed by her weight.

Furthermore, Lori's health was at risk. Her doctor had told her that, with a BMI of 42, her life expectancy was low. She was five foot three and weighed 292 pounds. She had a precursor to type 2 (adult-onset) diabetes, high cholesterol, and legs that hurt all the time.

Lori knew that she had to do something drastic to take off the weight. So the year after Kristin's suicide, she opted to have gastric bypass surgery. It was a difficult decision for her and her husband to make, because the procedure cost tens of thousands of dollars. But they agreed that it would be worthwhile—if it worked. "I had tried a lot of diets my whole life," Lori explained. "I went to Weight Watchers for the first time when I was just 10 years old. But nothing stuck. I had to do something different."

Lori found the procedure difficult to cope with at first. "I was sobbing two weeks after my surgery, 'Why did I do this?' Your food comfort is taken away from you." But within six months of the surgery,

Lori had lost one hundred pounds. She lost another fifty pounds in the following six months.

Lori knew that the surgery wouldn't fix everything. After the initial weight loss period, people generally begin to regain their appetites. In order to keep the weight off, Lori established and stuck to an exercise program. In the beginning, she could barely walk from her front door down the driveway to the mailbox. But she joined a health club and gradually worked her way from five to seven to ten and then to forty-five minutes of exercise. She also watched what she ate, cutting back on carbs and consuming more protein and vegetables. With her determination to lead a healthy life, Lori has kept most of the 150 pounds she lost off during the five years since the procedure.

Lori is enjoying life more because she left her job to work in the emergency room of another hospital. She had always wanted to be an ER nurse but, before the surgery, felt she wouldn't have been able to move quickly enough or keep up the energy for the job. Today she loves her work in the ER, which she finds far more stimulating. But best of all, Lori loves the freedom that her weight loss has given her to enjoy her family. They go to the park or take hikes instead of always eating or going to the movies together.

In addition, Lori said that her husband, Mark, was proud of her. About a year ago, she showed him a picture of her former, much larger self and asked, "How could you ever have been attracted to me when I looked like that?" Lori got choked up as she shared with me Mark's reply: "I never saw it. I didn't see a 'fat woman.' It didn't matter; I always saw who you are." Lori knows that she is blessed to have such an adoring husband. But she didn't make the changes for him—she did it for herself, her kids, and her sister, Kristin.

In November 2008, Lori celebrated her major milestones in physical fitness and her new healthy lifestyle by going on a women's bike ride through Southern California. She wondered when she reached the bottom of a particularly steep hill if she would be able to tackle it. But then she thought, "Kris is going to get me through this, just like she got me through my surgery." Lori added, "I know Kristin is looking down on me and smiling."

The Plastic Surgery Question

The fear of growing older is nothing new—women were trying anti-aging remedies as far back as ancient Egypt. But modern technology has given us more choices than ever before when it comes to preventative measures. While many women prefer to maintain their looks naturally through their lifetimes, others take more radical action with cosmetic procedures.

Some may argue that a woman's decision to change her looks through medical intervention is self-indulgent. What if, however, a woman had youthful energy but inherited genes that accelerated her aging process, thus clearly contradicting the way she felt inside? Because of her genetic makeup, she experienced loosened eyelids, sagging breasts, postpregnancy belly, and premature graying of the hair, while her energy level remained youthful, active, and lively. Would it be immoral, vain, or self-indulgent for that woman to receive plastic surgery, or to dye her hair, so that her physical appearance matched her internal energy?

Should we, as women, feel guilty if we elect to pursue preventative measures to preserve our beauty as we age? I don't believe that we should, given the societal pressure we face. It is tough to admit that youthful appearance doesn't last forever . . . and that we're vain enough to care. We can't deny that, as we move into the latter half of our 30s and on into our 40s, the physical manifestations of aging are sources of concern for many of us. At the same time, we can acknowledge the valid psychological underpinnings of our concerns about appearance, including a fear of no longer appearing attractive to potential or actual mates. The path you take—to have cosmetic procedures or not—is a personal choice, and it is important to make peace with your decision.

· · · ·

JACQUE FAIT, 53, is an inspiration. A ceramics artist, high school teacher, and mother of two, she started surfing when she was 51. Just two years later, she looks like a pro out on the water. Given how lanky and fit Jacque is, I was shocked when she told me that for many years she'd had body image issues.

Jacque, who has short-cropped blond hair and blue eyes, grew up in Costa Mesa and looks like the quintessential California girl. As a child, she always was a tomboy, playing football in the street with the boys, riding her bike to the beach, and boogie boarding. In high school and college, she ran track. As an adult, she has competed in triathlons and 10K races. "I'm very competitive," Jacque said, "to a fault sometimes. If I'm going to do something, I'm in 110 percent."

But in spite of her athleticism and confidence, the young Jacque felt self-conscious about her small breast size. The middle school boys picked on her for being flat-chested, and that experience left its scars. When she was a teenager, Jacque considered getting a boob job and she wore padded bras. But while she doesn't judge other women for making that type of decision, ultimately Jacque felt unwilling to put anything foreign into her body.

Nevertheless, Jacque didn't truly make peace with her body until a couple of years ago. Her teenage daughter, who has the same cup size Jacque does, said to Jacque, "I don't wear padded bras. I don't care, because this is who I am." Jacque thought, "From the mouths of babes," threw out all her extra-padded bras, and embraced her flat-chestedness fully.

Now that she is in her 50s, Jacque says, several of her friends have had breast reductions. "I am happy not to be swinging those bags of fat around!" she said with a twinkle in her eye. "I think it is better to be small-breasted when it comes to most sports anyway. I've realized that, whether I'm running or surfing, I don't want to have that extra weight to lug around. My 'girls' have done their job, and my husband adores them just like they are. I've reached a turning point in my life."

• • • •

SUSANNA GREEN LIVES in New York City. When she was growing up, she had a "Jew-fro"—a wiry, uncontrollable mass of black hair—and a prominent, crooked nose. While she felt fairly comfortable with her looks, some of her family members did not. Her appearance became such a powerful issue for her that, at age 43, she decided to make a documentary film about it.

Throughout her childhood and adult life, Susanna received many unsolicited, negative messages about her nose and her hair from her mother and her mother's sister, Aunt Marge. For instance, Aunt Marge once left Susanna a voice mail saying, "Honey, the bump is nothing. Just go to the doctor, and they'll give it a tap." On another occasion, Marge called Susanna's hair "a nest for low-flying birds."

But it wasn't until after her father passed away, when Susanna was 31 years old and single, that she felt the two older women's focus on her appearance turn pathological. Susanna remarked, "They were well-intended, but the pressure to improve my looks and find a man was a heavy burden. It made me feel more alone and more pathetic than I actually was, and I spiraled into a depression."

Eventually, something snapped, and Susanna realized she could choose to see the entire situation as quite humorous. She resolved to take her "weighty, depressing circumstances and turn them into something amusing and ultimately positive." Although she had no prior experience as a filmmaker, Susanna began making a documentary about her nose, her hair, and Aunt Marge.

During the summer of her fortieth birthday, Susanna took a documentary filmmaking class at the School of Visual Arts. Then she began to shoot. Susanna wondered, Who is Aunt Marge? What about her past had led Susanna's aunt to have such strong opinions about such superficial things? Why was she so preoccupied with Susanna's looks? What did this say about the way Marge thought about herself? "Answers poured forth, and I recorded," Susanna said with a laugh. "As Marge delved into the details of eliminating the bump in the middle of my nose, you would have thought she was discussing a peace treaty between Israel and Palestine before the United Nations."

With the help of an experienced editor and friend, Susanna's film is now nearing completion. The process has been both cathartic and therapeutic. She said, "The more time I spent really getting to know my eccentric aunt, the more I felt empathy for her ambitions and struggles. While she seemed preoccupied with the superficial, beneath it all I can now see the genuine concern and love she was expressing. And she never tells me to change my nose or my hair anymore." Furthermore, Susanna feels better than ever about herself.

Aging Gracefully

Aging gracefully means not clinging to what we *did* or *could* or *should* look like. You would think that if anyone would struggle with this issue, it would be a professional model. You might feel as if she had a valid excuse for resenting the relentless advance of wrinkles and corresponding decline in her social status. You might doubly excuse her for being bummed about turning 40 if you knew that a newspaper had recently, and rather meanly, posed the question, "Where did it go wrong?" about her. Frankly, I would have expected a former supermodel in her fifth decade to be at least a little bitter, jaded, arrogant, and depressed about her diminishing beauty. But then I met a remarkable woman who busted every single one of those stereotypes—a woman who personifies graceful acceptance of the aging process.

In 1990, George Michael came out with the video to his song "Freedom," which included the supermodels Naomi Campbell, Cindy Crawford, Christy Turlington, Linda Evangelista, and Tatjana Patitz. According to *The Guardian*, he'd been inspired by a *Vogue* magazine cover from January of that year featuring a stunning—and still iconic—black and white photo of these five women.

Flash forward twenty years. If you're like many women in their late 30s and 40s, you've probably been on a first-name basis with Naomi, Cindy, Christy, and Linda since you were a teen. But nearly all of us have forgotten the fifth member of the party: Tatjana Patitz. So had I, until an old friend from Duke who knew Tatjana mentioned her in the context of this book, and I set up a lunch date with her.

Into the café walked Tatjana, in some ways as intimidating as I'd feared. She was a five-foot-eleven leopardess with broad, slanted blue eyes, sandy blond hair, and exquisitely pronounced cheekbones. But she didn't wear oversize sunglasses or a fancy outfit, just jeans, a sweater, and flip-flops. There was no evidence of plastic surgery, only a natural sprinkling of wrinkles. And when she smiled, she radiated warmth.

Tatjana Patitz grew up in Sweden, leading a normal, quiet life with her parents and her sister until a talent scout discovered her at the age of 17. Suddenly, she found herself walking catwalks in Paris and Milan, hobnobbing with the rich and famous, and being shot by some of the top photographers in the fashion industry. In her 20s, she went on to win numerous high-profile ad campaigns, including Versace, Calvin Klein, and Chanel.

When Tatjana recollected her days as a supermodel, she said that they were a lot of fun but also intense and sometimes overwhelming. "I didn't know what to think," she told me. "There I was, a farm girl dressed in grown-up clothes, being told to act as if I didn't care. Deep down inside, I was shy and scared, but I guess I went along and enjoyed it." She shared the downsides as well, such as never having the time to furnish or decorate her New York "bachelor pad," breaking out in hives from stress, and developing a fear of flying. Furthermore, she said, "as a model, you are always judged, in ways that can be brutal. I remember going to go-sees (where you meet the client or photographer). They look you up and down, and it feels that your whole world and everything about who you are is being judged only by the way you look. That can be tough, no matter how secure you are." Amazingly, it seems that Tatjana managed to maintain a healthy self-esteem through it all. She laughed. "I always felt that I was a bit odd-looking, so in a sense I just thought, The joke is on them."

In her late 20s, Tatjana began spending time in L.A., modeling for the photographer Herb Ritts and dating a surfer. She found being in nature a welcome respite from her hectic, urban life. While the other top models settled in Paris or New York City, she opted for a beach house in Malibu where she could keep horses and dogs. She would fly places for gigs, and photographers would come to her. But she also gradually fell out of the supermodel circuit. That was a sacrifice she was willing to make. She remained in California and now has a son and is active on the board of a wild horse sanctuary.

When I asked her how, at age 42, she had been able to find peace in her life, Tatjana responded, "When I realized that my career was not going to hold my hand in my deathbed, I had to dig deep to find what I needed. That need was to connect with other women, on whom I could rely as mentors and who could show me the love and nurturance I did not receive from my own mother, from other models, or from men."

As for her looks, Tatjana stated that she was not interested in invasive procedures. "I believe in aging gracefully because it celebrates me as a woman. If a man wants the 20-year-old, he should have the 20-year-old. I know who I am, and what I have to offer. In the end— for me, as for every woman—beauty is what one emanates. It comes from feeling good about who you are with your flaws (and we *all* have them), and being at peace with yourself."

Reclaiming Beauty

It is time for us, as 30-, 40-, and 50-something women, to reclaim beauty. The process has already begun. But now that we have this opening, we women must back it up with our own fortytude. We must declare our presence and make it known that we are worthy of appreciation at all ages. We must not allow ourselves to become, as Tatjana put it, "invisible."

The changes to your beauty will come, even if you do your best to stave off signs of aging. It is your attitude toward the inevitable aging process that matters most. Can you let go of how you looked in your 20s and embrace the face that greets you in the mirror today? Can you see past the wrinkles and the stretch marks to the beauty that lies beneath, the beauty of your soul? Can you feel good about who you are and enjoy being in your body the way it is right now, imperfect as it is? Can you focus on your health and wellness as a primary motivator for taking care of yourself, rather than simply your appearance? Can you release your fears that your husband will leave you or men won't date you because you're over 40, and realize that you *want* only a partner who appreciates the divine, mature, powerful being you've become?

Let's start a movement. By looking good, feeling healthy, and reveling in our deep-felt security in who we are, we can shout out to the world, "I am alive and thriving!" We can admire ourselves and each other for all the experiences we've bravely faced, every wrinkle we've earned, every pound we've shed, only to regain it again. Rather than being fiercely competitive about our looks, we can cheer each other on.

Two

THE CLOCK IS TICKING

. . . .

AS WE NEAR 40, we become acutely aware of the fact that our clocks are ticking. We have had ingrained in us from a young age the idea that bearing children after 35 is a poor choice. And, to a certain extent, these warnings are accurate. From a biological standpoint, we have only until menopause sets in (between the ages of 45 and 55 on average) to conceive a child naturally. But the chances of having a successful full-term pregnancy begin to shrink even earlier than that—from our 20s onward—since egg quality starts to decline. By age 35, we already have passed the "peak fertility phase." What does that mean, exactly? Well, consider this: it takes a woman in her 20s an average of thirteen attempts to get pregnant. Between the ages of 30 and 40, our fertility becomes about half as efficient.

Nearly every childless woman I know from age 35 to 45 will experience moments of discomfort about her fertility—confusion, anxiety, depression, frustration, and fear. (The exceptions, of course, are women who have made the choice not to have children, or to embrace their stepchildren as their own, and who are genuinely at peace with their decisions.) These days, we have several options in terms of how to conceive and raise a child. Even so, for many of us who have put off or struggled with having children, fertility can be one of the greatest challenges as we approach our fifth decades.

Like many single women, I have dated numerous men in the search for a suitable partner. And I haven't totally immersed myself in my career and neglected other dimensions of my life, as some onlookers might presume. I just haven't met the right person yet. I still hope to have a traditional family (in the sense that, ideally, I'd like to be married to the father of our biological children), but I'm also beginning to explore my other options.

Some women ignore the fertility issue completely, waiting until their early to mid-40s before they try to get pregnant. When they visit the doctor and discover the hard truth that their chances of conceiving after age 43 are slim, they may feel devastated. They realize that, if they had acknowledged the issue sooner, they might have been able to do something about it, which only adds to their sorrow.

In addition, there are many women who try to have children for years but encounter difficulties along the way. During one of my internships in graduate school, I worked with women in the high-risk pregnancy ward at Mount Sinai Hospital. My primary responsibility was to provide support to the women who had miscarried. The one feeling that they all—regardless of age, race, or socioeconomic status—expressed was their sense of failure as women. They would talk about the fact that producing offspring is the most primal female task. They felt as though their bodies had betrayed them. Ultimately, they had to come to terms with what had happened. This proved an easier task for some women than for others, and I grieved with them.

When we confront our fertility issues, we must move forward with grace. The truth is, we have very little control over how things turn out. As our lives unfold, can we be grateful for what we do have rather than whip ourselves into a frenzy about what we lack? Can we be generous in sharing our knowledge and experiences with others? Can we be compassionate with women who have not seen their dreams for motherhood fulfilled in the way they had hoped? Can we travel down our unique paths with courage and acceptance?

Reactions and Responses

Jennifer graduated magna cum laude from an Ivy League university, climbed the ranks in her high-tech industry job, and maintained an enviable physique through a regimented fitness schedule and healthy diet. Yet at 41 she found herself single and without the child she had always dreamed of. Determined to turn her "perfect family" fantasy into reality, she married the next guy who came along, even though something "felt off" right from the start. Nine months later, when she was 42, they had a child together. Jennifer's dreams had come true . . . or had they?

Jennifer adored her child, but she was miserable in her marriage. For a few years, she managed willfully to blind herself to her husband's long absences, which he claimed were for business. But eventually she couldn't bear the blatant lies and disrespect any longer. She knew that he was having an affair. She confronted him and got him to admit that, in fact, he was leading a duplicitous life in another state with a woman who was the mother to *two more* of his children. "It was a positively wretched situation," Jennifer said. She left the marriage and began her life as a single mom.

The story has a happy ending, however. Jennifer, who is now in her mid-50s, has progressed by leaps and bounds not only in her professional life but also in her personal life. She fell in love again at the age of 46, remarried at 47, and is happily married to this day. When she hears younger women express concern over the ticking clock, she advises them to proceed with caution: "Don't act out of desperation just because of your age," she counsels. "Consider all your options. There are lots of ways to have children other than doing what I did and marrying the first guy who turns up. I got out of the marriage, but he's in my life forever as the father of my child. You might be happier having a baby on your own!"

• • • •

SITA IS A PETITE, perky 56-year-old. Born in Trinidad to "very traditional" Indian parents, she moved to Bozeman, Montana, for college. There, she met the love of her life. "Everybody in my family expected that I should marry an Indian professional," Sita told me with a grin. "But I married a blond-haired, blue-eyed, six-feet-seven-inches-tall basketball player." Her father was understanding, but her mother wouldn't speak to her for two years. Eventually, Sita and her husband traveled to Trinidad for a traditional Hindu wedding, which made her mother happy. "Now they like Brian more than they like me!" Sita said and laughed.

After graduation, Brian and Sita tried to get pregnant for several years but failed. IVF didn't work, either, so they decided to adopt. Their tall, blond-haired, blue-eyed daughter has Brian's coloring and Sita's braininess. Sita doesn't let it bother her that she looks so different from her husband and daughter. "I forget that, when people look at me, the first thing they see is my brown skin. I just think of myself as Sita, and my family as my family." Her decision to adopt has been one of the best she ever made.

My Fertility Story

The fertility issue is not a theoretical discussion for me. Hands down, it is the number one source of stress in my life right now. The question of whether I'll ever have biological children has caused me anxiety, particularly over the past three years, as I have witnessed friend after friend having children of her own. One minute we were happily single, or, as I like to say, we were all "playing in the playground." Then, one by one, each of my friends took off for the greener grass of family life, leaving me with the ball and no one to play with. While the metaphor might seem childish, it does describe my feelings about the loss of youth and the brevity of time. However, those regrets were eclipsed by my relief when I chose to take action. I talked to many women about their choices; I shared my fears with my friends and family; and finally, I consulted a fertility specialist. I am doing my best to respond with grace to the ticking clock.

I'm incredibly grateful to my sister Andie for delivering the wake-up call when I was 37. Several of Andie's friends had seen Dr. Jamie Grifo, a fertility specialist at New York University, because they were having difficulty getting pregnant. She said to me, "Sarah, you need to get your fertility checked out, have some tests done. You're not that young anymore." I was so disconnected from reality that I imagined myself as still having the body of a 25-year-old. I was healthy, energetic, athletic, and I took excellent care of myself. But so did Andie's friends, a point she would not let slide. "Just do it," she said. "What do you have to lose?" Her approach was so persistent and matter-of-fact that I took her advice.

But I still had my head in the clouds. I made the appointment with Dr. Grifo on autopilot. I was not paying attention to what any of it meant. Even though, as a therapist, I worked with many women in their fifth decades who were coping with their fertility struggles, I didn't picture myself in the same boat. Infertility is like cancer in that way: you know it's out there, but you don't think you will experience it— until you do. Most of us function as though the rules don't apply to us. We imagine that we're somehow invulnerable, but we are just as susceptible as the next person.

Andie came with me to my appointment. I walked into Dr. Grifo's office with a smile on my face, trying to be as stoic as possible. I let him know that I was just there to ask some questions. Then I briefly explained my situation: 37, single, and eager to have biological children of my own someday. Dr. Grifo said, "Let me show you some graphs." He presented the evidence like the scientist that he was—no drama, no judgment, just the facts. His charts clearly demonstrated how much easier it is for a woman to get pregnant at 27 than at 37. He did not candy-coat the truth. He didn't say to me, as so many people had in the past few years, "Don't worry, you have time." He discussed my chances with each passing year of having a healthy child. And the odds weren't great, especially after 40.

I burst into tears. This is not my typical style, to start sobbing in a physician's office, but I could not help myself. All I could think was How the hell did this happen to me? I had broken up with a serious boyfriend the year before but had no real prospects on the horizon. I hadn't thought 37 was that old, yet here was the incontrovertible scientific evidence, spread out on the table in front of me. I had never imagined myself in this position. From the time I was a little girl, I'd pictured myself as the mother of five rosy-cheeked children. Suddenly, I realized that I would be lucky to have even one.

My private practice was going well at the time. I had been working with all these women to solve their problems, thinking nothing could affect me. Then, smack! there I was, confronting one of the primary issues that I counseled people about. I realized that I could not allow myself to live in denial any longer. I had to embrace reality—as daunting, depressing, and frightening as it was at first glimpse.

Fortunately, my extremely practical, compassionate sister was there by my side. She and Dr. Grifo let me cry. Once I had calmed down, Dr. Grifo gave me a great deal of encouragement. He told me that truly, when it comes to fertility, nothing is cookie-cutter. He said, "You are never the population; you are an individual. In other words, population is a guideline—*not* a predictor." He reminded me that I had plenty of options and praised me for coming in to see him while I was still young enough to preserve several of these options.

Then Dr. Grifo did something that, to this day, I find truly extraordinary: he told me the story of his own fertility struggles with his wife. "What I learned from my personal experience was the best education I ever got," he said. "I find it's really helpful to my patients when I share my story. That way, you know I've been through it and I understand things from your perspective."

Dr. Grifo had three children with his first wife. After seventeen years, they got divorced. Some years later, he remarried. His new wife, Anne, was 40 at the time and had never had children. In fact, she'd had breast cancer and gone through fertility treatments with her ex-husband, so she and Dr. Grifo went straight to IVF when they decided to try for children together.

Unfortunately, Dr. Grifo and his wife had an arduous journey ahead. They tried one round of IVF when Anne was 41, but then her breast cancer recurred. After a lumpectomy and radiation treatment, she recovered. But during her treatment, doctors couldn't address her fertility issues, so she was 43 years old before she could try IVF once more. It didn't work.

Finally, the couple decided to use Dr. Grifo's sperm and an anonymous donor egg. They chose a different woman than the egg donor to serve as the gestational carrier, to keep the process less emotional for all parties involved.

Nine months later, they were blessed with a beautiful baby girl, and since then they've had a second child in the same manner. Dr. Grifo got misty-eyed as he spoke. "When our first baby was delivered, we were right there in the room. We took her in our arms. My wife said, 'It wasn't my egg, and it didn't grow in my uterus, but this really is my baby.'" He paused to wipe the tears away. "My wife is the most amazing woman in the world. Anyone who can do what she did . . . She's my hero." Dr. Grifo concluded his story with this thought: "We all assume that we have the privilege to bear children. We don't respect how much of a gift it is."

I couldn't believe it: my fertility doctor was tearing up as he told of his own experience with infertility. It disarmed me. It also made me think, This is exactly who I want to have on my team, helping me through this process. He totally gets it, not just as a doctor but as a human being. He could identify with my uncomfortable mix of anxiety and hope.

I told Dr. Grifo that I was ready to move forward, so he reviewed my options:

1. Have a baby with someone you know as a friend or co-parent right now, even if you're not sure you want him as your life partner.
2. Get into a relationship and start trying to get pregnant within the next year.
3. Freeze your eggs to use for IVF further down the road, either with a partner or with a sperm donor. Freezing your eggs buys you time to meet a guy or prepare yourself for being a single mom.
4. Even further down the road, use your partner's sperm and a donor egg (as Dr. Grifo himself did).
5. Adopt.
6. Don't do anything, and come to terms with the idea that you might not have biological children.

"At the end of day," he said, "if you want a baby, you'll have a baby. It just may not come about in quite the way you'd planned. But it doesn't matter. Your baby is your baby, and you'll be thrilled to have this little being in your life, regardless."

I looked him in the eye and asked point-blank, "What should I do?"

Dr. Grifo said, "I can't make the decision for you; you must make it for yourself. We don't know what might happen. You may or may not have trouble getting pregnant. You might meet someone next month and get pregnant right away. You might meet someone in four years and decide then to have a child together, in which case your frozen eggs will be in much better shape than your 41-year-old eggs. But I do recommend, if you're serious about wanting a child of your own, that you deal with this issue immediately. That way, you're preserving your options."

I looked at my sister. She was so comforting with her calm acceptance of the situation. But she wouldn't tell me what to do, either. All she would say was, "Great, you have options!"

I asked what the next steps would look like. Dr. Grifo told me that first, regardless of whether I decided to freeze my eggs, he should perform a fertility checkup. He needed to find out if all my parts were functioning properly and my hormone levels were healthy. If they were, then I would have a solid chance of getting pregnant within the next year should I start trying right away, and I would be likely to produce a good number of viable eggs should I take the freezing route. I left Dr. Grifo's office hours later, feeling far more peaceful about my situation than I had in months. I was moving forward; I was taking control.

On our walk from his office back to the subway on that blustery New York day, Andie and I talked further. It seemed clear to me that I should freeze my eggs. Yes, it was expensive, over ten thousand dollars, but it seemed worth it. I am a leave-no-stone-unturned type of person, so I was attracted to the idea of keeping my options open. I also felt certain that having the procedure would alleviate much of my anxiety about meeting Mr. Right.

I told Andie that there was just one problem: I wasn't sure I would have the time in the next six months to go through the hormone shots and minor surgery, because I was training for a triathlon. She looked at me like I was crazy. "Sarah, you're talking about having a child, yet you don't want to stop your life for two months because of a triathlon? You're making an investment in your lifelong happiness! Which is more important to you: fulfilling the dream of being a mother or appeasing your ego? Anyway, if you have a baby, it's going to change everything. Missing your triathlon training will be the least of your worries, believe me. You've got to decide where your priorities lie." I realized right away that Andie was right. I committed then and there to having my eggs frozen as soon as possible.

At that point, what concerned me most was how to address the subject with my parents. I scheduled dinner with Andie, her husband, and my mother for the following Wednesday night (my father couldn't make it). After we'd finished eating, I said, "I'm going to freeze my eggs. I'm ready to do this. And I might end up having a child on my own in a few years." My sister and her husband, of course, expressed their agreement. But even my mother reacted positively, with no hesitation. She told my father the next day, and he, too, expressed his approval of my decision. I felt very blessed to have such an open-minded, supportive, and loving family.

The good news is, when I decide to do something, I do it. So after a month of injecting hormones, I was in Dr. Grifo's office again to have the procedure. We were both pleased when he confirmed that he had retrieved a generous quantity of healthy eggs.

I immediately felt a huge sense of relief. My mind-set shifted completely. I was no longer frantically in search of a partner. I was no longer a victim of my aging body. I had time, and I had options. And I noticed an impact on my behavior as well. I didn't feel pressure to date every guy who came along. I could be more cautious, and I exercised better judgment. Since then, I have encouraged over a dozen women to have their eggs frozen. I feel that this experience is a gift I can share with others. I invite women to be incredibly honest with themselves, and to educate themselves about their options.

I'd like to offer one added word of caution as you engage in this process. As I explored my options, it seemed that everyone in my life held a strong opinion—and was eager to share it with me. My sister Andie was onboard with my decision to freeze my eggs. My other sister Jennifer's first instinct was "Adopt." My mother expressed concern that I might not ever be able to carry a child to term, given the fact that

I have scoliosis. I knew they only wanted me to be happy, but I listened for a moment, then politely asked them to keep their thoughts to themselves. I found it crucial not to focus on anyone's opinions other than my own.

Single by Chance, Mother by Choice

Societal norms are shifting. Just a few decades ago, women still felt harsh judgment for being divorced. Today, single moms account for about a quarter of all households with children; many of these mothers have never been married. Yet making the decision to be a single mom from the start is still a relatively new phenomenon, and women still can encounter prejudice when they consciously opt to become mothers without a father as part of the equation.

Let's put an end to this bias. Most of the women I know who have chosen to have children on their own wanted to find partners; they just didn't succeed in time. They all were racing against their biological clocks. And all of them are still hopeful that they'll meet a man soon who wants to be part of their family, whether or not he has kids of his own. Why should we judge women who choose this path in life? They are fulfilling their dreams.

•   •   •   •

KIM ALLEN, 44, has dark hair, freckles, and a permanent smile. Raised in a traditional, close-knit family in the Midwest, Kim always thought that she would have a family of her own. Her parents met in grade school, started dating in high school, got married at age 22, and have been together ever since. When they dropped her off at college, her mother cried, "This is where you're going fall in love and meet your husband." Only it didn't happen that way for Kim. She finished her undergraduate degree, moved to Boston and then to L.A., began a successful career in advertising, traveled, bought a house, and enjoyed a rich life with her friends. But she didn't meet the love of her life, get married, or have kids along the way.

Soon after she turned 39, Kim broke up with yet another boyfriend who told her, "I love you, but I'm just not ready to move forward with a family with you." She found herself without a partner—but not quite ready to have a child on her own. "It was crazy," she said. "I kept thinking, How did I end up here? But people do." Her ob-gyn convinced her to see a fertility specialist. Much like me, Kim said that she didn't feel 39. But when she saw the statistics and realized how rapidly her odds of having a successful pregnancy were decreasing, she decided to freeze a few embryos, using sperm from an anonymous donor—just in case her dream guy didn't come along. (Back then, egg-freezing technology had yet to be perfected—now it is as reliable as freezing embryos.) Then she gave herself two years to meet someone.

And yet, two years later, Kim was still without a partner. She was about to take the plunge into single motherhood and implant an embryo at age 41 when she met a fantastic guy. They dated for four months, but the relationship didn't work out. Kim gave herself some time to heal. Then, just one month shy of her forty-third birthday, she realized that she definitely was ready to have a child on her own. She thought, "I know exactly who I am and exactly what I want. I'm tired of letting other people's lack of ability to be happy make me unhappy." She had two of her frozen embryos implanted, and one of them took.

Kim's pregnancy wasn't easy—she had to go on bed rest for six weeks—but she never questioned her decision. Her friends took excellent care of her, and she realized that she wasn't really having the baby on her own; she'd spent years developing a loving, supportive community. She delivered a healthy baby boy three and a half weeks early, surrounded and nurtured by not just her friends but also her parents, who had completely accepted her decision.

Kim is thrilled with how things have turned out for her. She told me that everything has gone incredibly smoothly since her son's birth. She even feels grateful to be on her own, rather than parenting her child with an unworthy partner. "Thank heavens things didn't work out with that guy I was dating at age 41," she said. "I love every moment of this new life!"

In fact, even after Kim got "job-eliminated" when her baby was six months old, she didn't panic. She said, "I honestly am convinced that this little bump in the employment road is just the jolt I needed to take me to the next phase of my career." Having the little guy waiting at home put it all into perspective, and kept her from freaking out, as she might have done before having a child. "Honestly, I just feel lucky that now I get to spend more time with him," she reported. "I think a lot of what has carried me through the whole experience is the feeling that I am moving forward in the direction I'd wanted to for so long."

Kim mentioned a few hurdles she's had to cross, like going to parenting class alone when everyone else there had a partner. Or traveling on a plane with her baby for the first time and thinking, "Wow, I'm not just doing this alone today; it'll always just be the two of us. You can't deny that it's a struggle." Nevertheless, Kim has felt almost exclusively full of gratitude and happiness since the moment she found out that she was pregnant.

Kim summed up her experience in this way: "I would never presume to advise anyone regarding what they should do about their fertility. If you take this path, you have to be prepared and have a plan. But I can tell you that I am so overwhelmed with joy that I've made this leap. Nothing about it has felt sad, like, I'm 44 and single . . . On the contrary, I think how sad I'd be right now if I *hadn't* decided to become a mom on my own. I have no doubt that it is the best thing I have ever done. If you really want to have a biological child, it's a wonderful gift to be able to do this for yourself."

Kim is definitely open to the possibility of meeting someone and having a partner to help her raise her child, but she is prepared for that

Three

BREAST CANCER:
THE PITILESS BULLY

. . . .

I WAS 35 YEARS OLD when I learned that my high school class-mate Anna LoBianco had breast cancer. The news upset me, but I thought, If anyone is going to survive this disease, it's Anna. Everyone I knew agreed that Anna was a ferocious woman—in a good way. She was a force of nature, strong and opinionated. In high school, I'd been in awe of Anna. My admiration for her only grew when, as an adult, I reconnected with Anna and learned that she was on a crusade to im-prove public school education in New York City.

I had the opportunity to see Anna at a friend's birthday party. At the time, she was in remission and living in Manhattan with her two young children and her boyfriend, working in Harlem at the Bank Street College of Education. After a double mastectomy, she'd had her breasts reconstructed. She had undergone months of chemother-apy and was having radiation treatments. Yet she seemed just as full of energy, spunk, and attitude as ever. Except for her lack of hair from the chemo—which looked to me like a typical gutsy Anna fash-ion statement—you never would have guessed that she was ill. Anna didn't seem too worried about the breast cancer, either, even though it had spread to her lymph nodes before she'd had surgery. She talked about how she would bike to Sloan-Kettering in the middle of winter to receive her chemo treatments.

Then, less than a year later, I got word that Anna had died. The cancer had come back with a vengeance, spreading to her bones. She had fought heroically—never complaining, never adopting a victim mentality—but the cancer had won. Anna had just turned 36.

When I heard the news, I thought, My God, cancer is the cruelest bully. While I've always known that it was out there as a threat, breast cancer didn't seem real until my own passionate, powerful friend lay slain by its cold touch.

A Common Enemy

Starting in our teens and 20s, we see our gynecologists yearly for a Pap smear and routine breast examination. But as we move through our fifth decades and into our sixth, a new, important component is thrown into the mix during our "well woman" checkup: the mammogram. Tragically, most of us will know someone close to us with breast cancer, if we are fortunate enough to escape the diagnosis ourselves. Out of the 350 women I talked to while writing this book, every single one could identify at least one woman in her life who had fought this pitiless enemy.

The statistics are sobering. According to the National Cancer Institute, 12.7 percent of women born in the United States today will be diagnosed with breast cancer at some point in their lives: that's one in eight of us. Other than skin cancer, breast cancer is the second most prevalent type of cancer in women. As of September 2008, there were about 2.5 million breast cancer survivors in the United States.

The good news is that recent research suggests breast cancer rates are declining slightly, thanks to increased mammography screening and improved treatments. And, fortunately, breast cancer is highly treatable. Many women not only have survived it in their 30s or 40s but have continued to thrive into their 50s and 60s.

．．．．

CHERI PITCHER and Deb Stransky belonged to the Church of Jesus Christ of Latter-day Saints community in Orange County, California. They worked in the same office when they were diagnosed with breast cancer, one year apart. According to their boss, while both women experienced moments of struggle, they did so with "admirable grace," never acting like victims or becoming resentful of those in better health.

Deb was 44 years old when we met. When you looked at this outspoken mother of two with beautiful blond hair and sparkling blue eyes, you never would have believed that, approximately a year before, she had been engaged in a depleting war against breast cancer. Deb particularly detested chemotherapy, which she described as "excruciatingly difficult" because of the physical pain. In fact, she said that the chemo was so challenging it had forced her to "surrender everything to the will to live."

For Deb, surrendering everything meant, among other things, letting go of her vanity. Deb admitted that she had a difficult time with this at first. A few weeks after she started chemo, she'd had eyelash extensions put on to conceal "her sickness." Unfortunately, her eyelashes then fell out. But even worse was when she started to lose her hair. Deb always had seen her lovely locks as her "crown." Even as the hair began to fall out in chunks, she did not want to let it go.

One day, Deb was complaining to a friend who was a cancer survivor about her hair loss. Her friend said, "Deb, you need to surrender. It's time to shave your head."

Deb replied, "Surrender? I *have* surrendered! I have cancer. I'm having chemo. I've had no choice but to surrender." But she also heard what her friend was saying: Deb had to stop attaching so much importance to her looks. The next morning when she woke up, she found her hair matted to her head. Then, as she ran a comb through it, all but one patch fell out. Deb looked in the mirror and said to that patch of hair, "You have been my faithful friend, so loyal to me. So you are not going anywhere." Her bald head with that little poof sticking out may have looked funny to others, but it kept Deb's hope alive—and made her giggle every time she caught a glimpse of it.

Before being diagnosed with cancer, Deb admitted to judging individuals with the disease. She honestly felt that they had gotten cancer as a result of not taking care of themselves. On her first day of chemo, she saw many other people in the treatment room who were far sicker than she. Deb immediately thought, "This is a club I don't want to belong to." But after several weeks of watching her fellow chemo patients live with dignity and courage, she completely changed her perspective. She said, "I realized that I didn't even deserve to be in that club—a club full of such strong, inspirational people." Deb added that the hardest part of having cancer itself was raising her children and praying to God that they would be okay if she didn't survive.

Cheri was more soft-spoken than Deb. She, too, had shimmering blue eyes and a warm smile. Her hair, still growing out from her three weeks of chemo, was cropped short. A 38-year-old mother of four, Cheri had been diagnosed with stage two breast cancer a few months before meeting with me, and she had had a double mastectomy. As was Deb's, Cheri's biggest fear was not about dealing with cancer but about orphaning her four children.

Cheri had a more advanced stage of cancer than Deb, and she had only just completed her final round of chemo. She was still mid-process with her reconstructive breast surgery and was not yet out of the danger zone. Yet already, she was looking on the bright side of her illness. "I voice my opinion more now," Cheri said. "I guess I feel that I am worth being counted for the first time in my life."

I was crushed when, just two months after my interview with Cheri,

I got an e-mail from Deb saying that Cheri's tumor had returned and she was undergoing further radiation and chemo. Yet recently Cheri informed me that she has made a strong recovery and is delighted to be back at work. Cheri offers a powerful example of resiliency.

Facing Our Fears

All sorts of fears are aroused by this disease; it forces us to confront our mortality head-on. Many of us have heard the nightmare tales about both the experience of cancer—the pain and suffering it entails—and the arduous, unpleasant nature of the treatments. The very word "chemo" elicits negative associations, even if we haven't been through it ourselves.

But when it comes to reproductive cancers, it is not just our fears of illness and death that get activated; it is also our fear of losing those parts of ourselves that make us feel most female—our breasts and ovaries. Many survivors say that it can be excruciatingly difficult for a woman who has had her female organs removed to continue feeling sexy and sexually viable.

Yet numerous individuals have demonstrated their ability to live with grace after cancer. They express their femininity through their compassion for others, their passion for life, and their openness and honesty about how they are feeling. They have told me that they continue to connect sexually with their partners. They find ways to enjoy their new bodies, letting go of worrying about the extra five pounds on their bellies and instead reveling in just being alive.

•　•　•　•

IMAGINE DECIDING TO HAVE your breasts and ovaries removed even though you are perfectly healthy, in order to avoid the risk of ever getting a reproductive cancer. It might seem an overreaction. But when Jessica Queller asked her doctors to perform a preemptive double mastectomy and oophorectomy, although she showed no signs of cancer at the time, hers was a carefully considered, thoroughly researched choice.

Jessica was just shy of her fortieth birthday and eight months pregnant when we met in her Los Angeles home. A successful writer and a striking beauty with a petite frame and long brown hair, she smiled easily and exuded calm. She spoke with no pretension about the bizarre series of events that had unfolded in her 30s, inspiring her to have the surgeries as well as to write a controversial *New York Times* op-ed piece and a memoir, *Pretty Is What Changes,* about her decision. "My proactive stance comes from the trauma of watching my mother's death. I did it to honor my mother, and to prevent other women from suffering the way she did," Jessica explained to me.

Jessica's mother died of ovarian cancer when Jessica was 33 years old. Her mother had fought off breast cancer six years earlier and lived a healthy life since then. But the ovarian cancer killed her in just two years—a trauma from which Jessica has never recovered.

Jessica's eyes welled with tears as she spoke. "For those two years, my sister and I were constantly at my mom's side, watching her slowly deteriorate towards death. I managed to maintain my job as a writer for a television series, but basically my mother moved into my apartment. She even shared a bed with me during the final six months. My mother had been glamorous, beautiful, and vivacious. The suffering and pain her cancer caused her were indescribable. On her last day, her eyes were filled with terror. Ultimately, the doctors gave her morphine that kept her unconscious until she died."

At the time, the doctors had no idea that Jessica's mother had an abnormality in her BRCA gene—a gene that naturally suppresses tumors but loses this ability when the mutation occurs. This made her susceptible to more virulent strains of the reproductive cancers at an earlier age than most women.

Jessica first heard of the mutation from a high school friend who happened to be on the board of a nonprofit cancer prevention organization. But Jessica was too busy putting her life back together after her mother's death, trying to date, and wanting to start a family. She thought, "Maybe later I'll get tested for the BRCA gene abnormality."

After a year had passed, Jessica decided to take the test. She was shocked by the results: she had tested positive. "I couldn't believe it. I thought I was putting my mind at rest by taking the test, and never guessed I'd have the abnormality. I asked the doctor what it meant. He said, 'You have up to an 87 percent chance of developing breast cancer, and a 44 percent chance of ovarian cancer. But you're also at risk for developing the most virulent strains of reproductive cancers. And you're more likely to have a second incidence of the disease.'"

Jessica initially went through a denial phase. "I have to find a husband and have babies before I can deal with this!" she thought. But then her best friend from college, Kay, gave Jessica the opportunity to write a *New York Times* op-ed piece addressing whether such medical knowledge is power or indeed ignorance is bliss. In the course of researching and writing the article, Jessica became convinced that she needed to take action. "I spent a year obsessing over the question, Do I remove my breasts or not? The doctors told me that I could do surveillance and hope to discover the cancer early on, but all that would do is catch it, not cure it. I already had been through the experience of chemo and radiation with my mom, and I knew that I didn't want any of it. The only way to prevent someone from getting the reproductive cancers is to aggressively remove all the target cells in the breasts and the ovaries."

And that is how, at the age of 35, with no signs of cancer in her body, Jessica ended up having a double mastectomy. "I thought, My life is over. My sexuality and beauty are going to be destroyed, my natural body gone. But I was so wrong. I found myself with a boyfriend shortly after the surgery. We stayed together for a year and a half, and he helped me recover from the trauma of losing my natural breasts. He always made me feel sexy and beautiful. The fear before the surgery was the worst part. It wasn't really that big a deal afterwards."

During the course of her surgery and recovery, Jessica realized that one of the things that mattered most to her was being the mother of her own child. So at age 38, single and eager to have her oophorectomy at age 40, before her ovarian cancer risk skyrocketed, she decided to have a baby with a sperm donor. She went to the sperm bank, got pregnant, and was expecting her child only weeks after we spoke. Jessica said that she was filled with joy, because she had always wanted a baby. "I'm an eternal optimist. I do believe I will fall in love and I'll have that partner; it's just happening in a different order," she commented.

Jessica credited her Buddhist practice with helping her stay grounded. She added, "After my mother's death, I saw the whole world differently; I felt nothing could be worse than what I witnessed her going through with cancer. That put everything else in perspective. As long as I'm not ill, everything else is manageable. Yeah, I'm disappointed that I'm not in love, and that I don't have my mom, but I have my health and my baby, so I can handle the rest."

· · · ·

BEFORE WE MET in person, Beth Goodman ended every phone conversation with the same enthusiastic cry: "Sprinkles!" I had no idea what that meant, but it seemed clear that this breast cancer survivor was full of joy and determined to share it with others.

Beth was running the Atlanta, Georgia, chapter of Sisters Network Inc., a national organization of African-American breast cancer survivors. We agreed to get together at their annual meeting, held in 2009 in Memphis, Tennessee. When I arrived at the hotel where the conference was taking place, I called up to her room. A few minutes later, a gorgeous, slender yet curvaceous woman with a dazzling smile walked out of the elevator. "Sarah!" she screamed and ran across the lobby to give me an engulfing embrace. I couldn't stop grinning for the next two hours as we talked. Beth's joie de vivre was contagious.

Beth was diagnosed with breast cancer in 2007, when she was 39. Her story might be an ordinary one—she got breast cancer, treated it, and has been living cancer-free ever since—except Beth Goodman is no ordinary woman. She relied on humor and her unquenchable vitality to not only survive but thrive. Throughout her journey, she found strength in the divine, genuine acceptance of her circumstances and a desire to help other women. In other words, Beth handled her cancer with exceptional grace.

While Beth's breast cancer initially was designated as stage zero, the classification kept escalating. It ended up at stage two because the cancer had invaded a lymph node. Beth asked her doctor, "Why do you keep upgrading me? Is there a sale on?" Her husband told her to get serious, but Beth said, "I have to laugh at this in order to get through it."

The doctor recommended a mastectomy with the option of reconstruction. Beth chose to have her new breast made with tissue from her own body. "I got a tummy tuck *and* a boob job out of it!" she cried with glee. "My body may be over 40, but this here is the 2008 model."

After the surgery, the doctor told Beth that there was a 30 percent chance that the cancer had spread. She could decide whether to have eight rounds of chemotherapy. Beth replied, "I don't want to live in percentages, let's go for the chemo." And that's when her passionate personality kicked into high gear.

"One of the pivotal points in my life is when I deemed myself the Pink Diva—which is what I started calling myself when I went to chemo," Beth explained. She decided that, since chemo was what she had to do to heal, she was going to make the best of it. "Day One, I brought pink pom-poms and an oversized clapper that lit up to the oncology ward. From the moment I got off the elevator until I reached the chemo area, I was clack-clack-clacking. People there were looking cancerous, for lack of a better term. I thought to myself, I have got to change the energy in this place. The staff said, 'Ms. Goodman, you're amazing, but you're crazy.' I said, 'I'm not Ms. Goodman, I'm the Pink Diva to you.'"

From then on, the Pink Diva showed up for all her chemo treatment sessions dressed in high heels and "a Fortune 500 suit," fully made up, wearing a wig and false eyelashes after she started losing her hair. She'd bring cupcakes and place a pink carpet under her chair. But her favorite part about chemo was the other patients. So one day Beth brought a video camera with her and shot videos of people sharing their stories. "I called it the *Boprah* show," she said. "That's Beth plus Oprah."

The last time Beth went in for chemo, a middle-aged gentleman whom she recalled having waved at a few times from across the room told her that he had purposefully been scheduling his treatments to coincide with hers. "You have no idea what an impact you've made on me," he said. Beth couldn't recall any specific conversations with this man, but he said, "I was about to give up before you talked to me. That's why I've wanted to be here when you were here ever since. You gave me the will to live." Beth picked up her napkin and dabbed a few tears from her eyes. "I had no idea how I'd lifted up that man. . . . That helped me realize that you never know what other people are going through. And it proved to me that, even if some people aren't accepting of my Pink Diva energy, I still have to give it out."

When Beth's hair began to fall out, she cut it off, "Halle Berry–style," and asked her hairdresser to give her a weave over the bald spot. While her five-year-old accepted her new look, her teenage son didn't like the idea of his mom being bald. "He said, 'People are going to know that you're sick with cancer.' I said, 'Well, that's okay.' But I agreed to wear a wig for his sake." She took her two sons wig shopping and let them help choose her new look.

Beth believed that her connection to Sisters Network came about divinely. She had already decided to go to one of their conferences to promote her sparkling apparel line before she had been diagnosed. The day Beth got the news of her breast cancer, she called Karen Jackson, the founder and CEO of the organization. Karen immediately went into action, asking Beth to fax over her results, informing her of next steps, suggesting what to read and how to prepare. "Karen was a real sister, pun intended," Beth said. "And when I went to my first conference, I met all these incredible women who have been an inspiration to me." She was delighted when Karen asked her to start up the Atlanta chapter of Sisters Network shortly after Beth had recuperated from her surgeries.

I asked Beth what the secret was to keeping up her spirits throughout breast cancer. She said, "Well, I've always suffered from PMA—positive mental attitude. Since the cancer, I suffer from PMA squared. I wouldn't act sick. I wouldn't allow the people around me to be sad and upset for me. People said, 'Why you? You're healthy, you exercise.' So I asked God, 'Why me?' He said, 'Why not you? You have the faith to get through this.' When you hear 'cancer,' most people hear death. I heard, 'Can, sir.' I knew I could do this.

"God blessed me with breast cancer so that I could be a blessing to others. I encourage people to live. I kept their spirits up in chemo. I encourage them to do their monthly self-exam. I give motivational speeches now, too. I have a slogan, which I love to share with people: 'Live life on purpose, for purpose, and with purpose, because it's that purpose in which you will have a life to live.'"

Beth added that the most challenging part of her experience was having had to rely on other people. Her husband and friends nursed her back to health, but it was a humbling time for Beth, who told me, "I felt like a burden. After a while, I found that it helped me to see how the other people in my life *wanted* to help me; they even felt blessed to be there for me."

As we wound up our meeting, I had to ask, "What's up with 'sprinkles'?" Beth howled with glee. "That's my word. Think back to your childhood. Adding a few sprinkles to your ice cream made all the difference in the world. Sprinkles change your mind-set. They bring us back to a place of youthfulness and joy. So I say 'sprinkles' all the time to give encouragement and lighten things up. And it becomes infectious—you have to 'sprinkle' back."

Adding It All Up

Both Jessica and Beth have done an admirable job of coping with fear from the threat of cancer, as well as the loss of one or both breasts. They have maintained positive feelings about their bodies and their sexuality throughout the process. But it can prove challenging to accept ourselves when we don't look the way we want, or when we feel we've lost our connection to our bodies. I don't specialize in cancer recovery and therefore can't claim to be an expert. However, I find this exercise useful in therapy sessions with women who are struggling with a negative body image—whether the cause is a recent breakup, a childhood trauma, or an illness. It also has proven effective in helping me let go of negativity about my forty-degree spinal curvature from scoliosis, which has haunted me since I was a child.

Look at each part of your body, starting with your feet and moving upward. Ask yourself, What is the benefit of my toes? What is the benefit of my legs? What is the benefit of my stomach, my fingers, my ears, and so on? This exercise helps you to reestablish your relationship with every single part of your body by recalling how it serves a function.

What happens, especially if we are ill or fighting changes to our bodies, is we tend to get so caught up in what we've lost that we forget to appreciate all we do possess. Many breast cancer survivors have told me that they become distraught at the perceived loss of their femininity. If you are in this position, I invite you to focus on the other parts of your body: Where else does your femininity reside? Close your eyes and conceive of what makes you feel sexual. It might be your playful eyes, your seductive voice, your gentle, arousing touch, the curve of your hips, the subtle depression between your collarbones, or the delicate arch of your foot. You can find great wonder in every part of you, and in the whole that these parts combine to create—a beautiful, powerful, capable you.

We often speak in our culture about how terrible cancer is. We live in dread of this pitiless bully. So another exercise I recommend is reflecting for a moment on the benefits of your situation. I once was counseling a diabetic. I said, "What gifts has your illness brought you?"

"No one has ever asked me that," he replied. He thought for a moment. "It's made me really conscious of everything that I put into my body. And it's made me more appreciative of being alive." A breast cancer survivor easily might have offered the same reply.

Whether your body is healthy and strong or you're fighting for your life against cancer, your vitality hasn't necessarily expired. You still can be sexy; you can be beautiful; you can be inspirational. The strength you possess and the challenges you face all add up to make you the woman you are. Once you own that fact, you'll have taken a huge step in the right direction.

PART II

CONNECTEDNESS

. . . .

Human beings are social animals. Just as wolves prefer to live in packs, birds in flocks, and dolphins in pods, so we generally thrive in the context of belonging to groups. We tend to identify ourselves by our membership in various social collectives—family, company, neighborhood, nation, tribe of friends, sports team, religious organization, college alumni association, rock band fan club, sewing group, breast cancer survivor status, and Facebook friend. We seek out ways to establish and enliven connections with others in order to give our lives meaning.

Connectedness means empathetic laughing with friends and loved ones as a way to keep going during the most challenging times in our lives. It means mentoring and being mentored by people, as well as simply cutting loose and having fun.

Female friendships, relationships with co-workers, and intimate partnerships are critically important to women. When and if we lose our sense of connection in one of these three key domains, we feel at a loss, experiencing loneliness, distress at lacking the support and insight other women provide, and unease in the workplace. Connectedness is critical to every aspect of our health and well-being. When we connect in a positive way, we share love, we learn, and we grow.

Four

FEMALE FRIENDSHIPS

. . . .

WHAT IS IT about female friendships? Scientific research, which until recently barely touched on the subject, now tells us that friendships are even more critical to our health and well-being than family relationships. For example, a study of nearly three thousand nurses with breast cancer found that those without close friends were four times as likely to die from the disease as women with ten or more friends. The proximity of the friends did not seem to be a factor. In other words, it wasn't a case of friends being able to provide hands-on support in the form of a cup of soup, a ride to the doctor's office, or emergency child care—even a phone call or e-mail would help. Surprisingly, the researchers discovered that, in sharp contrast to friends, having a spouse was *not* associated with survival.

When I think about my female friendships, the word that comes to mind is "nourishment." Girlfriends feed each other's souls. We tend to each other's wounds in times of need, celebrate each other's successes, and simply make day-to-day existence more fun. I find that I can drive myself crazy by getting caught up in my own thinking process. But when I'm with my girlfriends, I get out of my head and operate more from my heart. Friends also help me make sense of my purpose on earth—and of course, they make me laugh.

Laughter is one of the most important ingredients in a healthy, fulfilling life. Laughing with your friends can be your life support during your most trying times. Some of my favorite moments as an adult have been spent sitting around the dining room table in one of my girlfriend's homes with a gang of fabulous women, eating a simple meal of spaghetti carbonara and chocolate. If nothing else, we get to *vent*, which always feels good—even if our friends tell us, "Your life isn't as chaotic or as terrible as you think."

When we're with our girlfriends or a best friend, we let each other know our secret fantasies and our dark thoughts, as well as our most tentative dreams. We are likely to go to our female friends first when we are making a choice about whom to marry, where to live, which job to take, or what to say to the new neighbor who leaves trash in his yard. When our lives spin out of control, our girlfriends give us perspective, and come to our rescue.

As a psychotherapist, I have people coming into my office because of conflicts with spouses, children, parents, and other family members, even co-workers, but rarely with friends. That doesn't mean we don't have disagreements with our girlfriends—we do. Sometimes we cross each other's lines, accidentally insult each other, flake one too many times on plans, or don't pay close enough attention. But perhaps thanks to women's high emotional intelligence, it seems that generally we are able to work things out. We talk openly about our hurt feelings. We explain misunderstandings. We forgive, and we move on.

When it comes to meeting life's challenges with fortytude, our female friendships are linchpins. A close friend of mine once said that you can judge the quality of a woman by looking at her friendships with other women. And it's not necessarily the longevity or the quantity of friendships that give them value; it's quality. Friendships may endure for a moment or for a lifetime—and provide a powerful connection either way.

• • • •

JOAN HUBBELL IS a 43-year-old single mother and public defender in Los Angeles. If you met her now, you never would guess where she came from and how different a person she used to be. She attributes most of these changes to her friendship with one woman: Jessica Barmack.

Joan grew up in Dearborn, Michigan, in an evangelical Christian family. She and her family attended church twice a week. Her parents would not allow Joan to go on a date with a boy until homecoming of her senior year in high school, when she was 17.

Joan attended a Christian college in the Midwest, and, during those years, she started to feel depressed. She began to suspect that the life of a devout Christian in the Detroit suburbs might be in line more with her parents' values than with her own. So by her senior year, Joan had hatched an escape plan—apply to Radcliffe College's Publishing Procedures Course.

When she gained admission to the program, Joan was surprised and delighted. At the age of 22, still "as pure as the driven snow," she excitedly packed her bags and ventured to Cambridge, Massachusetts. There, she met Jessica—and her life changed course.

Jessica Barmack came from the opposite end of the spectrum in terms of upbringing. Her mother was in a committed relationship with a woman. Her father had remarried a physician from Kashmir and converted to Islam. Not only that, but in 1973, Jessica's parents had won the first joint custody case in the state of Massachusetts.

Joan and Jessica became friends in the publishing course and began spending time together. Jessica loved how Joan made her feel like a smart, wise person. Jessica said, "Joan had tremendous belief in me. I'm not sure why, and I'm not sure it was well-founded, but I also believed in me when I was with her."

Joan, meanwhile, said that Jessica made her feel understood, supported, and embraced. "I had so many fears when I left Michigan," she explained. "Would I be able to relate to anyone outside of my world? Would I be corrupted and ruined? Would I lose my family? Jessica had so much confidence and passion for life. In her presence, I felt like I could let go and jump in. Her complete acceptance of me, and her joy in our friendship, allowed me to believe that others might also regard me as an interesting person and not just a sheltered oddity."

After completing the Radcliffe program, Joan and Jessica decided to move to New York City, the hub of the publishing world, even though Joan originally had planned to return to Dearborn. The young women saw each other at least once a week and had a great deal of fun playing together in Manhattan. After Jessica later moved to Hawaii, the friends remained close and visited whenever they could.

It was during this time that Joan truly found herself, thanks in large part to Jessica's influence. Joan left the evangelical faith, attended graduate school, and became a social worker. If not for Jessica, Joan believes she probably would have gone back to Dearborn and remained an evangelical her whole life.

When they were in their 30s, Joan moved to Los Angeles, and Jessica moved back to Boston. They lost touch, but Joan's life continued on its Jessica-influenced trajectory. Joan now lives in Los Angeles with her three-year-old son and works in the district attorney's office. Jessica lives in a suburb of Madison, Wisconsin, with her second husband and six-year-old son, and works from home as a freelance editor and copywriter.

After being out of touch for a decade, Joan and Jessica recently reconnected on Facebook. Jessica had been trying to contact Joan for years but simply couldn't find her. The women had missed each other, and both had felt deep loss and sadness. Now they are excited to rebuild their friendship. They feel certain that they will get along as well as ever, especially since they both have young children.

Joan and Jessica were fortunate to find such a close connection at a young age. It is clear that they have influenced each other profoundly. And even if they slipped out of contact, one truth I've found is that women seem to be able to reconnect with ease after long separations. It is one of the beauties of female friendships—their power to endure.

Adult Friendships

By the time we've hit our 40s, we may feel as though we've already made all the friends we need. Between childhood and college, co-workers and other moms, our plates are full. Our network is solidly established, and we simply don't have the time or energy to add new people to the mix. But there can be moments when everything changes, and a wonderful new presence comes into our lives. This is especially likely to happen when we experience unexpected life events—negative or positive. And sometimes, those friendships that would never have happened otherwise prove to be the most powerful of all.

Livia and Aileen became friends later in life, brought close by a crisis. They met in graduate school, when both women were nearly 40.

Livia Iskandar has shoulder-length, curly brown hair and light brown skin. She was born in Indonesia and grew up in Jakarta, with the exception of five years she spent in Australia. Because of her time overseas, even though Livia is ethnically Indonesian, she feels as though she belongs to a third culture. She met and married her husband when she was in her 20s. Their first child was born while they both were studying for master's degrees in London on prestigious Chevening scholarships. They had their second child almost seven years later.

Upon returning to Jakarta from the United Kingdom, Livia was determined to do something to help her people. In her early 30s, she established a trauma recovery and psychosocial empowerment non-profit called Pulih. The organization works with survivors of violence and disaster, focusing specifically on women. Over the years, it gained recognition, and soon Livia had over sixty employees at four Pulih offices across Indonesia.

After several years, Livia and her family moved to Washington, D.C., where her husband had gotten a job with the World Bank. But after three years there, she realized that, in order to move forward with her career, she needed a doctorate. And so, at age 39, she decided to advance her education by completing a public health program in Honolulu. Her family opted to stay in D.C., with Livia visiting them every month or two.

The East-West Center program began with a two-week orientation, which included seminars as well as studies of Hawaiian culture and field trips. During this time, Livia became friends with another program participant, a 38-year-old Filipina woman named Aileen. Livia was surprised; she didn't think that she would have time to make new friends. She had assumed that she would be too busy with schoolwork and frequent trips back east.

Aileen Maypa grew up in a rural village in the Philippines and earned bachelor's and master's degrees in marine biology from Silliman University, a top-notch school there. She had been doing research on coral reef ecology and fisheries for over a decade when she came to the University of Hawaii on a Fulbright scholarship. The East-West Center then granted her a degree fellowship for the fourth year of her Ph.D. program in marine biology.

Aileen found Livia to be a charismatic woman with a deep passion for her ideals and humanitarian work. Aileen said, "Livia has an unyielding inner strength that may not be obvious to many people at first glance." Livia was fascinated by Aileen's work with fish, which required her to dive almost every day. The women shared several commonalities, although Livia was married with two kids and Aileen was single: they were both graduate students of the same age from the Asia-Pacific region, and they both had been involved in advocacy work in their home countries.

Livia and Aileen had known each other for only a few weeks when Aileen began preparing for a trip back to the Philippines to continue research for her dissertation. Livia imagined that Aileen might be excited to go, but one night Aileen shared with Livia that in fact she was terrified. A distant relative had been battling Aileen and her two siblings over a piece of land they had inherited from her grandfather and had hired hit men to assassinate them. Livia was shocked.

Aileen felt that she could trust Livia in part because she was a psychologist who had a lot of experience dealing with traumatic situations. As Aileen's departure date approached, she and Livia talked about what Aileen could do to be safe. Then Aileen gave Livia copies of her data and important papers and the keys to her office, as well as important contact information—in case anything should happen to her.

After Aileen got to her house, in a remote area of the Philippines, she realized that the situation was worse than she had anticipated, and her life was truly in danger. She was terrified, even though her brother had hired three bodyguards and she herself had black belts in three styles of martial arts. "I realized that politically connected families in that area can rule with guns and goons, disregarding the law," Aileen said. For the next thirty-nine days, she communicated constantly with Livia by e-mail, text message, and instant messaging. "Livia helped me keep my sanity, focus on my work, and maintain hope," Aileen told me.

Nevertheless, by the end of her fifth week at home, Aileen wasn't sleeping because she was constantly hyperalert. In addition, her asthma had acted up because of the stress. Livia decided that she couldn't keep the information about Aileen's situation to herself any longer—she was too worried that her friend would be hurt. She encouraged Aileen to tell her adviser what was going on, and Aileen agreed.

Livia and Aileen's adviser together convinced Aileen to return to

Hawaii early, even though doing so meant that she wouldn't be able to complete her research. Both Livia and Aileen felt tremendously relieved. "Livia was instrumental in pulling me away from harm," Aileen explained. What's more, in the weeks that followed, Livia helped Aileen to process the trauma of "being hunted."

Since then, Aileen and Livia have remained very close. They feel the Philippines episode made their friendship that much stronger. Livia was able to offer Aileen stability and guidance when she needed it most. Aileen said, "It showed me that there was somebody out there who would do everything to save me, no matter what."

These days, Aileen helps Livia deal with statistics. She has also shown Livia what single life is like. Livia said, "Aileen is able not only to concentrate on her studies but also to work full-time. She can be as workaholic as she wants to be. And there are many other talents she's been able to pursue, such as martial arts. Recently, I suggested that Aileen start a self-defense class for women, and she did. She's an inspiration!" Aileen commented, "We take turns listening to each other's academic, emotional, and cultural challenges, and support each other however we can." The two women, who'd met only a little over a year before I spoke with them, already had brought many blessings into each other's lives.

· · · ·

LIKE AILEEN AND LIVIA, Claire Mood formed a strong bond with another woman as an adult—and the friendship affected her life profoundly. Six feet tall with closely cropped hair, ebony skin, and huge brown eyes, Claire has a formidable presence. Within moments of meeting her, you are guaranteed to see an immense smile spread across her entire face, lighting up her soul. She opens her mouth and you hear her laugh—a totally free and uninhibited sound of joy, and you simply must laugh with her. You can feel her dynamism, and it draws you to her. You instantly want to be her friend.

I met Claire in Manhattan in 2006, when I was working as a therapist at the prestigious counseling, research, and training center, the Ackerman Institute for the Family. She was 45 years old at the time and came in for family counseling with one of her teenage daughters. Claire's four children had grown up in the care of Claire's mother while Claire lived on the streets, addicted to crack. As I got to know her better, I came to respect Claire deeply, not only as a client but as a woman. So when it came time to write this book, I asked her if she'd like to be interviewed, and Claire enthusiastically agreed.

Claire was born in New York City. Her father was in the military, so her family moved around a bit, living in South Carolina when Claire was a teenager. Throughout her childhood, Claire's mother verbally abused her—more than the other kids, she suspected, because Claire looked the most like her father. So when her mother abandoned the family and moved back to New York, Claire, 13 at the time, didn't know how to feel. She was both relieved and devastated.

Tragically, around the same time, Claire suffered sexual abuse at the hands of a few family members who lived nearby. The entire experience left her feeling empty, distraught, disconnected, and unhappy. As many survivors of incest do, Claire blamed herself for what happened.

By the time her father remarried and moved the family to Texas, a few years later, Claire had begun a downward spiral that lasted for more than a decade. She got pregnant at age 17 by a military colleague of her father's who wanted nothing to do with the baby. At age 19, she decided that she couldn't stand El Paso anymore and moved back to New York in a wishful attempt to reconnect with her mother.

After a few tough years as a single mother on welfare and failing to gain her mother's financial or emotional support, Claire turned to drugs. "I was 24 when I started using, right here in the Bronx," she said. "This was back in the eighties, when drugs were fierce in New York City. There was a rumor that the government had dropped crack cocaine out of a helicopter onto the Bronx to kill all the black people—it was that cheap, plentiful, and easy to get."

For a while, Claire used lightly, mostly smoking weed and occasionally shooting up heroin. She was able to hold down a job. But slowly, she started using more and more. "I was so lost at that time," she said. "Drugs were numbing. I was looking for love, looking to be wanted and needed. But really I was looking for who I was, searching for Claire."

One day, after giving birth to a second child, Claire was institutionalized for putting her hand through a glass window. That's when New York's Administration for Children's Services (ACS) took her children away. By the time she had her third and fourth daughters, Claire had decided to ask her mother to take care of the children. She figured at least that way she would know the girls were together, and she could get them back someday. Furthermore, Claire didn't think her mother would verbally abuse her children as much as she'd abused Claire herself, since her mother was now financially stable and married to a kind man.

As her drug addiction worsened, Claire began to prostitute herself. "Sleeping with men was the number one sure shot; they'd give you drugs in exchange. It was nothing," Claire said, tears coming to her eyes. "Anyway, in a way, my body was already numb from that bad stuff that happened to me in South Carolina as a girl."

After a while, Claire found that the using was "just insanity." She was doing the drugs out of habit—not even to get high anymore. Also, the comedown from a crack high was unbelievably difficult. She would become psychotic and start hallucinating if she didn't get another fix.

Eventually, Claire hit bottom and decided to get sober. "I was just tired," she recalled. "If you saw me then, you would grab your pocketbook, although I never did steal—I was that scary. I was maybe 32 at that time." In July 1997, she signed herself in to a ninety-day treatment program.

At the halfway house, Claire discovered an incredible support group. She said, "We called ourselves the Day One Sistahs because we became friends the first day of being sober, when we started our new lives. Most of us wanted to be in treatment, but we knew that getting sober is really about finding yourself as a person. We knew that we were quietly fighting for our lives and needed each other's support in order to win. Every day was a fight to attach to the 'normalcy' of sober life that we had long forgotten or never had. How do you get your life back together after you've been doing drugs and living on the streets for years? Every day was a struggle. All those women in the Day One Sistahood—we helped each other to grow."

Claire met her best friend, Ellen, at the halfway house, too. Ellen was there on relapse when Claire arrived and openly talked to the new arrivals about what that meant. She told the women to take it one day at a time, and Claire admired Ellen's strength and honesty.

For ten years, Ellen and Claire kept in constant contact, calling every day and getting together regularly. And while the other women relapsed, Ellen and Claire never did. In fact, Ellen went on to become the director of a drug rehab center. Claire admired the way Ellen could look at the reality of a situation and not falter but build new hope and take responsibility for what she'd done. Ellen told Claire to get her kids back. Claire had signed off on them at the time, but Ellen reminded her, "Those are your children. You should fight for them." And so she did.

After she got sober, the first thing Claire wanted to do was get a job. She found work helping people who were HIV positive, though miraculously Claire herself never had contracted the disease. She worked double shifts. In 2002 she started college, and she graduated magna cum laude in 2007. In 2006 she won custody of her children. Today she works as a supervisor and caseworker serving the homeless and is considering going back to school for a master's in nutrition.

Claire said to me, "You know, at first the Day One Sistahood was just for us girls who were getting sober together. But now I realize that every woman I meet is a Day One Sistah, if we can grow and learn from each other. Whenever I meet somebody, I try to give her something. So I look for all the women in my life to be my Day One Sistahs. You're a Day One Sistah, Sarah. It means, I know we have something to exchange. Your color doesn't matter—it comes from the heart. Being a Day One Sistah is something about being genuine. It's women who show character in its purest form. I just know when you are one."

Strength in Numbers

Another critical way in which women nurture each other through connectedness is in groups of friends. Women know that relationships do not have to be one-on-one to be influential and meaningful. Whether it be with a book club, knitting gang, support group for parents with kids in the same school or with similar disabilities, childbirth preparation class, or professional association, we find many ways to bond and support one another in groups.

One example is the Moonlight Mamas, a monthly gathering of new mothers in Livingston, Montana. Founded in 2006 by K. Lee Subik and Chantelle Braham, the group of fifty-odd women also reach out to each other regularly by e-mail and phone. But it's at their get-togethers that "they really let their hair down." K. Lee said, "Our purpose in starting the group was to be able to get out of the house, have a drink, and socialize. Chantelle and I were both new moms and felt like we needed more adult time. I came up with the name Moonlight Mamas because I envisioned us getting out at night under the energy and light of the moon."

The group meets once a month at a different member's house. Their ages range from mid-20s to late 40s—what brings them together is motherhood. They use the group as a networking system for buying

and selling baby stuff, finding babysitters, making event announce-
ments, and even job hunting.

Beyond simply enjoying socializing and networking with other
grown-ups, members offer each other a great deal of support. At and
outside the gatherings, they share tips for child rearing and validate
each other's feelings. "We all seem to be on the same playing field when
it comes to motherhood, regardless of our age or what we do or where
we came from," K. Lee said. "Knowing that you are not alone is very
reassuring."

· · · ·

ONE OTHER WOMEN'S GROUP I've really enjoyed getting to
know is the Whistle Creek Women. Composed of my mother, Meredith Brokaw, and three other women in their 50s and 60s—Nan, Laurie, and Julie—the gang gets together for an annual outdoor adventure
as well as regular horseback riding near Bozeman, Montana.

The group gave itself the name Whistle Creek Women after taking
a camping trip at Whistle Creek a few years back. Now they make a
weekend-long journey there every year. Twice, they have rented ca-
noes and gone down the Missouri River with no guides, retracing the
route of Lewis and Clark.

I had the opportunity to speak with both Nan and Meredith about
their experiences with the Whistle Creek Women. They immediately
emphasized the point that what bonds this group is not motherhood but
horses. "I've always thought the world could be divided into two
groups: people who love horses, and all the rest," Meredith explained.
"The history of the world was forged on horseback—all the wars were
fought on horseback . . . You have to appreciate what horses have done
for us humans." Nan explained that horses have been pivotal in each
one of the group members' life transformations, and in their friendship
as well.

Meredith didn't meet up with horses until she was in her early 40s and first went to Montana. But she knew instantly that she needed to make the animals a priority in her life, despite the fact that very few people in her city world had any idea why. She stood up for what felt essential for her happiness at the time, and she hasn't stopped since.

Each member brings her own unique personality and skill set to the group. My mother is very even keel, and she helps to get things organized; Nan contributes poetry and aesthetics. Julie is a nurse who takes recently expired medications—which are no longer legal to sell in the United States but still potent—to Ecuador as donations for the underprivileged. But while she dares to go to remote places, she is also very centered. Laurie lets loose when she is with the group. "You can always count on Laurie to have fun—she has the most contagious laugh ever," said Nan. "And she is by far the most expert horsewoman of our foursome."

Meredith explained that, in addition to bonding over their love of horses and the outdoors, the group members enjoy acting like they're 18 years old again, before they had husbands or kids. They talk about books they are reading and other passions.

Once I asked my mother just after she'd returned from a Whistle Creek Women's trip how it was. Without hesitating for a moment, she answered, "I'm 64, and I'll be doing this until I'm 80."

Loss and Gain

A woman I admire greatly, Najla Ayubi, a 38-year-old Afghan lawyer and women's rights activist, once said to me, "In order to achieve something, you have to lose something." The statement resonated deeply with me. I believe having that attitude is a fundamental part of fortytude.

As we approach our fifth decades, we will lose our youth. Even if we maintain our vitality, creativity, beauty, sexuality, and joie de vivre, we must accept the fact that we will continue to grow older. In order to stay positive and embrace life, we must stop focusing on what we lose and shift our emphasis to what we have to gain. And one of the greatest gifts we have to gain in these latter decades is the possibility of deepening and strengthening our female friendships.

As we grow older, the challenge becomes taking the time to nurture our friendships. We can become so caught up with our careers, families, and other commitments that we stop calling, e-mailing, or visiting our friends. Yet we should be careful not to give our friendships short shrift, especially knowing how powerfully they impact our happiness, health, and well-being over the long term.

There are plenty of ways to reconnect. Set up a lunch date. Make the phone call to the college roommate who keeps popping into your mind. Compose an entertaining e-mail for your moms' group. Or even just take a few minutes to review the status updates on your friend's Facebook page to see what she's been up to, then send her a message. No matter how busy you are, you can create time in your schedule to touch base with your girlfriends. These relationships will sustain and guide you during your most troubled times, so that you can endure and thrive.

Five

MENTORING

. . . .

THE FEMINIST MOVEMENT may have succeeded in many regards—today, women represent approximately half the workforce and can make their way to the top despite the still-existent glass ceiling in many professions. Yet, as Alice Eagly and Linda Carli pointed out in their article "Women and the Labyrinth of Leadership," we continue to find evidence of discrimination against female leaders: men are promoted more rapidly than women with equivalent qualifications, even in historically female career settings, such as nursing and teaching.

This pattern is attributable in part to the fact that traditionally female traits, such as compassion for others, sensitivity, helpfulness, and a communal orientation, are not necessarily considered qualities of a powerful leader, while the traditionally male traits of aggression, dominance, control, and self-reliance are. Yet when women do rise to managerial positions—perhaps in part because they have adopted some of the typical "male" traits—they tend to be perceived as more deceitful, pushy, selfish, and abrasive than male managers.

It's a catch-22 situation. Some of our greatest strengths as women are our intensity and understanding of emotion, and our ease in forming deep interpersonal bonds. Unfortunately in the workplace, we can feel pressured to cut off our feelings and maintain a "professional" distance from our colleagues. Many women I've worked with feel as if they have to compromise their relational and emotional qualities in order to get promoted to positions that men have typically held. Instead of being supportive and nurturing of other women in the workplace, they've had to compete with each other to get to where they want to be.

Fortunately, the workplace is changing. More and more women are rising to positions of power, and more evidence is accumulating that we can do every bit as good a job as men in top leadership roles. In fact, the forceful, aggressive management style of men may be falling out of favor. Studies show that women generally demonstrate a more inclusive, team-building leadership style. Also, in general, employees of female managers report feeling more understood, supported, and valued. Some management gurus speculate that the female leadership style may flourish in the twenty-first century, as humankind comes to realize that we must cooperate in order to thrive—and perhaps even to survive.

Mentoring Relationships

We often devote the majority of our attention to connections in our personal lives—our relationships with our parents, siblings, children, partners, and friends. Yet most of us spend at least one-third of our waking hours at work. If we nurture these professional relationships thoughtfully, they can afford us an opportunity to enhance our support network and our own well-being.

In particular, I'd like to emphasize the value of mentoring relationships, both formal and informal. When we were younger, we may or may not have benefited from having a more senior individual take a genuine interest in helping us find our way. Regardless, as we enter our fifth decades, we can pick up the mantle and be of service to the new generation just entering the workforce. The specific challenges and rewards women face when forging such connections may vary by place of employment. But without a doubt, we all can benefit from committing to becoming mentors, selflessly sharing our wisdom and expertise with others.

· · · ·

STEPHANIE MACK, a powerhouse of petite stature, has drawn upon the support of a mentor in creating a successful small business. Stephanie's mother's parents emigrated from the West Indies; her father was from the South. Her parents raised their five children with a strong belief in goals and education, and they taught their kids to carry themselves with pride.

Stephanie was born and raised in the Bronx. From a young age, she wanted to be a nurse, but the thought of being a doctor never even crossed her mind because no one spoke to her about how she might attain such a degree. Therefore, after graduating from high school, she followed her childhood dream and went to nursing school at Bronx Community College. She has worked as an R.N. ever since.

Over the years, Stephanie moved up the ladder as a nurse. Eventually, she was promoted into a managerial role and went back to school for an M.S. in public administration. Once she had assumed leadership responsibilities at work, Stephanie felt a powerful drive to strike out on her own, but she didn't know what she wanted to do.

Then, as she was approaching her fiftieth birthday, Stephanie came upon a business idea. New health care regulations were going into effect, requiring hospitals to shred all confidential records. In her managerial role, Stephanie had to figure out how to solve that problem. She ended up hiring a commercial shredding company to do the job—and saw an opportunity to provide similar services. "I immediately went online," Stephanie said. "I was astounded to find that there was a document destruction industry. I saw a real market that I could tap into, given my nursing background."

Stephanie shopped a business plan to friends and relatives, asking if they'd be willing to invest. One of her aunts, who had just retired, gave her a loan, as did a cousin and several neighbors (most of them female) who had known her for years. By 2001 Stephanie was ready to incorporate Just-N-Time Dynamics.

Next Stephanie had to figure out where and how to buy a shredder and a truck, which she could take around to local hospitals to destroy their paperwork. While searching for assistance, she made an important and unexpected connection with another woman who helped her to succeed.

When Stephanie went online to find shredders to purchase, she came across the contact information for Cherie Bartell, a woman in Pittsburgh who was running her own document-shredding business, called All Safe Document Destruction Service, Inc. Cherie, a 50-year-old retired teacher, had been in business for years and had built a million-dollar company working out of her kitchen. The two women spoke several times on the phone, with Cherie playing a mentorship role.

Before Stephanie had even bought one piece of equipment from her, Cherie invited Stephanie to visit her in Pittsburgh. Stephanie accepted. Cherie then shared with Stephanie everything she knew about how to run a successful document-shredding business. Stephanie said, "Cherie was very friendly, very open, and very supportive. She was happy to see another woman coming into the industry. She took me to lunch, to dinner, and to the plant. She showed me all aspects of the business." When it came time for her to purchase, Cherie showed Stephanie the ropes and stuck with her until Just-N-Time was up and running.

As soon as her business was turning a profit, Stephanie was ready to expand. A friend told her about Acción, a nonprofit organization that provides microfinance loans to small business owners. While Stephanie probably would not have qualified for a bank loan, Acción lent her the funds she needed.

Stephanie worked her tail off those first few years to get her business going strong, manually loading boxes and feeding paper into the shredder. These days she has an automatic truck that lifts and dumps the boxes for her.

Stephanie definitely finds it challenging to run her own business. She was the first in her family to take on such a task. The hardest piece, she found, was managing the financials. Stephanie said, "I may have given the company the appearance of being professionally run, but inwardly it was a struggle." Meanwhile, she continues to work full-time as a nurse supervisor at night. "You know why I do it?" Stephanie asked. "Because I don't want to take a salary out for myself. I put all the money back into the business. I will do whatever it takes for my company to make it."

Mentoring in the Military

Another venue in which women connect professionally is the military. Today women make up 15 percent of the U.S. armed forces. More than 230,000 American women have served in the wars in Iraq and Afghanistan. However, women are still underrepresented in military leadership positions, and their role in combat remains largely underappreciated by the general public. Although the Department of Defense does bar women from serving in assignments where the primary mission is direct ground combat, modern-day conflicts have no clear front lines, and female soldiers therefore often end up in the middle of the action. Also, women suffer from a higher rate of sexual trauma in the military—sexual harassment, assault, or rape. In this high-stress environment, women can offer one another critical guidance and support.

• • • •

BRIGADIER GENERAL LOREE SUTTON is one of only 57 women among the 875 total flag rank officers serving in the U.S.

military today. While her appearance is intimidating, with rows of medals and a star pinned to her dress uniform, complemented by short-cropped red hair and piercing blue eyes, her manner is instantly sincere and engaging.

Sutton, who grew up in Southern California, applied for an army health professional scholarship after gaining acceptance to medical school. While she never intended such a long career in the military, she has stayed with it ever since because she has grown to love and respect the profession, and those courageous enough to join it. As an army psychiatrist for over two decades, Sutton speaks as someone who "has been steeped in learning how to better foster resilience and mitigate the impact of trauma with respect to the human mind, body, and spirit."

As the head of the Defense Centers of Excellence (DCoE) for Psychological Health and Traumatic Brain Injury in Rosslyn, Virginia, Sutton feels blessed to be working on the cutting edge of cultural change. She is supporting military leaders at all levels in transforming their historic "suck it up and drive on" mind-set. Rather she encourages them to embrace a public health model that emphasizes strong partnerships—on both the battlefield and the home front—with peers, families, units, and communities. She explained, "Our message is simple, yet powerful: you are not alone; the unseen wounds of war are real; treatment works, and sooner is better; and lastly, reaching out is an act of courage and strength."

This daunting mission tracks its origin to the growing recognition in 2007 that, thanks to medical advances, the military was saving the lives of those who would not have survived previous conflicts. Complex conditions resulting from improvised explosive devices employed in both Iraq and Afghanistan comprise myriad injuries, including internal organ damage, traumatic brain injury, and other unseen psychological, moral, and spiritual wounds of war, which often turn out to be the most deadly of all. Committed to eliminating stigma, Sutton and her team lead a holistic effort, harnessing integrative approaches such as yoga, acupuncture, meditation, nutrition, and animal-facilitated therapies, as well as more traditional treatment options.

Her voice intensifying, Sutton stated, "I am impatient. This is not business as usual—the suffering is real *today*, so we must deliver what we have now, and continue to improve every single day. To paraphrase Churchill, never in the history of our republic have we placed so much on the shoulders of so few on behalf of so many for so long. Anyone who questions the strength of these remarkable individuals needs to visit our wounded warriors. It breaks my heart to see what they and their loved ones are experiencing, but I always leave humbled, inspired by their intrepid spirit, courage, and dedication to each other."

Brigadier General Sutton admitted to me that she grimaces inside when reporters ask her what it's like to be a woman in uniform. "The smart aleck in me is tempted to retort, 'It's hard to say, given that I've never experienced being anything else!' There's truth to that: I don't know. What I bring to all my missions is who I am, Loree Sutton as a human being. Yes, I'm an officer who happens to be a woman. And as a senior leader, I accept responsibility for educating, mentoring, and coaching at all levels to mitigate the unique stresses of being a woman in uniform. Yet I also work to strengthen cohesive bonds regardless of gender or, for that matter, religion, race, or sexual orientation. In the end, we are fellow warriors; we are brothers and sisters; we are human beings, learning to live, love, and serve on this small planet of ours. Truly, we're all in this together."

While Sutton strongly prefers seeing herself as an officer and physician in uniform, as opposed to a woman in uniform, there can be no doubt that she has forged inroads on behalf of all women in the military. Yet especially in matters of warfare, peacekeeping, national security, community resilience, and psychological well-being, Sutton is right: in the end, we are all just human.

Mentoring Through Volunteering

Yet another important venue for forming connections outside the family domain is through volunteering. According to the Bureau of Labor Statistics, about one-quarter of Americans volunteered through an organization at least once in 2009, with women volunteering at a slightly higher rate than men. The average amount of time spent on volunteer activities was fifty-two hours per year.

Marianne O'Grady is a stout, matter-of-fact woman in her mid-40s. She has mentored people through her volunteer work. Through years of dedicated effort in Afghanistan, she has even founded her own nonprofit, School Is Open.

Marianne has been teaching second grade in San Francisco for twenty years. She had always wanted to work overseas, but as an elementary school teacher, she felt that she had nothing to offer. Then, about five years ago, around her fortieth birthday, Marianne sat down to consider her strengths—and she had an epiphany. She realized that kids around the world need teachers. Marianne had already been training teachers for years, working nights at a graduate school of education. And she had a perfect schedule to do such work overseas, since she got off all school holidays, including two months over the summer.

So one day, Marianne started searching the Internet for places that needed more teachers. She figured she might as well go to a war zone halfway around world, because she'd surely find "a slight level of adventure" there. She came across some information about a program in Afghanistan—a country where, for thirty years of wartime, people basically hadn't gone to school, much less been trained as teachers. Many teachers had eighty to a hundred students in their classrooms at a time, with multiple classes rotating through each day for just three-hour shifts.

Six weeks later, Marianne was on the ground volunteering. She brought college teaching courses and supplies to people in rural villages who, for reasons of poverty and remote location, couldn't otherwise get training. After making a few visits with the educational nonprofit she'd discovered online, Marianne decided that she could do a better job on her own and founded School Is Open. Although it required mountains of paperwork and serious elbow grease, Marianne soon triumphed in getting her organization not only 501(c)(3) status in the United States but also official registration in Afghanistan.

Marianne said that she never would have set out to conquer such an immense task in her 20s or 30s. "Getting this done was a matter of life experience. In my 40s, many things in my life have gotten wider—my hips, my vision, my skill set, my idea of how the world functions, my career, and my life through volunteering. Everything is wider."

Men and women come together for Marianne's training sessions, which she enjoys tremendously. "I watch the people I teach in Afghanistan. They look really old, although they're not; they're just worn. They have nothing modern—no electricity, no cell phones, no computers. So I'm watching this guy with a big gray beard and a giant turban, who I've been told for a long time is probably a terrorist, play around with a two-dollar magnifying glass I've brought with me. He is a science teacher, and he has some education, but he has never seen one of these in his whole life. He acts like a five-year-old playing with the magnifying glass. He's so excited! He holds it up to his eye, and then to another person's eye, and nothing of the thirty-year war is left there in his aura. It's gone, for him and for everyone else there. They're turned on. They're empowered. And I'm just standing there, giggling and crying and gazing on in awe. So I try to get back there as often as I can."

Breaking Down Barriers at Work and Beyond

Many of us worry about drawing boundaries at work. We want to maintain a professional distance from our colleagues, imagining that, if we get too personal, our behavior might be considered inappropriate, or we risk exposing our weaknesses. Certainly it's important to ensure that our co-workers feel as though we are trustworthy, and we don't want to fail to maintain a professional demeanor. But, at the same time, we can become too fearful, too constrained, and too hesitant to reach out to those who surround us at work and in volunteer settings. As a result, we can miss out on valuable opportunities to connect.

The responsibility for forming mentoring ties falls on us, as women approaching midlife. We can capitalize on our strengths as relational beings to reach out. I therefore invite you to make an effort to break down the barriers between you and your more junior colleagues—the female ones, especially. We women are still at a disadvantage relative to men in the working world, so we must make a conscious effort to build our networks and enable other women to succeed.

Six

INTIMATE PARTNERSHIPS

. . . .

MANY YEARS AGO, I was reading the newspaper when a marriage announcement caught my eye. A preacher had said to the newlyweds: "Marriage, in effect, is with a stranger about whom you have a magnificent hunch." Days later, I found myself perplexed by this quotation, and still pondering what it meant. I thought, How can that be? Most people spend so much time getting to know their future spouses before making such a serious commitment . . . How could they ever look at each other as strangers?

So I started to pay close attention to and ask questions of couples who had been married, seemingly happily, for years. I soon realized that what the preacher had said appeared to be true. Sure, these individuals might have had laundry lists of requirements for potential mates, including education, looks, intelligence, height, values, hobbies. But once the proverbial boxes had been checked, what determined how people selected their mates? I could not uncover any scientific formulas or magical secrets. Mostly, it seemed to be their intuitive sense that this was "the one." They would tell me how much they had learned about their partners since, which they hadn't known at the time they got married. They would point out that you never know how people will grow and change. Most of them considered themselves lucky to have chosen so well.

Naturally, I consulted my mother and father for their opinion on this subject. Together for forty-seven years, my parents may be an anomaly when it comes to modern-day love. Though they've always led frenetic lives, they are still completely in love and remain committed to one another. They met in high school and got married when my dad was 22 and my mom just 21. They concurred that they'd had little more than a "magnificent hunch" about each other at such tender ages.

Intrigued by what brings and keeps people together, I took classes in couples therapy in grad school. As I earned my master's in social work at New York University, I conducted fieldwork on the dynamics between spouses. Eventually this led to my work at the Ackerman Institute.

During the eight years of my internship and employment at Ackerman, I observed my colleagues and they watched me through a one-way mirror as we facilitated couples therapy sessions. We would then give each other feedback. I found this a fascinating way to learn about relational dynamics. I gradually incorporated couples work into my private practice and have since had the opportunity to work with people in all stages of their relationships, from first encounter through dating for just a few months to married for years.

You might think that, having worked for nearly a decade as a couples therapist, I would have become jaded. But the opposite is true. While I've always understood and appreciated that my parents' situation is rare, and while I've had my own interesting moments when it comes to romance, I've nevertheless held firm to the idea that marriages do not have to end in divorce or deep-seated discontent. It's true that, by the time many couples come in for counseling, they are teetering on the edge of a breakup. Yet I have witnessed enough success stories and am enough of an optimist myself to believe that, ultimately, an intimate partnership can provide the opportunity for sharing an incredible life adventure with another person.

In this chapter, we explore connectedness within the context of an intimate relationship. But before we get started, I'd like to make one thing clear: I am not talking about marriage per se. Whether you are married or not, in a long-term relationship, living with a boyfriend or girlfriend, just starting to date someone, gay or straight or somewhere in between, relationships are relationships, and the issues are serious for everyone. We'll meet couples whose relationships have stood the test of time and discuss factors that sometimes undermine partnerships. I'll present cognitive-behavior exercises designed to facilitate a more powerful connection. And we'll also talk about infidelity, a challenge that many women have faced—and one that most certainly requires fortytude to handle well.

The Four Horsemen

In my search for the "magnificent hunch," I may not have found the secret to selecting the perfect mate. But my investigations *did* reveal how successful partnerships endure. Especially when compared with people who have suffered greatly in their marriages, I found that the most content couples consistently demonstrate a great deal of curiosity about and respect for the other person.

My parents serve as wonderful models of this quality. Throughout the decades that their marriage has survived and flourished, I have witnessed them engage with interest in the other's career and personal pursuits. They ask questions, share insights, and inspire and support one another without fail. They may have moments of frustration with each other, but they always treat each other with respect.

My conclusions were confirmed during my training as a couples therapist, when I studied the work of Dr. John Gottman, a renowned relational therapist. He argued that conflict in intimate relationships is inevitable; what matters is how we handle it. Gottman famously described "Four Horsemen of the Apocalypse" in long-term relation-ships: criticism, defensiveness, contempt, and stonewalling. If he observed signs of these behaviors and emotions during a couples therapy session, he found, the partnership would be unlikely to endure.

Criticism occurs when people believe that there is something "glob-ally wrong" with their partners. Instead of focusing on specific behaviors that are troubling, critical people attack their loved ones' personalities and characters. Defensiveness is defined as making excuses, refusing to take responsibility, or offering up another complaint in response to neg-ative feedback. Contempt, in Gottman's words, is "any statement or nonverbal behavior that puts oneself on a higher plane than the other partner." It is a blatant sign of disrespect. Stonewalling takes place when the listener withdraws from the interaction, leaving the partner isolated and blocked out.

Gottman noted that, for most couples, the four horsemen inevita-bly show up from time to time. It is when they take up permanent residence that a partnership is seriously jeopardized. Also, in the work I've done with my client couples, I've discovered that, in gen-eral, these issues do not appear all at once. Rather there are moments or even whole days when a particular challenge or two rears its ugly head.

Battling the Four Horsemen

I've found that a powerful step in getting people to work out their rela-tionship issues is to have them identify for themselves when the four horsemen appear. We talk through the concept, and I provide a written description of the four horsemen as a way to help them recognize these bad habits later. I then assign them the task of observing and noting on paper the moments these qualities show up in their interactions with one another. At first, it can prove easier to identify the issues in your partner's behavior. So I encourage individuals to reflect honestly on how their own behaviors might exemplify one of the challenges, and to make note of these incidents, too.

Most of the time, I find couples very interested in examining the ways they might be undermining their relationships. They take their homework seriously and quickly become motivated to rebuild respect and demonstrate curiosity about each other's lives. Gottman identified several tactics for doing just that, including the following:

- Cultivate a friendship with your partner by taking time every day to confide in one another, listening attentively to each other's feelings and ideas.
- Actively nurture respect by paying attention to your partner's positive qualities. Focus on what attracted you to each other in the first place.
- Always behave respectfully toward one another. Never call each other names, belittle each other, or make unkind comments in front of other people.
- Validate each other. Pay each other compliments. You have the power to tear each other down, but you also have the power to build each other up.
- Listen to each other. Men, in particular, may not let their partners influence them. Yet Gottman has shown that healthy couples share power.
- Forgive. You won't survive if you can't move past harm the other person has caused. It may take some time, but find a way to work through it together.
- Take a break. When a conflict heats up, issues are more likely to appear. Step away for twenty minutes to calm your body down, and then resume the conversation.
- Pick your battles. Not everything is worth fighting for; some things you just need to let go.

- Keep things positive. Gottman's research has shown that a five-to-one ratio of positive to negative interactions makes a relationship last.
- Work on yourself. Don't put all the responsibility on your partner's shoulders. You are half of the relationship.

Reigniting the Flame

While Gottman's research has proven tremendously valuable in my work, I've also discovered that not all couples are battling the four horsemen. Some of them simply find themselves bored with or disengaged from their partners. I've counseled a number of women who had been married since their early 20s. Their typical complaint was "When you've been married for this long, you get so wrapped up in the daily lives of others—your children, your in-laws and extended family, your friends, your co-workers, and even your spouse's colleagues from work—that eventually you lose the emotional connection to one another."

In response to this issue, I introduce several exercises that I learned during my years at the Ackerman Institute. All are based on the belief that you can reignite the flame in your marriage or long-term relationship with the use of rituals. I invite the women or couples I'm counseling to think of three rituals that they would be willing to perform with their partners and make a commitment to doing them on a daily or weekly basis.

An example of a ritual is to take a piece of information from, and leave a piece of information with, one another every day. In the morning, check in before you both take off for your day's activities. Tell your partner about something that will happen during your day, such as "I'll be taking the kids to the zoo" or "I've got to submit a report by noon." Ask about something that will happen during his or her day. When you reunite that evening, recall what your partner said to you, and ask how that particular event went. Have your partner do the same for you. It may seem like no big deal, but this simple ritual can offer a straightforward, effective way for you to stay closely connected.

Another example of a ritual is to celebrate each other's triumphs, big and small. Sherri complained that she felt like she was in a rut and didn't know if her husband recognized it. I asked her to describe what she meant by "rut," since we can experience such malaise quite differently. She immediately stated, "Well, for instance, when Tim and I were newlyweds, we would always do active things together. I also used to run in 5K races, and Tim would come cheer me on. Now, fifteen years into our marriage and two kids later, the only running I do is around the house like a chicken with its head cut off, trying to maintain order."

When I asked Sherri if she felt motivated to run 5K races these days, she said in a defeated tone, "Yeah, but who is going to watch me run? Part of the fun is having someone cheer you on from the sidelines. Tim used to, but now we have all this other stuff going on in our lives. We go to our kids' sporting events, but I can't imagine that Tim still would want to come to mine."

After hearing Sherri express her frustrations, I invited her to think about the possibility of creating a ritual with Tim in which they celebrated a small daily personal triumph together. I suggested that they could build up to bigger triumphs from there. For example, if Sherri started to train for a 5K race by running again on a daily basis, Tim could celebrate that success by running with her some days. This would serve a twofold purpose by also providing a way for Tim and Sherri to spend quality time together. They could have an even bigger celebration together after she had run the 5K, perhaps inviting the kids to join in. In return, Sherri would celebrate one of Tim's successes every day, such as getting an eagle on a long par five on the golf course. When Tim participated in a local golf tournament, they could have an even bigger celebration.

A third ritual I recommend to my clients is trying something new together on a weekly basis. This can take the form of anything that piques both partners' curiosity. For example, one couple in my practice expressed an interest in rock climbing, so I encouraged them to take lessons together. They found classes at a local gym and started going once a week. They loved it. Rock climbing not only improved their physical fitness but also boosted their enthusiasm for life and each other. Furthermore, it gave them something to bond over. When I used to attend weekly boxing classes in New York City, I noticed many well-seasoned couples who seemed to enjoy nothing more than sparring with each other in the ring. What better way to get out your marital frustrations? As long as you refrain from harming the other person, sparring actually brings you closer together.

If there are no gyms near you with rock-climbing walls and/or boxing rings, you may need to work together on coming up with creative ideas. You don't have to participate in something physical together. The point is to find a stimulating activity that you both can enjoy. You might consider taking a cooking class and learning to make a new dish every week. Perhaps you'll schedule a weekly visit to a local museum or nightclub. Or maybe you'll just agree to establish one night a week when you both stay home and watch a movie that makes you laugh or read a book together. The options are infinite.

Regardless of which of these activities you choose—or if you decide to make up one of your own—the point is that establishing shared rituals can help you emotionally reconnect with your spouse or partner. It starts with the simple commitment to spend time together. Then you take things a step further by truly using that time to connect, pay attention to your partner, appreciate his or her best qualities, and enjoy each other's company. They require effort and determination on each end, but taking these steps will lead you down the path to reestablishing a healthy, positive bond with your partner. If you realize how much fun you're having together, who knows where your creative energies might take you next?

Infidelity

So far we have been discussing long-term relationships in which, we presume, both people want to stay connected. But what happens when one or both partners choose to stray? A graduate school professor of mine once said that affairs are more permanently destructive than most people realize. They are traumatic to those who are cheated upon, and they wreak havoc on the person who cheats, generating feelings of guilt and shame.

There is room for reconciliation and forgiveness. Occasionally, an affair even serves to bring a couple closer together by helping them resolve issues that had been festering, untouched, for months or years. However, this is not generally the case. According to research conducted by the National Opinion Research Center at the University of Chicago, 17 percent of women and 20 percent of married men report having been unfaithful. And only 35 percent of unions survive infidelity.

In my practice, I've observed that many people cheat at moments when they feel vulnerable, for instance after the death of a parent. This is when we, as relational beings, most need to connect with others. Also, women tend to have affairs after their partners have lost their jobs. Perhaps they feel that their husbands are no longer fulfilling their roles as providers.

In addition, many people face a conflict between their desire to stay in a committed relationship and their equally powerful desire to stray from it. From a neurological and psychological point of view, human beings are attracted to continuity and sameness, to safety and a sense of being home. Yet, at the same time, we feel a powerful pull toward adventure. We fantasize about escaping from home to find our true selves and live out a grander destiny. Our comfortable, safe, cozy houses can turn into prisons. How do we resolve this dilemma? Often, the answer is: have an affair.

Women Who Cheat

In 1976 Gail Sheehy's book *Passages* became the go-to source for adults experiencing crises at various points in their lives. The back cover copy read: "Sheehy shows a new generation how to embrace change and achieve productivity and fulfillment at any stage in life." When I looked at the chapter entitled "Catch-30" and the chapter on the 40s, I could see how some of the issues had changed. For example, Sheehy assumed that, for the most part, men would have careers, whereas women would be housewives struggling to form their own identities. However, many of the concerns people face during those two decades—including infidelity—have remained the same.

Without a doubt, both men and women have affairs. In many cases, this decision is driven by the biological urge to have sex, along with the desire for adventure and "something new" that we discussed. But another factor enters the picture for women as they approach their fifth decades. While Sheehy identified this phenomenon in the 1970s, it has been my experience as a therapist and as a woman in her late 30s as well: 40 is a dangerous age for infidelity among women.

Why are women particularly susceptible to cheating when they are in their late 30s and early 40s? The reasons are the same as they were thirty-five years ago. Sheehy argued that, as women hit the age of 35, they believe they have only a five-year window left in which to have an affair. They feel that, once they are older, men will no longer find them desirable—so they had better take advantage of their sexual allure now. You could call this "the second biological clock." I have found that the subject of infidelity arises frequently in my sessions with married women aged 35 to 45: "Should I or shouldn't I?" Or "Now that I have, should I stop?"

An affair can be incredibly alluring to many women in committed relationships. It offers external validation of our physical attractiveness. It proves that we are still worthy of male attention. It's an ego boost. And it's a way to stave off that creeping, dreaded sense of our own mortality. Yet most women—like most men—caught up in the panic of midlife do not want to give up the comforts of their marriages or risk being alone.

For single women over the age of 35, having an affair with a married man may present a more attractive option than ever before. As we get older, we may fear that all the "good men" have been taken, and therefore married men are our best bets.

• • • •

MOST WOMEN WHO CHOOSE to have an affair are seeking connectedness—with their new lovers, with themselves and their youth, perhaps even with their original partners through a rekindling of sexual desire. So that we might learn from their stories, I offer here two examples of women who traveled varying distances down the path of infidelity, with different outcomes.

Betsy began an affair around the age of 35. Married when she was only 22, Betsy had two kids by the time she was 27. As her fortieth birthday loomed closer, George, an old friend from high school, moved back to her small town. "We kept bumping into each other, and it didn't seem like a coincidence. It felt like fate was bringing us together," Betsy told me.

Betsy came to see me for counseling when she was mid-affair. She said it surprised her that, when she started sleeping with George, her marriage wasn't falling apart. "It wasn't how I imagined things would be," Betsy said. "I always thought women who cheated must be miserable at home. But my husband and I were quite content." While she still loved her husband, and wanted to keep the family together for the sake of the kids, she was torn because George made her feel "so good."

"Is this affair about you and your husband outgrowing each other?" I asked. "Or do you think it might be more about how you're relating to yourself?" When she looked deep inside, Betsy admitted that she had been feeling as though aging had set in rapidly, and she thought this might be her last chance to enjoy her sexuality. But the more she thought about it, the more she wanted to recommit to her marriage.

So we explored ways that Betsy could find more fulfillment and that sense of vitality she'd had with George within the context of her marriage. To reconnect with herself, Betsy began attending pole-dancing classes, which she loved. "There are only women in there. Funny, but I realized that, because I am not attracted to the other women, nor do I want to turn them on, I just focus on me and my gangly legs wrapped awkwardly around the pole." She giggled. "Believe it or not, this makes me feel sexy and sensual."

• • • •

MARY ALSO MARRIED young, at age 23. Her husband, a highly paid attorney, put her down constantly, claiming that she was overweight and not smart enough for him. So by the time Mary began seeing me, at age 38, she had no self-esteem and suffered from an eating disorder. We worked hard to rebuild her sense of self and find ways for her to take control of her life. Mary chose to take up spinning classes and manage her diet, and as a result she lost a lot of weight. The mother of four, she had not worked in years, so she also decided to begin volunteering.

Once Mary was feeling better about herself, she found men attracted to her. This boosted her self-esteem even further. Eventually, she started an affair with a man from the nonprofit organization where she volunteered. Mary's husband had belittled her for over fifteen years. When she was with him, she became quiet as a mouse. Here was a man who told her that she was sexy, smart, beautiful, and fun. She blossomed around him. Mary wasn't sure that she wanted to make her marriage work. She felt that she and her children might be better served by her separating from her husband, and sometimes that is the case.

Have you, like Betsy, lost touch with your sexuality? Are your physical and/or emotional needs not being met, as was the case with Mary? If either of these scenarios rings true for you, I invite you to slow down and reconsider your actions before you go looking for a new lover to "solve your problems." Begin by seeking the answers inside yourself. Ultimately, we are responsible for our own self-confidence and fulfillment. There are many ways to find excitement, experience stimulation, and build your sense of self without having an affair. You might choose to stay in your relationship, or you might choose to leave. But if you stray in the meantime, you are likely to do more harm than good—to your partner and to yourself.

Men Who Cheat

Of course, women are not the only perpetrators of infidelity. Men cheat, too. As we have seen, what motivates many women to have affairs as they enter their fifth decades is the desire to feel vital and desirable again. Men also have affairs because they want to feel vital and desirable. Yet, in my experience, they are less motivated by age. They simply don't have the same biological clocks as do women, nor do they feel the same societal pressure around hitting 40. They want to feel desired by other women at any age!

When it comes to our partners being unfaithful, the question is not so much why they do it but rather how we choose to handle it. Sandra West offers an example of someone who faced her husband's affair head-on.

Sandra, 43, and her husband Phil, 44, had been together for ten years, and they had two children under the age of ten. They met through their work at a biotech company in San Francisco, started dating, and moved in together not long after. Three years later, they got married.

Within two years of tying the knot, Sandra and Phil were pregnant with their first child. "It was the happiest time of our relationship. On a scale from one to ten, we were at an eleven," Sandra told me as she pulled her glasses off and wiped the tears from her eyes. "We were at this dinner party where people were describing the most intimate things they'd ever done. Most people talked jokingly about their wildest sex acts. But when it came to Phil, he said, 'Having a child.' And it was so true. It made us so intimate. We were incredibly connected during the first few years of our baby's life. We had so much fun."

Five years later, baby number two came along, and things changed. Phil had been reluctant to have a second child, but Sandra had felt strongly that their first child needed a sibling. Eventually, Phil had caved to Sandra's desire. So when number two turned out to be a real handful rather than the easy, peaceful baby their first had been, Phil expressed little empathy for Sandra's plight. "I was complaining one day about how exhausted I was, and Phil just said, 'Well, this is what you wanted.' I shut down after that. I couldn't talk to him about anything related to my stress and strain with the kids from then on."

As Sandra and Phil struggled to provide for and raise their two children, their connection to one another grew more and more faint. Meanwhile, Phil made a new friend, Amy, an attractive woman ten pounds slimmer and eight years younger than Sandra, who also was married with three kids.

Sandra exploded when she discovered that Phil and Amy were having an affair. She ordered Phil to pack up his bags and leave. Phil started crying, saying, "I'm so sorry" and "It was a huge mistake." He had slept with Amy only once, he claimed. The whole emotional affair had lasted only eight weeks. Couldn't Sandra find it in her heart to forgive him?

"I was enraged," she said. "Then, all of a sudden, as he was putting his suitcase in the trunk, I thought, Where do I want him to go? Am I sending him right to her arms? So I changed my tone and said, 'You should stay.'"

At that moment, Phil and Sandra committed to working things out. A key part of Sandra's approach was not making the affair into a bigger deal than it needed to be. "I didn't have to tell some sob story," she said. "I chose to view it as an unfortunate but forgivable transgression. And he's genuinely sad and remorseful about it." Meanwhile, Phil agreed to go to therapy to work on his issues. As a result, he's been learning to take better control of his temper. He is doing things, like losing weight, to boost his self-esteem. He's also focusing on paying Sandra more compliments and being kinder to her.

In addition, Sandra has come to understand the role she played in the affair. She did not make Phil feel sexually desirable, she discovered. "I was too hard on him," she can admit now. She has been working in therapy to focus on Phil's positive qualities and to express feelings of love and appreciation more often. She's loosened her control of their calendar and is allowing more spontaneity to arise.

Nevertheless, Sandra understandably has experienced frequent moments of frustration, uncontrollable anger, sadness, and vindictiveness. She admitted that things have been far from perfect in her relationship with Phil since the affair. They both snap and say mean things to each other. Sandra feels waves of venomous rage toward Amy. "I struggle with feelings that I hope she'll get a virulent form of cancer," Sandra said.

I have noticed that Sandra's wanting Amy to disappear is a common sentiment among the women with whom I have worked on infidelity issues. Why do wives tend to hold "the other woman" primarily responsible for the affair rather than their husbands? It's easier to direct their anger at a third party outside the intimate relationship, especially if they want to work things out with their partners. This is a natural tendency. But while I do invite forgiveness when infidelity occurs, I also believe it's best to lay the accountability where it belongs—on both parties involved. Don't let your partner off the hook too easily. If you do, you may avoid the very work you need to do to help you survive the next alluring person who shows up in either of your lives. You may miss the painful yet valuable opportunity that infidelity can provide to shift yourselves and your relationship in a more positive direction.

Stay or Stray?

I use this exercise with clients who either are having affairs themselves or have caught their partners cheating. I find it helps them answer the question that lies beneath the anger, excitement, curiosity, sadness, and other emotions that arise in the event of an affair: Am I in or out of this relationship?

Before we begin, I let clients who are doing the cheating know that they're not criminals. People in our society are immediately demonized for infidelity. As a therapist, I take off the judgmental hat. If they're the ones being cheated on, I let them know that they are not alone—infidelity is incredibly common. It doesn't mean there is something wrong with them.

Next, I ask my clients to breathe. Yes, just breathe. Whether you're the cheater or the cheated one, the situation creates anxiety. Breathing deeply is the most effective and efficient way to open up an honest dialogue with yourself.

Once clients are breathing well, I do not dive into the reasons they or their partners had an affair. Instead, I ask, "When was the last time you were really happy?" I get them talking about what worked in their relationship at the start. How did they end up with their partners in the first place? This helps draw them out of the present moment, and reminds them that *now* represents only one tiny fraction of the entire relationship.

Then I encourage my clients to explore their feelings about themselves, especially if they are women approaching midlife. It can become so easy to focus on the other people involved in affairs—the partner, the lover, and the children. "Where are *you* in the midst of all this?" I ask. I invite my clients to tell me how they feel about themselves on a scale from one to five, with one being terrible and five being great. Then I ask, "How did you contribute to those feelings?" You can't place all the blame for your feelings—whether you're on a high from an affair or a low from being cheated on—on others. You do have control over your own life. Where do you want to take things from here?

Next, I suggest that couples who want to stay together follow Dr. Gottman's advice, as discussed at the beginning of the chapter, to try to recapture positive feelings and move forward. But if one or both partners aren't willing to do their work and make improvements, it may be time to get out.

Connected to Yourself

Throughout this process, stay connected to the most important person of all: yourself. Our focus in this chapter has been on connectedness to an intimate partner. Intimacy can prove critical to our well-being. Yet one of its greatest hazards is that we can lose ourselves in our relationships, becoming codependent.

Also, especially when it comes to affairs of the heart, other people love to chip in with their two cents. However, it is best to turn down the volume of others' voices. It's easy to look to others for answers when we're struggling with such major, life-altering issues, but we must examine ourselves fearlessly and come up with our own solutions. Therapists are not fortune-tellers or all-seeing gods; we don't necessarily know what is best for you. Relationships can appear totally different in the office setting than behind closed doors when it is just the two of you. I never tell my clients what to do, or if I think their relationships can or should not work.

Fostering a strong, loving connection with an intimate partner, especially over years and even decades, definitely takes work. I advise my clients to treat their relationships like part-time jobs: a long-term relationship is a responsibility to which you must devote time and effort if you want to reap the rewards. But the rewards—a powerful connection to another human being, a valued opinion when making decisions, a trusted partner during times of crisis, laughter, joy, shared memories—can be tremendous, making it all worthwhile.

PART III

ACCOMPLISHMENT

. . . .

Accomplishment is the third Core Value of women who flourish into their 40s and beyond. Most women who thrive at this stage of life feel like experts in some domain, whether that be maintaining healthy relationships with friends and family members, playing tennis or the guitar, cooking or painting, writing a business plan, pursuing a career, organizing charity events, or a combination of these. Of course, they attained this expertise only after many years of practice, and even after moments of humiliation when they felt they had "failed."

According to a recent article in More *magazine, a happy and surprising benefit of hitting our 40s is that we develop a greater sense of mastery. The Mills Longitudinal Study followed over one hundred graduates of the prestigious private women's college in Northern California for five decades, beginning in 1958. The study revealed that the women had a "surge of confidence" in their early 40s. They reported feeling powerful, productive, independent, confident, and competent. In their 20s and 30s, by contrast, they reported insecurities such as "I'll never get myself together." A separate, decade-long study of seven thousand U.S. adults aged 25 to 74 confirmed these findings. According to the lead researcher, women's "sense of mastery peaks in midlife." A third study, of 382 graduates of the University of Rochester, found that both industry* (defined as feeling competent) and identity (having a strong sense of self) soared as people reached middle age.

It doesn't matter whether the activity over which you have mastery is singing a child to sleep, counseling clients, baking cookies, writing a novel, managing an executive team, catching a softball, comforting a disgruntled partner, throwing a birthday party, resetting a broken leg, or soothing yourself during challenging times. Whatever you do, it can serve as a source of pride and contribute to a positive self-image.

However, there is a caveat here: while possessing a sense of mastery can prove critical to a healthy self-concept as we grow older, our relentless pursuit of achievement also can turn into a trap. The main challenge that women in today's world face isn't that we are expected to do too little; it's that we are expected to jam forty-eight or seventy-two hours of living into every twenty-four-hour day. We are held to such a high standard.

In that light, we can consider what it means to be an accomplished woman. Not necessarily a woman who has "the perfect" husband, house, car, and children. Not necessarily a woman who has founded her own multimillion-dollar high-tech company or climbed the ranks of the largest law firm in town. But a woman who knows and appreciates what she is capable of, and sees the strengths in other women as well.

Seven

WILL I EVER BE GOOD ENOUGH?

. . . .

I AM 5 YEARS OLD. My father, a 35-year-old, baby-faced White House correspondent, has been climbing the ranks at NBC rapidly. That year, he is promoted to anchorman of the Today *show, and off we go to New York City in our forest green station wagon, our most precious belongings and even our cat, Foggy, piled around us.*

In our new Manhattan apartment, I curl up next to my mother on my Indian-quilted bed, a reminder of my parents' humble South Dakotan origins. She reads me the timeless children's classic The Little Engine That Could. *The book tells the story of a small blue choo-choo train that struggles but ultimately succeeds in carrying its heavy load over an intimidating mountain by repeating the mantra "I think I can, I think I can." The moral of the book is obvious, even to a 5-year-old . . .*

Work hard and you will succeed.

This was a message that my parents subscribed to then and continue to embrace to this day. They indoctrinated my sisters and me with the importance of determination and discipline in pursuing goals, big or small. And, of course, they led by example—my parents' well-earned successes had a tremendous impact on us kids.

Once we landed in New York, I started to notice that my father was an important person. I didn't necessarily see him as a celebrity, but I realized that his status gave us access to big events and garnered us special treatment. For example, my family got to attend game six of the 1977 World Series, where Yankee Reggie Jackson memorably hit three consecutive home runs to defeat the Dodgers. Afterward, I sat on my dad's shoulders in the overwhelming crowd as people surrounded him, asking for his autograph. Meanwhile, my mother, an accomplished athlete and businesswoman when she wasn't raising her children, demonstrated the indomitable "I think I can" spirit as well.

As we were growing up, my parents made it clear that Jen, Andie, and I were blessed with the gifts of a superior education and exposure to opportunities that many individuals—including themselves—did not have at our age, if ever. Nevertheless, they emphasized that we Brokaw girls had to carve our own marks on the world; we could not rely on our last name and social status.

Here is an example to give you a real sense of how my parents imparted these values. After supper every night, my father would assign us girls to chores number 1, number 2, and number 3. Number 1 was to clear the dishes, number 2 was to put the dishes in the dishwasher and clean the pots and pans, and number 3 was to set the table for breakfast the next morning and take out the garbage. He did give us a weekly allowance as an incentive, but he made it clear that we had to earn our place at the dinner table through effort and discipline.

Yet somehow over the years, the "I think I can" mantra haunted me. Every time I confronted a failure—or even a success—I would face self-doubt. Had I tried hard enough? Had I done my best? Or was something wrong with me? Was I inadequate? I often felt that I fell short of my family's high standards. I wasn't "good enough."

My teen years were fairly typical. I went to school, participated in after-school activities, talked endlessly on the phone with my girlfriends about virtually nothing, and hung out with them on weekends. The one significant difference between me and most other kids my age was that I had scoliosis. From the age of 13 to the age of 16, I had to wear a plastic brace wrapped around my torso for twenty-three hours a day. Meanwhile, my sisters graduated from high school and left home to attend top-tier colleges. My father had become the anchor of *NBC Nightly News*, a position he held for the next twenty-two years. My mother wrote several party-themed books. They offered the perfect picture of success. It seemed obvious to me that everyone could see how *I* was the imperfect one in the family.

Of course, my parents did not view things this way. They gave me incredible support and encouragement. They also emphasized that I should hold my head up high and focus on all the accomplishments I could make, in spite of the hindrance of the brace and the risk of embarrassment. In other words, I wasn't off the hook for doing my best and making them proud.

But I was in my 20s when I really felt my "I think I can" mantra fade. Jen was on her way to becoming a doctor, and Andie was doing very well in her career in the music industry. Meanwhile, I felt myself swimming in a vast ocean without a life jacket. Uncertain of what I wanted to do with my life, I moved to Japan in 1993. Although I was learning a new language and immersing myself in a foreign culture, I lacked confidence and felt generally discontent. Was I being the little engine? Was I working hard to achieve my goals? No, I didn't even know what my goals were.

Then, at age 24, I had my first panic attack. I was in L.A. for the holidays to hang out with my sister Andie and visit relatives in Orange County. Cruising on the 405 freeway one afternoon en route to see my grandmother, I suddenly discovered that I could not breathe. I found my way to the shoulder of the highway and sat in my car, freaking out. As vehicles whizzed by, dangerously close, I contemplated going to the ER. Cell phones didn't exist, so I was on my own, wondering if I might be dying.

Eventually, I managed to calm myself down enough to drive to a pay phone. I called Andie. As soon as I'd described what had happened, she said, "Oh, you're having a panic attack."

Stunned, I asked, "What? How do you know? I could have a collapsed lung!"

"Nope," she said. "Jen used to get those all the time. Where are you? I'll pick you up and take you to the doctor."

I gave Andie the address, and, within fifteen minutes, she picked me up. The doctor confirmed her diagnosis. Finally, I was able to take a deep breath and escape from my moment of temporary hell. But what now? I wondered. I was supposed to return to Japan in two days. The doctor prescribed a couple of Valiums for the plane ride, and off I went. We didn't explore the deeper issues at play or the root causes of my attack.

After several more months in Japan, I was still at a loss. I could not understand or shrug off the anxiety that seemed to creep up on me at unexpected moments. In the spring, my mother visited me, and that was when I fell apart. I shared with her my uncertainty about life after college and said I felt at a loss for where to go next. My mother encouraged me to return to the States. And so, at the age of 24, I found myself living with my parents, jobless and overweight from all the White Russians that I had consumed in Tokyo—and feeling very unaccomplished.

I felt especially unworthy in the eyes of my family members, who continued on the road to greater and greater success. *The NBC Nightly News with Tom Brokaw* was now at the top of the Nielsen ratings. My mother had won the rookie reining (a Western version of dressage) competition after horseback riding for only five years. Not only that but Jen had become an ER doctor and married a wonderful man she met in medical school, and Andie was a cool rock-and-roll rep for EMI Records.

Let me be clear: my parents and sisters did nothing to put me down. On the contrary, they made many attempts to help me figure out my way in life. In hindsight, I could have listened to the myriad suggestions they offered. But I knew that I had to find my own path. I brushed out the old "I think I can" motto and took action. I went on the Jenny Craig diet and lost all the unwanted weight. I committed myself to graduate school. And a few years later, I found myself a successful therapist with a private practice in Manhattan. The panic attacks subsided.

Still, to this day, I can struggle with the sense of not being good enough, especially at moments when I'm feeling vulnerable after a blow to my ego. I worry that I'm not living up to my extremely accomplished family's standards. None of them has ever seen a therapist, so I can find myself devaluing my choice of career at times. I haven't had a family of my own yet, whereas both Andie and Jen have, so I can feel as though I'm falling short in my personal life as well. At my lowest moments, I think, What have I been doing with my life?

When those feelings come up, and the panic starts to set in, I remind myself to return to my values. What matters most to me? Am I following my heart? We all are on our own journeys, with our own sets of blessings and challenges. I focus on the areas in which I feel a sense of mastery, including working as a therapist and coach, completing triathlons, developing a secondary career in photography, surrounding myself with wonderful, supportive friends, and being the best owner I can be of my dogs, Inca and BB. Then I take a deep breath and tell myself that I'm doing fine. Generally speaking, the panic subsides.

Enough Is Enough

When it comes to accomplishment, the core question for many women is: How do we learn to appreciate that we are good enough just as we are, without compromising our standards in terms of what we want to achieve in life? We do want to feel a sense of mastery in some domains of our lives, because this sense contributes to psychological well-being and positive self-regard.

But at the same time, we don't want to undermine ourselves. If we become too achievement-oriented, we can get caught up in thinking that we have to accomplish a great deal in life in order to be worthy people. We might waste our energy and personal power on feeling inadequate. Or we might spend so much time concentrating on climbing the next mountain that we forget to stop and appreciate the view from the hilltop we're standing on right now.

Societal expectations about what we, as modern women, ought to be, do, and have in order to deem ourselves "good enough" have only become more complicated in the past few decades. We receive mixed messages about what we should be striving to achieve. Call it the dark side of women's lib. We have remarkable freedom to do whatever we want, but, as a result, we can find ourselves struggling to define what it means to be "accomplished."

It's easy to become confused by these contradictory messages. That is why, ultimately, we must turn inward and develop our own standards for what it means to be good enough. We can begin by asking ourselves, "What do I want to achieve in life?" "What makes me feel good about myself?"

●　　●　　●　　●

KITTY PROVIDES AN example of what can happen to someone who doesn't feel good enough—even to deserve love and kindness. Yet she also proves that it is possible to shift that energy over time, realize you are worthy, and transform your life.

At 22, Kitty married a man who was emotionally and occasionally physically abusive. He would yell at her, belittle her, and disregard her emotions completely. They had two children together, so Kitty stuck with him for a long while. But eventually, when she was 44, she'd had enough. She told him that she wanted a divorce. When she did, her husband tried to kill her. Kitty had to endure a brutal trial to have her ex sent to prison, even though she was experiencing post-traumatic stress disorder the entire time.

But Kitty's troubles with low self-esteem weren't over yet. Four years later, she married a man whom she believed to be her Prince Charming, only to find out that he was a sex addict who snuck off into the woods to take pictures of women he paid to "model" for him. "I filed the paperwork for the divorce myself," Kitty announced with pride.

Meanwhile, Kitty's two teenage kids were "going crazy." They both experimented with drugs, skipped school, forged notes, treated her with total disrespect, and made her life miserable. Her son, like his father, became abusive, pushing around his sister and Kitty herself. She had to throw him out of the house. "It was a tough love thing," Kitty said. "It was horrible."

Kitty was nearly 50 when these events came to pass, inspiring her to take a long, hard look at her life. At that moment, she decided she'd had enough of being the victim. So she went to counseling to turn her life around—and it worked. "When I started therapy, a lightbulb went off," Kitty said. "I'd always been told I was stupid, worthless, couldn't do anything. But the therapist showed me how, in reality, I was already doing everything!" The therapist also gave Kitty exercises to do with her kids. "I'd follow her instructions, and it would work," Kitty recounted. "She'd say, 'You're my success story.'" For the first time in her life, Kitty felt good enough.

Today, at age 59, Kitty proclaims with a smile, "I've come a long way. You'd never know what happened to me back then." She has a job that she loves as an office manager in a public school. She was able to save enough money to buy her own house a few years back. She has developed a close network of girlfriends who stand by her. She looks great, keeping in shape through regular exercise. Above all, she feels positive about who she is and what she has achieved in life.

Kitty had this to say to other women who might be in a similar position, struggling to love themselves and truly believe in their worth. "Get counseling! Whether it be Al-Anon or whatever. Just do it." She paused for a moment. "Also, I'd like to say this to women who don't feel good enough. 'You know what? You're a strong person. You're stronger than you think you are. You've got to believe that. You've got to believe in yourself.'"

The Impostor Complex

For many years, I have recognized that I suffer from an impostor complex—underestimating my expertise and worrying that someday the whole world will discover that I'm a fraud. For example, even though I have a master's degree in social work and ten years of counseling experience under my belt, when I got the publishing contract for this book, I thought, They'll see right through me! They'll realize I'm not an expert!

As a therapist, I learned that this tendency is a known phenomenon, commonly called the "impostor syndrome." Here is another way in which women feel not good enough. Apparently, it is not unusual for achievement-oriented women to believe that they do not deserve what they have accomplished, even though they have earned it through their own hard work. We often feel like phonies.

Part of the problem lies in the fact that women tend to attribute success to external factors, such as a friendly boss or a lucky break. However, we internalize our failures, attributing them to our innate flaws, such as a lack of intelligence or self-discipline. And so, we must make a conscious effort to revise our thinking. We must choose not to fall into the trap of thinking that we haven't earned our hard-won accolades, or that we deserve failure. We must deliberately concentrate on making ourselves feel like we're good enough.

• • • •

MARY KIM BREWSTER, an attractive, warm, graceful 52-year-old half-Korean, half-Caucasian mother and Ph.D. in psychology, is keenly familiar with the feeling of not being good enough—in spite of her many achievements. Her story offers particular insight into the role that cultural expectations and societal messaging can play in a person's sense of accomplishment.

Mary's father arrived as a Korean immigrant in the United States after World War II. A doctor, he moved to Minnesota and built an anesthesia practice. He was a pioneer in that he was one of the first Asian physicians practicing in the Midwest. He was also a workaholic. Until the age of 70, he carried both anesthesia and pain management practices—full-time. When he retired, three physicians were required to replace him.

Meanwhile, Mary's mother was a child of the Great Depression who grew up on a farm in rural Minnesota. For her, waking up before dawn to milk the cows was merely the precursor to a long day of physical labor.

Mary's family set the standards for accomplishment very high. Mary said, "The three common themes in my family were work, work, and work." For her father, work was the expression of the Confucian ethic of his Korean culture, as well as an immigrant success strategy. For her mother, work was hardwired as a means of survival. "The combination of the Confucian and Depression-era mind-sets of my parents was like the Protestant work ethic on steroids!" Mary recounted with a laugh.

In addition, Mary had to contend with her father's inherent disappointment in her—simply because she was a girl. Having grown up the oldest son in a family in Korea, her father believed that males come first. While other American fathers in his generation also were raised before the feminist movement, Mary felt that the messages her father inherited were "literally medieval." His sense of male entitlement and gender privilege drove her crazy. It also prevented him from raising Mary as an equal to her brother and engendered tremendous anger and resentment toward him from his wife and his daughters. Mary understood that her father's male chauvinism was cultural, but she didn't feel that was an excuse.

Mary believes that this sentiment is common to Asian-American women. She said, "I see that Asian-American women—and here I speak in gross generalities—grow up with cultural proscriptions about achieving and competing while simultaneously carrying messages that value women for being pleasing and deferential. The two messages collide. There is a great deal of anger—often unconscious, always unspoken—around the devaluation Asian-American women experience growing up in their families and communities. Underneath this, however, there is a craving, sometimes on the level of starvation, for love and approval from their fathers. There is the irreconcilable desire to please 'Father' as the achieving alpha woman as well as the devoted caretaker of men. This can create a mind-bending role conflict."

Mary continued to explain that what she sees in many women, but in Asian-American women in particular, is a driving, sometimes debilitating perfectionism. Basically, to be valuable, validated, and visible, they feel that they must please everyone and achieve on all fronts. They must be the impeccably dressed, socially savvy, sexually pleasing, professionally accomplished community activist who also is raising perfectly well-adjusted children who are headed to Ivy League schools and professional degrees. "The stakes are high," Mary said. "To let go on any of these fronts is to risk being disapproved of, or to be disappointing and to lose your value as a woman. Many women get caught on a hamster wheel, searching for approval and validation from their fathers. And if getting Father's attention is impossible, then gaining control over one's body, food, et cetera can become the next best thing. Of course, this becomes a recipe for anxiety, depression, eating disorders, and relational conflict."

Mary still struggles not to get caught up in the need for approval from others, even though she has spent years working as a professional therapist. She offered these words of wisdom. "I guess my wish is for Asian-American women to take a step back and look at the contextual, cultural factors that create the sense of 'not being good enough.' I do think that it gets started early in life, oftentimes with the familial disappointment at the birth of the girl (not a boy!) in an Asian-American family. My hope is that women will examine how the cultural messages create this internalized sense of inferiority, and with this knowledge: resist, resist, resist!"

Eating Disorders

One common way in which women manifest their tendency to feel "not good enough" is through eating disorders. Six percent of women in the United States will struggle with anorexia, bulimia, or a binge-eating disorder at some point in their lives.

Most of us think of eating disorders as young women's problems. However, recent statistics from the American Public Health Association indicated that from 1999 to 2006, there was a 48 percent increase in hospitalizations caused by eating disorders among patients aged 45 to 65. In my professional experience, eating disorders among older women are grossly underreported. The problem often goes undetected simply because these women are under less supervision from other people (they no longer live under the watchful eyes of their parents or in a college dormitory) and more skilled at hiding their disorders.

I've had a dozen clients over age 25 with eating disorders during my ten years in private psychotherapy practice. All were bulimic. Bulimia is more difficult to detect than anorexia because those who have it generally do not become extremely thin. Even though, over the long term, bulimia can cause damage to the stomach, teeth, and esophagus, and wreak havoc with blood pressure, its negative consequences are not as evident, especially to the outside world. These clients were practiced at running the water to hide the sound of their vomiting, binging only when alone, and otherwise keeping their secret.

There didn't seem to be any correlation between relationship status, race, or profession among my eating-disordered clients. One characteristic that I observed, however, was that they were all hard-driving, achievement-oriented individuals. The same holds true for younger women with anorexia and bulimia—they tend to be quite accomplished people.

For women with the drive to be successful, and to prove to the world that they are "good enough," weight can be one of the easiest factors to control. No matter how hard we try, we are not necessarily able to determine when we get a promotion at work or how well our children perform in school. But we have direct control over what we put into our bodies and how hard we exercise every day.

Occasionally, a client's eating disorder is so severe that I recommend hospitalization. But in general, the combination of individual therapy and a support group proves effective. When I work with clients struggling with this issue, we begin right away to build their self-esteem, constantly returning to the theme of accomplishment. I often find that if they can ground themselves in a strong internal sense of being "good enough," these women can gain control of their eating-disordered behavior.

• • • •

REBA IS A 41-year-old half Hispanic, half African-American bodybuilder. After suffering from bulimia for most of her life, she finally acknowledged and decided to address the problem at age 29 by seeking counseling and attending support groups. She was able to rid herself of her bad habits and discover renewed passion for life.

Reba's height and finely toned body make her intimidating at first. But she quickly disarms with her openness and easy laughter. It's hard to imagine her growing up as one of the only "colored girls" in an upper-middle-class, white neighborhood in Michigan. There, she adopted white standards of feminine beauty—the desire to be unnaturally thin. In college, she had a Caucasian roommate who taught her to throw up after meals. That's when she got hooked on bulimia. "When

I got thin and ripped for the first time, in my late teens, I discovered that I could earn respect from white women that I'd never had before," she told me. "Plus I loved the high I got from throwing up, and the sense of being in control."

For over a decade, Reba struggled alone with her bulimia. "I thought I was the only black or Hispanic woman who had an eating disorder," she told me. Part of the problem, in her view, was that no one ever mentions the existence of the disorder among minorities. When she eventually did research online, in her late 20s, Reba realized that her belief that only white women had eating disorders was false. "I've discovered that there are plenty of minority women dealing with these issues, and I feel it's important that our voices be heard," she said.

Since admitting to her problem and seeking help, Reba has come to appreciate how much pressure she had been putting on herself to be "good enough." "I'd always felt that I fell short," she said. "I knew that I could never be white, but I didn't fit in with other black women, either. I had to come to a place where I accepted myself exactly as I was. I'm so much happier now than I've ever been. I still love to work out and eat well, but I'm no longer destructive about it. I constantly tell myself that it's okay not to be perfect—I'd rather be alive."

Good Enough Right Now

The acclaimed analyst Carl Jung wrote that people don't complete the process of individuation—or psychologically separating from their family of origin—until they hit 40. With this perspective in mind, there's yet another reason for us to look forward to our fifth decade. The fact that we are establishing our unique identities as we age, and honing in on what really makes us tick, is likely one reason people tend to experience a surge in self-confidence after 40. Women with forty-tude have identified where their talents lie and know how to focus their energy on these arenas. They give up pursuing channels that don't serve their health and well-being. And they learn to appreciate that they're good enough exactly as they are.

Here is an exercise that I might use with a client who is stuck feeling she isn't good enough. I begin by asking her to close her eyes, take a deep breath, and think about the things she does. Then I invite her to assess her energy level while she is performing each of these activities. I encourage her not to judge how good she is at something—whether it be playing Scrabble, teaching soccer, or running a meeting—but rather to focus completely on her own enjoyment and satisfaction, without comparing herself to others. Finally, we discuss why she spends time on activities that she doesn't enjoy. I suggest refocusing energy as much as possible on those activities that feed her soul and give her the most positive feelings.

Many people, consciously or unconsciously, subscribe to the mantra "One day, I'll have *x*, and *then* I'll be happy." *X* might be a new house, partner, or job, or it might simply be losing ten pounds. Frequently, this belief centers on accomplishment, or not feeling "good enough." We are plagued by the idea that we need to be, do, and have *more* in order to be worthy of joy and contentment.

But this is no way to live. We have to take ownership of our vitality and well-being here, in this very moment. There is no later, only now. If we live for the future, we end up ignoring the many blessings that we already have.

Eight

THE ACCOMPLISHED PARTNER

. . . .

WHEN I FIRST contemplated exemplars of accomplished partners, I immediately thought of my mother, Meredith Brokaw. Not only is my mom married to an extremely accomplished man but she is also accomplished in her own right. Naturally, she has had her share of trials and tribulations as an adult, but she has exhibited grace through it all. She never seems to have felt burdened or constrained by her role as the wife of a famous television news anchorman, yet neither did she choose to rest on my father's laurels, as she easily might have done. Instead, she has succeeded in staying out of the shadow of her successful husband and has found her own fulfillment, both professional and personal.

However, my mother was reluctant at first to be interviewed by me because she does not consider her accomplishments anything special. Of course, I didn't want to overexpose my mother, either. But her very hesitation about being profiled in this book only reinforced how appropriate a choice she was. So while I considered other options, I kept coming back to this idea that I wanted her profile here. My friends, and others I spoke with who know my mother, all agreed. So after several months during which I tried and failed to find someone more appropriate, my mother finally acquiesced.

We sat down to have a conversation about this topic over dinner one night in Manhattan's West Village. Once we'd ordered our food and were contentedly sipping glasses of prosecco, she began to tell her story.

My mother was 33 when our family moved from California to Washington, D.C., so we girls were 3, 5, and 7 years old. Meredith's primary focus at that time was on getting us settled into the move across the country. She was not concerned about her own career, outside of being a mom. At the same time, she found Washington "a very tough place for spouses." Even women who were doctors, or very accomplished in other careers, would be treated as "just wives" if their husbands were in politics.

After two and a half years in Washington, Meredith started thinking that it would be tough for her to live there long term. Just then, my father got the job with the *Today* show in New York City. My mother was thrilled to make the move there. "I felt liberated," she said. "The role of women in New York was clearly different."

Meredith had been a teacher before having her three children, but she didn't miss working outside the home until I was about 5 years old. It was the seventies, and women were starting to feel a real push to have careers. She had several friends going back to law school and even medical school in their mid-30s. Meredith got excited about getting back to work herself. At 35, she began asking herself, "What am I going to do next? What's my career?"

My mother had always dreamed of opening her own business. She had two female friends who served as role models, having opened an educational toy store in D.C. So when she realized there wasn't yet any store like that in New York, she seized the opportunity to fill the niche. My mother said, "I had this idea that I could be an entrepreneur. Then I met a fabulous woman, Mary Slawson, who was interested in being my business partner. The rest is history." When my mother was 37 years old, she and Mary opened the first Penny Whistle Toys store in Manhattan. They met with success and later expanded to several other locations, including stores in Brooklyn and Bridgehampton.

Meredith believes that the most successful marriages, business partnerships, and good friendships are the ones in which people bring out the best in each other. She feels fortunate that the man she picked to be her husband at age 21 turned out to be so supportive. Without his backing, she doesn't believe that she ever would have accomplished what she did. "Tom's view has always been, 'Meredith can do anything.' I have to damp down his enthusiasm sometimes. For example, he thinks that I'm a champion bridge player and horseback rider, when I'm not. It's just that he admires me. He's really proud of the things I've done, including writing books and launching Penny Whistle Toys."

Conversely, Meredith is proud of all that Tom has achieved, though that might seem obvious. She said, "It has to be a two-way street. That's the reason why our marriage has endured for nearly a half-century. We both feel that, no matter what, the other person is great, and that we can figure out solutions to all sorts of problems. We have a really solid base."

It's true. My dad is incredibly supportive of my mom and admires her a great deal. But even so, I feel that she achieved a great deal. For example, when I was about 9 years old, at a time when few women were running it, she finished the New York City Marathon. I asked, "Where did you get the drive to accomplish so much?"

My mother took several bites of her fish before answering. "One time, I was being interviewed for an article, and the reporter asked, 'When did your life start?' I thought, What an interesting question. It's true that so many people are waiting for their lives to really start. Does life begin when you get married? Get your first job? Have kids?

"But I don't think of life like that. I don't ask, When did it start? I think life is more like taking a vacation: the trip is the whole entirety, including planning it when you're still back home, not just when you get to your destination. You have to know when you're in high school and you're working hard at the school newspaper that that's a valuable part of life. You're not waiting to finish school and begin your first job in journalism. Life happens all along the way. You have to stop and say to yourself, This is my life. You just continue to evolve."

I wondered if she had a sense of accomplishment now, given all that she has achieved. Meredith described feeling disbelief at how amazing her life has been. "If I have a sense of accomplishment, I wouldn't say that it's about my personal accomplishments but more about what we've achieved as a family unit," she said. "We've held together all these years. We've done interesting things and seen interesting places. Tom and I survived raising kids in a big city, whereas many people would find that completely daunting. But we didn't know any better, so we weren't daunted, and it all worked out."

Finally, I asked Meredith if she had any advice for women in their late 30s and 40s. She said firmly, "Women have to focus on their own selves, their own lives, distinct and different from those of their kids and husbands."

Powerful Women, Intimidated Men?

Establishing a solid, grounded intimate relationship can prove challenging enough in today's world. But the process can be even more complicated for women who are accomplished in their own right. According to a recent *New York Times* article, in 1970, 4 percent of husbands had wives who made more money than they did; in 2007, 22 percent did. Men are also increasingly likely to marry women with more education than they have. But many high-achieving women still worry that the majority of men feel threatened and undermined by our success. We fear that their fragile egos simply can't handle having a partner who equals or surpasses their level of accomplishment.

Well, there's some good news for us, ladies: it seems that men may not be as turned off by powerful women as many of us assume. According to an article in *Psychology Today*, many men are actively seeking partners who are just as accomplished as they are. In fact, they find the idea of having a wife who is nothing more than "arm candy" embarrassing. This shift may be partially driven by economics—households need two wage earners to compete in today's world. But it also seems that societal standards continue to move away from women as sex objects and toward women as equals. Men report that not only would they feel bored with "trophy wives" but that their peers would judge them negatively for making such a choice.

•   •   •   •

JULIE BLACKWELL IS a nonprofit executive, wife, and mother of two from Seattle. Her enthusiasm for life, accompanied by her infectious laugh, is contagious. In spite of taking a fairly conventional path for most of her 41 years, she has made an unconventional marriage work. She has done so by embracing adventure, demonstrating a willingness to compromise, and paying close attention to both her own and her husband's needs and dreams.

Julie was 31 years old and making a good living at a job in the high-tech industry when she met John, who couldn't have been more different. John was an intense person—an extreme mountain biker and ultramarathoner who pursued his passions, as she put it, "for love, not money." Plus he had long hair and a beard. Julie's parents—and many of her friends—were shocked when they realized that she was taking her relationship with John seriously. "John was not the ideal partner in terms of financial security," Julie explained.

But Julie felt "totally wowed" by how John had chosen to live his life. And so, two years later, she married him. She admits that this decision required a leap of faith—as it does for everyone. Nevertheless, if she had married someone more like herself, she would have felt suffocated. She said, "John meets my need for adventure rather than stability. Yet I also knew that he would put the same amount of heart and soul into his marriage and family as he did into racing, because that's the kind of person he is."

Julie and John's relationship has taught them both many things. John introduced Julie to a whole new level of pushing herself, mentally and physically. She now moves outside her comfort zone far more often than she did before. In turn, Julie feels that John benefits from her outgoing, social personality. She has shown him how to open up and let people in. Also, John lives at the extremes, so Julie's more even, practical approach to day-to-day living stabilizes him.

Not long after they got married, Julie and John had two children. During those years, Julie continued to work in tech and pay most of the bills, while John pursued his athletic career and shared the household responsibilities. But the imbalance in paychecks never bothered either of them. Julie wanted to work and enjoyed her job. And John was working hard, too—he simply wasn't earning as much. Julie said, "It isn't like I married a lazy guy. John just isn't driven by money; that's not what he thinks about. He's driven by adventure, pushing his limits. And he does things that no one else on the planet does, which I think is tremendous."

Julie also had faith that someday John would be able to allow her to follow her passions while he paid the bills. And in fact, about a year ago, Julie decided to quit her high-tech job and go to work for an environmental nonprofit. John wholeheartedly supported her decision, even though it meant a cut in Julie's paycheck. Over the past few years, John also has parlayed his passions into a career in the sporting-goods industry and is now earning almost as much money as his wife.

Julie readily admits that she and John have challenging moments. There are times when he is away for ten days on some excursion and she has to work, take care of the kids, and do all the housework, and it starts to feels like too much. During these moments, Julie intentionally practices letting go of her desire to do everything perfectly.

Sometimes money becomes an issue for Julie as well. She has no doubt that she made the right choice by marrying someone who was fundamentally happy with where he was and what he was doing, as opposed to marrying someone because of how much money he earned. At the same time, dealing with the bills—the responsibilities of owning a home and having two kids—can be stressful. "When I put money aside, I feel blessed that John and I both have had a lifetime full of amazing experiences," she said. "But when it comes down to the mortgage being paid, I wish I could have those same positive feelings all the time."

Julie offered to share with me a special practice that she and John do every year or two to keep their marriage going strong. "It's called a summit. We each come up with ten questions. Then we take the list of twenty questions, and we go away to answer them on our own. Some of the questions are fun, but some are quite serious, like 'Where do you see us in five years?' And 'What about me drives you crazy?' When we're done answering on our own, we go away for the weekend and talk about the questions for hours. It's really great because, in everyday life, we can forget to tell each other how terrific we think the other person is. So we also have questions like 'What do you love about me?'" It sounded like the type of exercise that I'd recommend to my clients in couples therapy.

When it comes to a successful partnership, Julie believes strongly in trusting yourself and not listening too much to the opinions of others. "My relationship with John isn't perfect," she said. "I've sacrificed financial stability in order to be with someone whose values and lifestyle I really respect. But we all have to make those sorts of choices when we commit to marriage or a long-term relationship."

Identifying Intelligences

This Identifying Intelligences exercise, which I use in therapy, is particularly relevant to couples struggling with the perception that one partner is more accomplished than the other. Based on the Harvard psychology professor Howard Gardner's theory of multiple intelligences, the exercise encourages people to think outside the box about the many ways in which they and their partners might be talented.

I begin by asking both people to identify their intelligences. Often, they assume that I mean book smarts or educational achievements. Those who've earned advanced degrees or do well on crossword puzzles generally feel confident of their intelligence in this domain, whereas those who didn't perform as well in school feel that they fall short. But after talking about how they stack up against others according to this conventional definition of intelligence, both people are likely to run out of ideas.

And so I say, "What about your other intelligences?"

At this point, the couple usually look at me like I'm a little bit crazy. "What do you mean?" they ask.

I then present a handout that lists the eight types of intelligence identified by Gardner: linguistic, logical-mathematical, musical, spatial, bodily-kinesthetic, naturalist, interpersonal, and intrapersonal. I explain how what we traditionally think of as our IQ, or intelligence quotient, represents only our abstract thinking capabilities and reading comprehension skills. Gardner said that our society has a very skewed and blindered perception of what intelligence is: we tend to disregard the many *other* areas in which we express talent and accomplishment. An athlete possesses fantastic kinesthetic intelligence, for example. Many women have rich capabilities in both the intrapersonal (self-knowledge) and interpersonal (understanding of others) domains. Fortunately, our culture has begun to place more value on these types of emotional intelligences, or EQ. But we still have a long way to go in recognizing the full eight domains as valid forms of intelligence.

Once they've had a chance to look over the handout, I ask the couple to identify the areas in which both they and their partners express their intelligence. Then I ask them to discuss how these various talents might be misinterpreted or underappreciated. For example, many women feel as though their husbands don't value their ability to keep the couple emotionally connected to children, parents, friends, acquaintances, and even co-workers.

I also ask the couples to talk about how they respond when they feel they don't measure up to other people in terms of a certain type of intelligence. For example, if you feel that you have no musical talent and you end up at a party where everyone is playing an instrument or singing, what do you do? Do you say, "Forget about it. I'm out of here." Do you get drunk? Do you act out, overcompensate, and seek to become the center of attention by emphasizing one of the skills that you do possess? When couples become conscious of their reactions to situations in which they feel vulnerable or inadequate, they are able to relate to each other more deeply. Perhaps you tend to behave in a way that seems brassy and dominant when, underneath the bravado, you really just want to feel valued.

Often I will spend several sessions with couples working through the list of intelligences, discussing the assumptions each person has about the talents he or she possesses, and encouraging the couple not to compare themselves with other people—or with each other. "What's the point in comparing yourself when no one's DNA is the same?" I ask. "Every person on earth possesses unique traits. The question is not how you stack up against some arbitrary standards of intelligence or success but rather can you identify and appreciate the particular talents that each of you has to share?"

I find that, most of the time, people are pleasantly surprised by this reframing of intelligence. We have such a powerful tendency to compete with others. If we pay attention to the many ways in which we excel, we generally feel much more comfortable with ourselves. "I thought I was a loser because I never did well in school," a client might say. "I never thought of my connection with animals as a talent worthy of recognition." I watch as the couples visibly become more relaxed, open, and content—not only with themselves but also with each other. Reevaluating their partners in this new light helps them develop appreciation for the others' special skills and contributions.

One couple I worked with in this way had struggled for years over the idea of accomplishment. Jennie and Paul came into therapy because Jennie was an alcoholic, but Paul had discovered this only after marrying her. Over the years, her alcoholism had grown steadily worse. Jennie worked as a teacher and recently had started sneaking drinks during the school day. Paul was furious and wanted Jennie to get her drinking under control.

We explored what triggered Jennie's need to drink. I asked her, "What brings you to that place of self-doubt where you want to escape with alcohol?"

Jennie responded, "Paul is so much more successful than I am. He's this corporate executive. He makes so much more money. He's always at business meetings and important functions. Meanwhile, I have this simple job of teaching elementary school students." It seemed clear that Jennie was acting out by drinking in response to her feelings of inadequacy. She didn't feel that she was an accomplished person in comparison to her husband.

I asked Jennie and Paul to evaluate their intelligences. Paul did indeed rate himself high on the linguistic and logical-mathematical scales. But initially, Jennie resisted identifying any intelligences of her own. "I just teach. So what?" she said.

We talked further about what Jennie did, her hobbies and passions. She loved teaching art and had a real talent, Paul said, for painting, sculpture, and pottery. "See, you have spatial and bodily-kinesthetic intelligence, Jennie," I pointed out.

Furthermore, Jennie was an excellent teacher. Her kids loved her, and she'd even won a teaching award. Paul said, "You definitely have interpersonal intelligence, too. You're so good with those kids. You really get them."

Jennie just beamed when she heard this praise from Paul. "I never thought of it that way," she said.

Completing this exercise helped Jennie to rebuild her self-esteem. But it also emphasized to Paul the ways in which she was an accomplished human being. It got them both out of the trap of measuring Jennie only according to her IQ and career pay scale, and placed emphasis on her other wonderful qualities. "You're not in a competition," I said. They both agreed to stop spending so much time comparing themselves to one another and instead shift the focus to appreciating what each of them had to offer.

For the next several sessions, we continued to explore ways in which Jennie and Paul could capitalize on their strengths in building their relationship. Jennie began attending AA meetings and was able to quit drinking. Both Jennie and Paul expressed feeling as though they had a whole new partnership as a result of our work together.

As we enter our fifth decades, most of us come to a point where we have a good grasp of what comes naturally to us, what talents and skills we were born with and which ones we simply don't possess. We discover that, while we all can continue to explore new activities and push our boundaries throughout our lives, honing in on a sense of mastery in certain domains can prove beneficial. We let go of pursuits that exhaust us and devote our time and energy to the activities that we find most fulfilling.

As you do this, however, I invite you not to judge your accomplishments within too limited a framework. Remember all the types of intelligences Howard Gardner identified, and see if you have some talents—hidden or not so hidden—that you don't regularly recognize and appreciate.

Nine

THE ACCOMPLISHED MOTHER

. . . .

WE DON'T LIVE in the 1950s world of *Leave It to Beaver* any longer. Fortunately, we have made slow but steady progress in the past fifty years toward gender equality, especially in comparison with other countries, such as Afghanistan and the Democratic Republic of Congo, where women struggle daily for their dignity and even for their lives. We are blessed to live in an open society where mothers from many backgrounds, with varying personal situations, political viewpoints, and professional associations, all can find acceptance and support.

There are many ways to go about being a mother these days. You can take the conventional approach of getting married to a man and having a biological child (or two or more) with him. Or you can simply live with him and have kids without being married. You can partner with another woman and raise your children with her. You can struggle with infertility and decide to use in vitro fertilization, an egg donor, and/or a surrogate to bear your child. You can join a commune and raise your and other people's children collectively. You can adopt. You can choose to have a baby on your own.

Of course, not everyone has a choice in how her version of motherhood turns out. Partners separate, people die, and some women try to have biological children but discover that they aren't able to do so. Each approach to parenting presents its particular set of challenges and rewards. But the bottom line is, as long as you are able to provide for your children's basic needs, and ensure that they feel safe and loved, it's okay (sigh of relief). Most people will not judge you harshly, or try to take your child away, as they might have done in the past. What's more, you will be able to find a community of like-minded women in similar situations—online, if not also in person—to support you. You will find a way.

Stay-at-Home Moms

According to a recent article in *The New York Times*, women at elite colleges are shifting their attitudes about being stay-at-home moms. Whereas for the previous two to three decades, female college grads have expressed a desire to have full-time careers and families, these days they are increasingly willing to give up the career part of the equation. Sixty percent of female undergraduates informally surveyed at top schools indicated that they had already decided to suspend or end their careers when they had children.

The largest challenge stay-at-home moms face is to their self-esteem. Some suffer an ego blow as soon as they quit their jobs, feeling as though their contributions to society as moms are not adequately valued (and it's hard to argue with that point). Other SAHMs raise their children quite happily only to find that, once the kids graduate from high school and move on, they are at sea, uncertain of what they should do next.

Colleen provides an interesting example. She comes from a strict English and Irish-Catholic family with nine children. It was her mother's full-time job to raise them. "Mom was the CFO and COO of our household; Dad was the figurehead CEO," Colleen said. "He would give her his paycheck, and somehow she would make it all work out." But in spite of seeming content in her role, Colleen's mother encouraged her daughters not to choose her life path, urging them instead to pursue careers. Colleen dutifully went to college, got her law degree, and began practicing as an attorney. But she wasn't happy. "I realized that I was fulfilling my mother's dream and not my own."

When she reached her 30s, fell in love, and moved in with her boyfriend, Colleen decided to follow her heart. She gave up her high-powered career and began volunteering and applying for part-time jobs. "I just want to be home," she told me. "I want exactly what my mother had, even though she didn't want us to have that. I like doing chores. I think the life of a stay-at-home mom is pretty great."

The truth of the matter is, the vast majority of women don't even have the option to stay home—particularly in today's tough economic climate. *Time* magazine reported that over 70 percent of women with children under 18 are in the labor force. Single mothers nearly always have to work to support their families. But even families with two parents often require both to be wage earners simply to keep up with housing, education, and health care expenses.

But for those women who want and are able to choose the stay-at-home-mother path, the key lies in defining who you are, independent of your roles as mother and wife. This may mean pursuing other interests outside the family, such as sports and volunteering. Or it may mean simply making peace with your truth, knowing in your heart that you are contributing to the world in your own way.

• • • •

TANYA FREEMAN OFFERS an example of a woman who is, for the most part, content being a stay-at-home mother of four children. She doesn't seem to have the hard-driving need to seek other achievements and gain outside recognition to feel fulfilled. She does her job well, and she knows it. Therefore, she is able to derive from being a mother the critical sense of mastery and self-confidence that defines the Core Value of accomplishment.

After graduating from college, Tanya took a teaching job at a middle school in Columbus, Ohio. There, at age 22, she met her husband, Joe. They enjoyed several fun years of working, dating, and hanging out with friends before getting married when Tanya was 26. Then they had four children within eight years.

From the beginning, Tanya's decision to be a stay-at-home mom felt natural and enjoyable to her. Yet sometimes she does wish that she had accomplished more outside the home, especially when she was younger. "It's not cut-and-dried, but I think I didn't have the confidence that I could do anything other than be a middle school teacher and mom. I love doing this, but at the same time, I never tried for more, like being a college professor," she explained. She looks forward to the day, when her youngest is a bit older, that she can audit a course or two at a local university for intellectual stimulation.

Tanya also admits that she sometimes feels guilty about playing tennis in the morning and leaving the younger kids with a babysitter. But she points out that there isn't a mother in the world who lives guilt-free. When she occasionally gets frustrated or catches herself whining, "Oh, I've got so much to do," she stops and takes a moment to reevaluate. "Do I really have that much to do? Not really!" she says to herself. "I have it pretty good."

Every time Tanya sees one of her children, she takes the time to acknowledge him or her as an individual. Tanya recognizes that she won't have that opportunity forever, so she must make it a top priority every day. Her husband has told her that her eyes light up whenever her kids come into the room.

When her children all have graduated from high school, Tanya imagines that she might work full-time again. But she doesn't know what she'll do. She might go back to teaching, or she might try a new career involving project management. "I'm good at shepherding people. I'm very organized and can keep lots of balls in the air. So I think I'll find something," she said. "But I am afraid to go out into the world as someone who has been a mom for decades and say, 'Hire me!' I worry that they won't take me seriously."

Yet, even when those fears come up, Tanya never doubts having chosen the right path for her. She thinks it might be fascinating to have a career, and she struggles sometimes to value her contributions as a stay-at-home mom at the same level as a paying job, but, on the whole, she wouldn't change a thing about her life. "You get a lot of joy and love out of being a mom," she said. "I've had to accept that the house can't always be spotless, and dinner is not always on the table right at six. But I do a good job at creating a safe, stable environment for my kids, so I focus on that, and I feel proud of it."

Divorced Moms

Not all marriages last, and when they don't, mothers may find themselves having to cope with separation from their partners and complicated arrangements with their kids. Divorce puts immense stress on people. Therapists consider it one of the most traumatizing life events, along with the death of a loved one. But ending a marriage becomes even more challenging—emotionally as well as financially—when children are involved.

According to *The State of Our Unions 2009*, a report issued by the National Marriage Project at Rutgers University, only 67 percent of U.S. children grow up with two married parents. That's the lowest figure in the Western world, and it means that there are plenty of divorced moms out there. If you're facing this reality, you can take comfort in knowing that you are not alone.

In my psychotherapy practice, I have found that many women feel, at the time of their divorce, that they are failures as mothers. They express deep concern about the long-term impact the divorce will have on their children's psychological well-being. We spend time discussing the ways in which they can minimize negative consequences for their children and simultaneously work on rebuilding their own self-esteem. I am quick to point out that, while divorced parenting poses its own set of challenges, it is still parenting. The woman's fundamental role as a mother has not been compromised. This holds true for all of us: even if you are experiencing some trauma in your personal life as the result of a divorce, you still can provide a loving, safe, nurturing home to your children.

• • • •

JESSICA LAZAR IS a divorced mother of two who did an admirable job in handling her separation from her husband. She certainly struggled with the decision to leave the marriage, and worried about how her two daughters would handle the change. But she and her ex-husband also made it their top priority throughout the process to safeguard their children's happiness. All four family members have coped well as a result.

Jessica grew up in Evanston, Illinois. Although her family is Jewish, Jessica was raised in an urban commune on the north side of Chicago that was ecumenical. "The seeds were planted really early for me in terms of my spiritual practice," she commented.

After completing a master's of science and journalism degree, Jessica lived in Israel for many years as a reporter and English teacher. While there, she met and married her husband, Dan. Ten years ago, they moved to Washington, D.C., so that he could join a graduate program, and Jessica worked as a research editor on documentary films. During that time, they had two daughters, now ages 8 and 6.

When her second daughter was born, Jessica took a hiatus from work. Her editing job kept her at the office until quite late, and she felt as though she was missing out on her young daughters' lives. In search of work-life balance, she started teaching yoga full-time in 2004.

Jessica initially thought that she would teach yoga only until she burned out. But as the months went by, she found herself growing more and more passionate about her work. At the same time, she found herself less and less satisfied with her marriage. She felt that she was on her own evolutionary path. She and Dan had grown so far apart as lovers and intimate partners that they were more like good friends. Jessica tried for a long time to stave off the realization, but eventually she had to admit that they both would be better off if they parted ways as husband and wife.

Jessica and Dan agreed to make the divorce process as smooth as possible for their children and to be loving, communicative, and self-sacrificing as they parted ways. They spent time researching and discussing their options in order to determine what would serve their daughters best. They settled on what's known these days as a "nesting arrangement": they agreed to share one house and one apartment for the first year of their separation. The girls would stay at the house all the time. When it was Jessica's turn to parent the children, she would stay at the house while Dan lived at the apartment. Partway through the week, they would switch. As a result, the girls never had to pack up their stuff and move. Their family home and its rhythms were preserved.

In addition, Jessica and Dan made a commitment to help their daughters cope with the emotional impact of the divorce. They devoted time to talking about it, allowing the girls to process. They would say, "This is what you'll be losing; here is what we'll work to protect; and here are the new opportunities that might emerge." Rather than presenting the divorce as something catastrophic or horrible, they explained it as a moment of transition.

Finally, the couple had strong rules about exposure to lovers and casual acquaintances. New people were not allowed to come into the family home at all, and new intimate partners would be introduced only once a relationship was firmly established. "It's really up to the parents to set the boundaries for what's appropriate. We felt we ought to bear the burden. We would prefer to inconvenience ourselves at every turn rather than to put the girls through the wringer," Jessica said.

Jessica admits to having moments of deep darkness and sadness about the divorce. However, she has no regrets. She said, "I don't want to sound corny, but I have to say, everything that I hoped for and wished for is either in my hands or within my reach. What I wanted was liberation from a marriage that wasn't working, and in tandem with that to preserve a friendship with my ex-husband; for my daughters to be on solid ground; financial footing for my family; and newfound ignition around my work—and all of those things have happened."

Stepmoms

Yet another way in which women can enter the role of motherhood is through marriage to a man who already has children. How smoothly that transition goes depends largely on the circumstances and the personalities of the people involved. It's a highly individual process. Yet, in general, the key to bonding with stepchildren is being patient and flexible.

I have known several women in my practice and personal life who have found immense joy and contentment in being stepmothers. Jackie Smith is one. Jackie is 46 years old. She grew up on the East Coast and has spent most of her adult life in Boston, where she works as a surgeon. Jackie became a mother for the first time as a stepmother. Six years after meeting her husband, and four years after marrying him, she is thrilled to treat his two children—ages 13 and 16—as her own.

Jackie had been married twice before she met her current husband but had never had children—at first, she didn't want them; later, she found out that she couldn't have them. Although her parents never put pressure on her to have kids, because both of her sisters were having them, Jackie felt left out at family gatherings. Everyone else would talk about teething, inappropriate aggression for a 6-year-old, and the latest must-have toys. Jackie eventually would give up and say, "Can we go shopping?" That was the one thing she knew they could enjoy doing together.

After her second marriage ended when she was 40, Jackie became quite depressed. She thought, "Okay, so here are all the things I'm supposed to have done by now, and I've done none of them." She did have an impressive career, of course, but somehow she felt that didn't count because she hadn't had kids and "driven them around to soccer games." As a result, Jackie felt like a failure. "I kept thinking, This was not the plan."

That summer, Emma, a woman who had been one of Jackie's mom's best friends when Jackie was growing up, came to town. Jackie hadn't seen Emma in ten years, but when they went to lunch, Jackie admitted to feeling blue. Emma said, "So life didn't turn out the way you'd planned. Who gets everything they wanted, anyway? Deal with it. You can mope about it, or you can figure out how to fast-forward." Emma's words shook Jackie out of her stupor. Right then, she made up her mind to start enjoying her life. Within the next few months, she took rock-climbing lessons and Photoshop classes. And, lo and behold, she began to feel better.

Jackie could have adopted a child on her own, but she never felt a desire to be a single mom. She thought all that responsibility would be too much for her. However, that next summer, she met her current husband. Jackie and Andy were working on the same medical research project. They would have a cup of coffee from time to time and chit-chat about their weeks. Andy would talk about his two kids, whom Jackie thought sounded great. Jackie would share her hobbies and passions. A couple of months later, they started dating, and everything went smoothly from there.

Jackie met the kids after about a month, even though Andy initially had said that he wanted to wait at least three months to introduce her. She fell in love with them immediately. These days, the children spend alternate weeks with Andy and Jackie, and the other weeks with their biological mother and her new husband.

Jackie feels that, without a doubt, being a stepmother has altered her life for the better. For example, being a surgeon is very intense and demanding. Jackie used to work eighty to ninety hours per week, seeing patients and conducting research. Now she makes her personal life a priority. Jackie said, "Now I tell my boss, 'You can have me during work time, but the rest of the time, unless it's truly a crisis, I'm not there.' That's been absolutely huge."

Furthermore, her status as stepmother has helped her to reconnect with life in a more joyful and affirming way. Jackie commented, "I think it's easy to get jaded. But then, when you have kids, you watch them do things that you've long since taken for granted, like spinning around on the grass in the backyard. You see life through the eyes of someone who is still young, and it knocks the stuffing out of your cynicism."

Earlier this fall, Jackie's 13-year-old stepson was playing football for the first time. He made an open-field tackle that prevented the other team from scoring a touchdown, even though he doesn't play defense. Jackie got tearful as she described what happened next. "Afterwards, he was standing on the sidelines, and he looked over to the stands to see us—his mother, father, stepfather, and me. He smiled, and, oh my God . . . I saw that smile and thought, He'll have that kind of happiness stored in him for the rest of his life. It was a perfect moment."

Single Moms

Women end up as single moms for a variety of reasons: they leave their husbands, or their husbands leave them. Their husbands die. But more and more often these days, middle-class women are choosing to have children as single mothers. In the past, women basically had two options: marriage and motherhood, or spinsterhood and career. But today's women know that they can have both a career and children—and they don't even have to be married to do it. Whether through accidental pregnancy, adoption, consensual sex with a friend, or insemination with sperm from a sperm bank, an increasing number of women are making their way as mothers without spouses.

The challenges for single mothers are not insignificant. Aside from taking on the role of primary caretaker, single mothers also must act as breadwinners. The stress can prove overwhelming, and every woman I spoke with in this situation emphasized the importance of having a solid support network in place before they began the process.

• • • •

MARISSA RAUCH ADOPTED a child on her own from Russia when she was 40. Now 47, she lives with her 8-year-old daughter in Washington, D.C., where she works as a freelance photographer. And she couldn't be happier with her decision to become a single mother.

Marissa began thinking about adopting as a single woman when she was 35. On that birthday, she promised herself that she wouldn't turn 40 without having a child. She then ended up in a serious relationship with a guy for a couple of years, but they broke up when she was almost 39. As soon as that happened, Marissa started the adoption process.

Marissa chose to adopt rather than visit a sperm bank because she felt that going through a pregnancy without a partner would be lonely. Moreover, she never had had a burning desire to bear her own child. She always had known that she'd be a mom but didn't particularly care how that came about. She figured she might as well give a home to a child who needed one.

The adoption process was grueling. Marissa had to fill out reams of paperwork and then have everything notarized and certified. She kept thinking, "If a married couple had to fill out all this paperwork before they had a child, they'd never do it!" Marissa spent twelve hundred dollars on notary fees alone.

However, it took only nine months from the day she submitted her final paperwork until Marissa got her baby. "It was just like a pregnancy!" she exclaimed. The adoption agency called her the day after Christmas to tell her that a seven-month-old girl was available in Russia, although she had to get over her chicken pox before Marissa could pick her up. A month later, Marissa's mother flew with her to greet the newest family member.

"It was so exciting," Marissa said. "I fell in love with Daniela the moment I saw her. We were lying on the bed in Moscow just a day after my mom and I got her. She only weighed nine pounds at the time. And she just threw one arm on me and one arm on my mom, like we'd always been together. It all seemed totally natural. Life was really good."

Marissa had taken the time to prepare everything before she left. Still, her friends threw her a huge baby shower after she got back from Russia. Marissa laughed when she told me, "The UPS truck arrived every day for a year with a gift for Daniela. Strangers sent me presents, people I barely knew. People were like, 'Wow, I can't believe you did that! I could never do that. You're so brave.'"

Two of her friends later said that Marissa had inspired them to adopt on their own. "But I don't want people to see me as a role model," she commented. "I'm not out to save the world. I did this for me as much as for Daniela."

Marissa gets tremendous support from her family and friends. She also feels lucky, in that Daniela has been an easy kid. "We're a team now. I can't imagine my life without her," Marissa said, her voice cracking with emotion. "I hate to seem like a Pollyanna, but being a single mom has been great in every way."

Everything was going smoothly for Marissa and Daniela until about eighteen months after they came together. Then out of the blue, at age 41, Marissa started feeling sick. She noticed herself dragging at photo shoots and couldn't figure out why she was so tired. It turned out that she had cancer. Marissa said, "My doctor was crying when she told me, she was so upset. She knew my situation, that I was a single mom." Six weeks later, Marissa had surgery and discovered that her cancer was stage four, meaning that it had spread all over her body. Once a month for six months, she had to have chemotherapy.

Fortunately, everyone in her life rallied around Marissa. Her mother, sister, or the nanny would stay home with Daniela. People cooked them dinner. Marissa had just one bad day each month, on the third day of chemo, when she always felt sick. Her next-door neighbor said, "After the nanny leaves, I'll come over." So she would take Daniela to the park that day. "It was awesome," Marissa said. "I am really blessed to have had such an incredible support system."

Meanwhile, Marissa thought, "Thank God I have Daniela," because it was her daughter who kept Marissa going and gave her the strength to fight her cancer. Marissa most looked forward to taking a shower with Daniela in the evening, reading books together, and then going to bed early. It has now been six years, and, fortunately, there has been no new growth of Marissa's cancer.

On the whole, Marissa feels that, as long as you set up a good support system and can afford it, becoming a single mother can make life so much richer. "I have a really blessed life. I never take one thing for granted," she said. Then she added, "But you have to prepare your head more than anything. It's all about your attitude. You have to think, Yeah, I'm going to get through this. I'm going to be there for this kid no matter what."

The Accomplishment of Motherhood

While feminism may have brought women into the workforce and focused attention on our achievements outside the home, ironically, it didn't challenge the widespread assumption that women should have children. Motherhood continues to be seen as a sign of status in our culture. No matter how accomplished you are as a career woman, you still earn stripes for having children. Of course, some women choose not to become mothers at all, and they are not ostracized for their decision. But the vast majority of women still desire children and view them as the ultimate proof of worth and womanhood.

As a result, women can feel tremendous pressure to perform as mothers. They may feel a great portion of their identity tied up in the success of their children as students, athletes, and socially well-adjusted human beings. They may experience guilt about having to go to work, needing to take time off for self-care, or just plain getting bored and tired at times. This is all understandable. The point I would like to emphasize—and I hope it has come across clearly in this chapter—is that we do ourselves a favor by letting go of specific ideas of what it looks like to be an accomplished mother. As we have seen, there are many ways to approach modern-day parenting. Women—whether divorced, single from the start, or happily married; whether biological mothers, stepmothers, or adoptive mothers—all have reason to celebrate their achievement. Simply to be a mother who loves and provides for her children is an accomplishment in and of itself.

Ten

THE ACCOMPLISHED
CAREER WOMAN

. . . .

WE ARE STILL struggling to define what it means to be an accomplished career woman. Does it mean earning the largest salary or reaching the highest rank? Does it mean working for a cause that you truly believe in, even if that requires taking a pay cut? Does it mean achieving the most recognition and winning the most awards for what you do? Does it mean throwing everything you've got into your career, or does it mean finding a balance between work and personal life? And where does having children fit in?

I don't think there is any "right" answer, especially in these rapidly changing times. Rather, we all must take a close look at our lives and come to a personal understanding of what makes us feel most fulfilled. Some of us will choose the stability of a high-income profession. Others will gravitate toward careers in which we feel that we are helping to make the world a better place. Others are driven by their creative passions. Some women choose to have a family and work, others to stay home with their kids, and others not to have children at all.

Money, Money, Money

If I were to think about the one topic—other than sex—that seems most difficult to discuss in therapy sessions, I would have to say it is money. When new clients come to me, I find that it takes about ten sessions before I can create a dialogue about money. Discussing money is, for the most part, considered socially inappropriate in our culture. But in spite of the reluctance many people have to talk about financial issues, money often proves one of the greatest sources of stress in our lives.

Money has meaning for each and every one of us. In the past, men traditionally tied more of their self-esteem to income and bank balance than did women. Today, however, more and more women are feeling the same way—that their net worth determines their worthiness as human beings. Unfortunately, as we get older and become greater masters of our crafts, advancing in our careers, we also can become trapped in an obsessive need to accomplish more and earn more in order to feel successful. Psychologists call this the "aspirational treadmill." Think of it as a fancy way of saying "keeping up with the Joneses."

Many women I work with find themselves enmeshed in a triangulated relationship between money, career (either their own or their partners', or both), and their personal lives. They argue that it has become increasingly difficult to create work-life balance, and that it demands an ever-greater amount of money to sustain a comfortable lifestyle for themselves and their families.

Although without a doubt we need a certain basic amount of money in order to survive and thrive, it is also true that some people care more about their incomes than do others. What I find most critical to ask my clients is not how much money they make but rather how they define their self-worth. In a society where the emphasis is placed on dollars in the bank account, I ask, "How do you validate yourself in ways that have nothing to do with money? By quality of life? Adventurous experiences? Achievements and awards? Fighting for justice, human rights, or environmental protection? Creating a loving family?"

Some women who have committed their lives to their careers have told me, "I've been able to prove myself by doing well in my job and making a difference." This statement serves as an example of a healthy attitude toward career accomplishments—women measuring themselves by their contributions to the world rather than by the number on their paychecks.

Work-Life Balance

Many women entering their 40s have both a career and a family. According to the Bureau of Labor Statistics, over half of all mothers with children under the age of 3 are employed full-time. *Time* magazine recently reported that 40 percent of women say they are the primary breadwinners in their household. I have encountered more than a few new mothers in my therapy practice who were looking forward to returning to work several months after giving birth. They were eager to have adult contact and intellectual stimulation, and to feel validated as "more than feeding and diaper-changing machines." Then again, many other mothers have expressed reluctance and even despair at having to return to work shortly after having children. But regardless of her initial attitude, nearly every mother ends up struggling at some point with the ever-elusive issue of "work-life balance."

• • • •

JANET STERN HAS confronted the issue of work-life balance head-on and has come to some interesting—and perhaps surprising—conclusions. In her professional life, Janet has taken on one of the most male-dominated industries around: investment banking. As a senior-level director at a firm in Boston and the mother of two, Janet has found it critical to check in with herself regularly. She determines whether she's on track with what she wants in life and adjusts as necessary, but she also is realistic in acknowledging that sacrifices must be made.

Janet, 43, grew up in Colorado. After graduating from college, she immediately joined an investment bank in Chicago, taking off just two years to complete an MBA program. By the age of 30, she therefore already held a fairly senior position. She continued to excel, attaining promotion after promotion in her 30s and on into her 40s, even as she married and had two children.

You might suspect that, in order to succeed in such a male-dominated career, Janet had to adopt more masculine characteristics. But on the contrary, she finds that, these days, women who become "too male" don't do as well. "Admittedly, most of us who chose this career probably had a lot of 'male' traits to begin with," Janet said. She mentioned her own hard-driving competitiveness, abruptness, and lack of patience with others. "But there's a new generation of women in banking who are holding true to themselves and succeeding. We no longer feel the need to pledge our entire lives to the company."

While Janet does not feel that the women in banking are held to a higher standard than the men, she argued that the women do have to work harder. These days, women do have room for error, and the outright sexism that they saw in the seventies, eighties, and even into the nineties has declined. Still, men tend to have a natural affinity with one another based on common interests, such as football and golf, that women don't always share. And so women end up putting more effort into building the connections that naturally help men advance. "As a result," Janet said, "you need to outperform consistently as a woman to get noticed and promoted. There's no way around the fact that you have to work very, very hard."

Janet herself doesn't mind working hard. She theorizes that people with an inclination to be workaholics self-select into banking. She said with a chuckle, "I would've worked myself half to death in any other industry, too. A person is ultimately wound the way they're wound, and I was always wound to work hard. If you want real balance, then you don't choose a career in investment banking."

Although Janet has been able to have a social life, it definitely comes second to her demanding work schedule. She particularly regrets not having made more time for engaging in social activities with other women in banking. She has noticed that, in her industry, women don't network with each other as much as they might. In fact, Janet generally has found the men to be more supportive.

Asked about her work-life balance, Janet merely laughed. "I don't have it! Work-life balance is the million-dollar question, right? Well, I have asked every woman I know who has a high-powered career and a family, and the reality is, no one knows the answer. I struggle with it every day."

In Janet's view, the idea of "having it all" is a lie. "Having it all means messing up everything a little bit. It means accepting that a B from me is still better than an A from some people, and definitely better than a C from me. When you're used to nothing less than perfection from yourself, that's the hardest part. You have to get comfortable with trade-offs."

Janet gets up most days at 5:30 A.M., and is in the office by 7:00. She works until 5:30 or 6:00 P.M., and is home by 6:30. She keeps her kids up late so that she can make them dinner and put them to bed every night. They're asleep by 9:00, she has a few minutes with her husband, and then she goes back to work at her home computer until 11:00 (sometimes later), and then to bed. She doesn't work out much; she doesn't read, or watch TV, or see movies; and she rarely sees friends outside playdates.

The upside, in Janet's mind, is that she gets paid much better in banking than she would for working just as hard in publishing, fashion, or another traditionally "female" industry. She would rather get paid ten times as much now, while at the peak of her earning power, and take it easy someday in the future, "when they inevitably fire me."

Janet also mentioned that she makes enough money so that her husband can stay home to raise the kids, which suits both of them well. "He's happier being home, and I'm happier working. Even though I feel like a train wreck a lot of the time, I wouldn't change anything."

The biggest downside to Janet's chosen lifestyle is that she starts thinking people are expendable. "In my business, people leave and people get fired all the time. As a result, I find myself less able to resolve conflicts in my personal life. When friends or family piss me off about something, I immediately think about 'firing' them from my life rather than working it out!" Janet told me with a laugh.

In addition, she is always exhausted. "Most adults probably find me boring, unattractive, and impatient," Janet said and grinned, although I had to disagree. I found her wry humor entertaining, and she definitely did not look worse for wear. Janet argued with me but then said, "Well, so long as my kids and husband don't care, I don't much care. One day, I will be foxy and rested and have intriguing things to say. Whenever that may be."

As Janet stated, part of the problem is that, as women, we tend to set such a high bar for ourselves. We demand that we show up fully for all of our commitments, and we have trouble saying no to more. We erroneously think, I can multitask, schedule, and plan my way through this. And we do execute impressively well and efficiently much of the time. But many women end up sacrificing their own needs, and their own sanity, in the process of seeking to be accomplished career women. We need to remind ourselves that work does not define who we are.

Career Women without Kids

Many women entering their 40s are accomplished career women, in the sense that they've developed an area of expertise, feel mastery over their jobs, and are in a position to mentor younger women. Some of them choose to have children, and others do not.

Alison Thompson has put concerns about family and money aside in favor of volunteering. Alison, "43ish" years old, grew up on the edge of the Australian bush. Throughout her childhood, her older brothers led her on adventures into the untamed wilderness. Her father was a minister who engaged in missionary work, so she also traveled frequently with her parents to developing nations around Asia. As a result, Alison developed a courageous spirit (and impressive nursing skills) at a young age.

Alison moved to New York in her mid-20s. After trying a variety of jobs, she decided to attend film school. She had just completed her first feature film when the World Trade Center was attacked. She immediately joined the Red Cross as a volunteer and ended up spending the next nine months working at Ground Zero. "That experience really changed my thinking," Alison said. "I'd been making this silly comedy, and suddenly it just all seemed so stupid. Twenty-three of my friends died in the September eleventh attacks. I realized that I had to do things that mattered. I had a bigger calling. I knew that I wanted to spend my whole life doing that sort of volunteer work."

Eventually, Alison returned to her filmmaking career, but this time committed to making films with a message. Then, on Christmas Day 2004, she learned that an enormous tsunami had hit Southeast Asia. As she and her boyfriend, Oscar, sat glued to the television watching the death toll rise, Alison felt a calling to go help. She invited Oscar to join her, and he accepted. She then began calling friends to raise money and gathering medical supplies for the trip. A week later, they took off for Sri Lanka.

As she had at Ground Zero, Alison ended up staying far longer than intended. She and Oscar remained working in the village of Peraliya for over fourteen months, during which time they raised thousands of dollars, recruited many dozens of volunteers to join their efforts, collected dead bodies, rebuilt the school and supplied the kids with new school uniforms, ran a hospital that serviced thousands of the injured, and became part of the community themselves. Shortly before she left, Alison also established the Community Tsunami Early-Warning Centre (CTEC), a nonprofit organization that she still runs, which helps to set up tsunami warning systems throughout Southeast Asia.

Alison loved watching how volunteering filled people with confidence. They would forget all about their own problems. "People changed before my eyes. They'd blossom after a short time in the field," Alison said. "You don't know what you *could* do until you do it. You're in an adrenaline rush when you're in a disaster zone. It just keeps you going every hour, not thinking ahead. You deal with whatever comes your way. So you might think to yourself, I could never do that, but you can."

After returning to the United States, Alison and Oscar made a documentary film, *The Third Wave,* about their experience in Sri Lanka. It comprised footage that Alison and a Sri Lankan–Canadian man had shot on a basic, handheld video camera. She and Oscar spent months promoting the movie at film festivals around the world, including Cannes.

Alison made it clear that she doesn't expect everyone to just take off on some wild volunteer adventure to the other side of the planet for months at a time. Doing that isn't necessary to have a positive impact. "There's so much to be done right in your backyard. Even if you just take a week of vacation, or a couple of hours on a weekend, to volunteer, it all helps," she said.

As far as people making excuses that they have nothing to offer, Alison argued that we all have common sense. "Your skills are everything you've done since you were little. You don't have to be a doctor or a construction worker to be of assistance. Volunteers can do art or music with kids, or just play with them. They can dig a well or start a garden. They can teach English, sanitation and health, or offer small-business services."

I wondered if Alison wanted to have children, since children obviously would impede her ability to travel the world as a volunteer on a shoestring budget. She replied, "You know, all my life, I wanted four kids. But that changed around 9/11. I loved the freedom that I had to stay and volunteer there for as long as I wanted. And so the desire to have kids just gradually went away. I'm a mother to all those tsunami kids. I want to be a bigger mother."

I wasn't surprised to get word just two weeks after the January 2010 earthquake in Haiti, which killed hundreds of thousands of people and left many others stranded without water, food, or medical care, that Alison had arrived on the scene to help out once more. She plans to stay for at least a year.

• • • •

CONNIE RICE IS an extraordinary woman who has made an incredible impact on her community and the U.S. justice system at large. Like Alison Thompson, in addition to choosing not to have a family, she has forgone the opportunity to make far more money than she does. Instead, she has devoted her life to fighting for human rights. Her accomplishments are too numerous to list—she has won more than fifty awards for the advancement of multi-racial democracy—so we will touch only on the highlights of her career here.

Connie, age 53, was born in Washington, D.C., and grew up all over the world. After graduating from Harvard, she attended law school at New York University. She then earned a prestigious clerkship with a judge on the U.S. Sixth Circuit Court of Appeals. She worked for a few years at a law firm, but at age 35 joined the NAACP Legal Defense Fund (LDF). She became the codirector of the Los Angeles office just five years later.

Connie laughs easily and has a confident yet comfortable and welcoming manner. In response to my opening explanation of *Fortytude*, she said, "Oh, my 40s were great. My 40s were fun. I always thought

I'd hit my stride in my 40s, and I did. My 50s I hate, though. Whoever thought of hot flashes needs to be dug up and shot." We both laughed.

When she was approaching 40, Connie thought for a while about having children. Since she wasn't married, she even visited a sperm bank to explore her options. She picked donors based on their intelligence and height, not considering their race because she didn't care. The problem was, once she read their essays, she would say, "Oh no! He's no good." Her doctor teased her, "This isn't the Harvard Admissions Committee!" because she had served on that for a time. Eventually, she realized that she just didn't want to have kids.

Connie never has regretted her choice not to have a family. "I always thought, when I'm 90 and sitting on a porch, the thing I'd hate the most is to have those coulda woulda shoulda kind of feelings. So I asked myself, When I'm 90, what will I regret? Not having been married or had kids? Or not having devoted my life to a good cause? The truth is, my life is about my work. If you have kids, your life has to be about them. If I'd had children, I wouldn't have done half of what I've done in the world. I work 24/7, and it wouldn't be fair to them. So it was an easy choice for me, but I was brutally honest with myself. Maybe that's selfish altruism."

Anyhow, the way Connie looks at it, she has a million kids—all the poor, disadvantaged youngsters for whom she fights "like a tigress" every day. She builds them schools. She works to get the violent neighborhoods they live in reformed. She makes sure they have transportation. During a graduation speech, she once said to the parents in the audience, "You raise the children and I'll raise hell!"

Speaking to other women who don't want to be married or have kids, even though they feel that's what they are supposed to do, Connie said, "Be honest about what you want. If you want a husband and a child, you have to organize your life to make that happen. But recognize that you'll have to do most of the work. Don't make yourself miserable by having a kid when you don't want one. There are a million ways to live your life. There is nothing balanced about my life, and I'm very happy about it. No one imposed this lifestyle on me, and I don't feel I'm missing out on anything."

Evolving Our Careers and Ourselves

The women profiled in this chapter all are generally content with their chosen careers and life paths. But what happens if you're not feeling fulfilled by what you are doing in your professional life?

When clients of mine are struggling with their careers, I first encourage them to explore their fears and goals around money. Determining how important it is to earn a specific income, and how their financial situation will affect their well-being, helps them consider whether they are willing to make a change. I generally ask the following questions:

1. How was money discussed in your family? How did those discussions affect you growing up?
2. What do you feel is the ideal amount of money to have? And why?
3. If you were to have that "ideal" amount of money, would you pay more or less attention to the values in your life?
4. If you could teach a woman of the future generation something about money, what would you teach her? If a woman who is older than you could teach you something about money, what could she teach?

Try asking yourself these questions. If you take the time to really explore your answers, you might find yourself surprised at how much—or how little—money you consider truly necessary. Finding

out how much money you believe you need can prove valuable in helping you to set your priorities and define what it means for you to feel
"accomplished."

Next, I suggest that clients identify their skill sets. Not all of us are
going to radically change career at midlife. By the time we enter our
fifth decades, most of us have a pretty good sense of what we can do
well. I believe that we're hardwired to be better at certain things in life
than others—we are gifted at birth with specific types of intelligence.
Some people may never be musicians because they can't even tell if
they're singing off-key. Others will never be doctors because the sight
of blood makes them faint.

Nevertheless, I encourage people to get creative in their definitions
of what they do well. You are not a product designer but an artist. You
are not an office assistant but an organizational expert. Separate yourself from the particular role that you have in your current workplace
and pull back to see yourself as an individual with unique talents. Then
brainstorm all the arenas where you might apply those intelligences to
your work. Involve other people in your assessment, so that you don't
unconsciously limit yourself. Do some research online, reading de-
scriptions of jobs that appeal to you even if you think, at first, that you
aren't qualified to take them. And, of course, remember that you can
continue to evolve the skills you already have, or you can seek to develop new ones—because it really is never too late.

These days, many of us are committing to the path of awakening.
The upside to the economic upheaval and the environmental crisis is
that we're being forced to pay more attention to our values and our impact on the world. We are coming to realize that managing our natural
resources more carefully and finding ways to help other people are
critical tasks for us to devote our lives to, regardless of societal status or
annual income. This is what women with fortytude know.

For those of us who do wake up, the rewards are rich. We are able
to let go of many of society's prescriptions concerning what we must

own and how we must operate in our lives in order to be "successful," and instead to embrace our true callings. We move from seeking material gain toward celebrating spiritual pursuits. We stop comparing ourselves to mass media–created ideals of accomplishment and instead turn inward, asking ourselves how we can make the most of our time on earth.

PART IV

ADVENTURE

. . . .

Adventure, the fourth Core Value of women with fortytude, reflects a contradictory aspect of human nature. We have an urge to conserve, and to create nests for ourselves and those we love. Simultaneously, we feel a pull to strike forth in search of new experiences that foster our growth.

Adventure means not settling into a tired, old pattern but rather challenging ourselves to renew our interest in and enthusiasm for life by pushing out of our comfort zones. It does not necessarily imply recklessness, however. As several women in the Dallas focus group put it: "We all need to have excitement and new experiences without being irresponsible."

Here is the challenge that I set forth before you: Does your life right now seem mundane? If so, I invite you to step outside the routine for one or several days. Adventure can include the following: trying a new restaurant, a new sexual position, a new weekend activity beyond your habitual tendencies, or a new type of person to date. It can be anything that piques your curiosity—anything that you find exciting.

My sister Jennifer makes it a point to seek out adventure every five years. In her late 30s, she took up triathlons, despite never having swum or biked competitively. These days, in her 40s, she is addicted to open-water swimming. In fact, she just completed an *Alcatraz* swim in the San Francisco Bay without a wet suit!

While Jennifer battled several anxieties during her youth, she truly has decided to be fearless in her 40s. She hasn't conquered every fear (she still flees from moths), but she now looks to find adventure in all parts of her life. "The older I get, the more I realize that time spent being afraid is time wasted," Jen told me. "So I don't spend my time wringing my hands anymore. I know that I am challenging myself when I feel a flash of fear and have to be conscious of overcoming it."

As an ER physician, Jennifer has had to train herself to remain calm in the midst of panic, and she has carried over that ability into her personal and recreational life. A year ago, she started a business in an entirely new domain: private medical advocacy. This field has emerged to help guide people through the complex world of modern medical care when they are facing a serious illness.

Jennifer said, "Part of the reason I did this was to keep myself moving forward in my 40s. Being an ER doctor is kind of like being on a treadmill: after ten years, you master the skills. Even though you never know what will walk in the door, nine times out of ten, it's the same thing you've seen before. I wanted to try something new." Being a pioneer is very exciting to her. "Taking this step," she said, "feels a lot like rock climbing—terrifying and exhilarating at the same time."

My sister has taken fear and turned it into motivation to propel herself forward. Women with fortytude do this all the time. I invite you to challenge yourself to move beyond your routines and embrace the unexpected. Step into the adventure of your life.

Eleven

IT'S NOT TOO LATE

. . . .

ONE OF THE biggest mistakes we can make as we move past our 30s, through our 40s, and into our 50s, is to begin telling ourselves, "It's too late." Too late to start a new career. Too late to follow our dreams. Too late to have a family. Too late to run a marathon. Too late to volunteer for a nonprofit. Too late to learn to play a musical instrument. Too late to find happiness. Too late to be the people we most want to be.

Some of us may feel that there is something missing from our lives, in spite of our many achievements and blessings. Even if we are in a satisfying relationship, have enough money to pay the bills, enjoy our children, and feel accomplished in our careers, we might still sense that we're lacking vitality. But we can seek out novelty at any age. It is *not* too late to take on challenges, to push ourselves out of our comfort zones, and to find our way to true fulfillment.

Not Too Late to Connect to Your Body

With a grounded, powerful presence, Patty Ivey of Washington, D.C., is one of the most fit, youthful-looking 56-year-olds I have ever seen.

She serves as an example of how it is possible to find a connection to your body, and hence your self-confidence and strength, after the age of 40.

Patty grew up in Long Island in a strict, conservative Catholic family, and she married young to escape. Her husband was a kind man with a good sense of humor, a hard worker, loyal, honest, and true. "He's the kind of guy women dreamed of being married to," Patty said.

But Patty quickly began to realize her husband's flaws. He would become depressed and quite negative. Furthermore, he couldn't communicate about his emotions. Patty explained, "I need a deep soul connection with people. I've got to crawl inside and get to know you. I can't just talk about politics and sports. So as our marriage went on, I got more and more lonely."

Nevertheless, the marriage lasted for sixteen years. It survived a move to Washington, D.C., when her husband got a job there; Patty's discovery in her early 30s that she was infertile; and her opening a small baking business called the Cookie Lady at age 35. But eventually, Patty realized that she couldn't take the sense of isolation in her marriage anymore. She and her husband went for couples counseling. She asked him to open himself emotionally, but he said he couldn't do that. They left the therapist's office in tears and agreed that day to divorce. She was 37.

Many of her friends and family members told Patty that she was making a mistake—her husband was a great guy, they said, and she shouldn't let him go. Only years later did her mother pull her aside and tell Patty that she, too, had felt lonely in her marriage but never had the courage to do anything about it.

Patty struggled after her divorce. Since her husband had told her that he wasn't able to change for her, she had been left feeling as though she wasn't worthy of being loved. "It was the ultimate rejection," she said. "I was devastated. I couldn't wrap my head around it." Patty felt as though she had failed on several levels as a woman: to have children and to keep her marriage alive. She sank into a depression.

When Patty started dating at age 39, it only made matters worse. "Time and again, men rejected me when they found out how old I was because they wanted to date for a few years, then get married, then have kids. They were doing the math and saying, 'You're too old.' I hadn't even told them that I was unable to bear children."

So Patty started doing whatever she could from a physical perspective to look younger. She wore short skirts to attract attention, but they only made men think that she was easy. She also worked hard to get thin. Having always been a bit chubby, she went on diets and took up serious exercise for the first time in her life. Soon she had developed an eating disorder.

"I had anorexia," Patty explained. "I was pretty much not eating. I'd have maybe seven hundred calories a day, and I was running five miles a day. Plus I just had the anorexic mind-set—I thought I was overweight. I was a mess." When friends tried to tell her that she was getting too thin, she simply stopped hanging out with them.

In her early 40s, Patty found out that her mother was dying of a brain tumor. She sold her cookie business and began seeing a therapist. Within the next couple of years, things started to shift. Patty was recovering from her eating disorder. She also met a terrific guy, an artist who offered her support when both her mother and her dog passed away, and patiently helped her piece her life back together. "He nurtured me," Patty said. "I so needed nurturing."

Nevertheless, Patty still didn't love her body or who she was. Then, at age 47, she injured her knee and had to have surgery. Her doctor advised her to lay off the compulsive running and do yoga to heal. Around that time, a friend asked Patty to open a yoga studio with her—not because of Patty's minimal yoga experience but because of her business know-how. Patty agreed, and a few months later they had opened the first of three Down Dog Yoga studios in the D.C. area.

But there were more changes in store for Patty. "I'm a big believer that the universe puts you where you're supposed to be," she said. Six months after they'd started Down Dog Yoga, her partner quit and left Patty with the business. At that point, Patty still "didn't know the first thing about yoga or how to teach it," but she had to start learning fast. She hired a bunch of teachers and took a teacher training course. It didn't take long for her to fall in love, and for her new business activity to become her passion.

Patty spoke with absolute conviction when she said: "Yoga changed my life. After I started teaching yoga, I really came into my body with love and compassion for the first time. And I realized that this is my work in this lifetime. Yoga for me is power. As my body got stronger, my mind got stronger, and I became a stronger person."

I wondered what advice Patty might have for women who hadn't found a connection to their bodies, and who perhaps felt intimidated by yoga or other physical activities. "Just show up and keep showing up," Patty counseled. "I remember when I was going through the divorce, there were days when I felt that I couldn't get out of bed. I just had to put one foot in front of the other. Exercise is the same. Just keep doing it. Show up. Connect to your breath. Don't worry about wearing cute little outfits, either; wear whatever you want. But be committed. Stick to it. Hold on to faith, believing in what you can't yet see. Change will come."

Not Too Late to Become a Mom

Samantha Loehman, age 50, lives in Seattle, where she works as an oceanographer. Many aspects of her life are adventuresome, from her exciting career aboard research vessels to her passion for mountain climbing. But perhaps her greatest adventure was adopting her first child at 44 years old, and her second at 48.

From a young age, Samantha was interested in nature, science, and how things work. So she chose to major in biology as an undergraduate. But after working in a lab stress-testing cardboard boxes to see how much pressure they could withstand, and feeding cows at 3:00 A.M. to study milk production, she decided in her late 20s to get an advanced degree in marine science.

During and after grad school, Samantha found herself in an exhilarating job, working day and night with fabulous people aboard ships, drinking coffee, listening to music, and making fascinating scientific discoveries. She joined expeditions to Hawaii, Tahiti, Barbados, Senegal, and throughout the Atlantic Ocean.

Samantha envisioned herself as married with three children, but although she dated several fantastic guys, she never completely clicked with any of them. However, she feels now that things happened that way for a reason. Had she married one guy she had fallen in love with, she might never have come across many of her current life opportunities. "I think the family part would've accelerated and the career part would've slowed," Samantha said. "But anyway, I didn't meet the person who would've made the mom option possible."

Samantha moved to Seattle for work when she was in her mid-30s. There she joined a climbing club, where she met her husband, Max. They got married one day after her fortieth birthday.

Although Samantha and Max tried for some time to get pregnant, they did not succeed. Eventually, when they sat down and considered their options, adoption seemed right. "Just look at the problems the world faces, and the number of kids who don't have a place to call home, or a mom and dad. It felt like adopting was a good thing for the world—for us as parents, and for the kids."

When she was 44, Samantha and Max adopted their first child, a six-month-old boy from Guatemala. Four years later, they adopted a seven-month-old girl. They chose Guatemala because they found a wonderful orphanage there where the children all were held, cared for, loved, well-fed, sung to, and kept in good health.

Samantha expanded upon the process. "At the time I was going through the fertility stuff, I was sad not to have a biological child. But ten years down the road, if I ask myself, 'Am I still saddened by my infertility?' the truth is: I'm not at all. These children I've adopted, I mean, they are a gift! They were joyful, laughing, and happy from the moment we got them. Of course, all children are a gift. But I honestly can't imagine feeling any closer to my kids if they were biologically related to me."

Samantha still works, and continues to love what she does. She'll go on three-week-long research cruises at times. She leaves the kids with her husband, and gets help from her sister-in-law, climbing friends, and a babysitter. She feels able to balance work and motherhood, and has no regrets about her choices. In sum, she said, "Life is pretty fantastic."

Not Too Late to Change Careers

Susan Wayne left an impressive corporate career to pursue a very alternative one after the age of 40. Susan grew up in what she described as a "WASPy, well-to-do, white suburb of Chicago." Her father was a doctor, her mother a stay-at-home mom. While her parents had no expectations of her going into business or having a particular career, they were very achievement-oriented.

After college, Susan worked briefly in corporate finance. She then got an MBA and switched to a career in advertising. She worked hard and did well. At age 28, she bought her first condo and met her life partner, Diane. For the next decade, Susan's life continued fairly predictably, as she made significant career advances and gained more responsibility each year.

At the same time, Susan started taking classes in spirituality and training to be a Reiki healer. "It was my side passion," she said matter-of-factly, as if energy work were the norm for any high-ranking advertising exec.

When she was 38, Susan got a terrific job offer from another company, which brought her and Diane to San Francisco. And that's when something shifted for Susan. The couple went to Hawaii for her fortieth birthday. After her stressful year of moving and taking on a new job, she just wanted to sit on the beach and relax. But then, the day before her birthday, she took a book that her assistant had given her called *In the Footsteps of Gandhi* to the beach. The book contained profiles of inspirational people such as Cesar Chavez, Joan Baez, and Thich Nhat Hanh. As she started reading it, Susan burst into tears.

"I was sitting under this little umbrella chair looking out at the ocean and just sobbing," Susan said. "I couldn't stop, either. The meltdown lasted the whole day. I wasn't grieving; it wasn't sadness. It was my soul speaking to me, saying, 'You need to pay attention.'" Susan went back to the hotel room and told Diane, "I'm not doing what I want to be doing with my life."

A year later Susan left her job, and she and Diane took off to travel the world. Susan found this a challenging time. While she was relieved not to be in the corporate world anymore, she also was stressed about what she would do next. "It's a dilemma both being spiritually inclined and having a type A personality!" she said and laughed.

Eventually, Susan decided to become an interfaith minister. While studying to be ordained, she is doing energy/Reiki and shamanic healing work, teaching spiritual growth classes and giving talks, and developing a book/training project involving archetypes.

Susan has no regrets about having spent so much time in a corporate career; she feels as though she was meant to do what she did in her "previous life." Because of the money she earned at that job, she has been able to live for three years without a steady income. Also, she developed skills in leadership, strategic thinking, visioning, teaching and mentoring, and business—all of which she uses every day in her new career. "I consider myself a spiritual entrepreneur," she explained.

Susan feels that "success" means doing work that is meaningful and joyful, and that she can support herself with. "Due to my pay cut, especially since the economy crashed, Diane and I have had to dramatically ratchet down our lifestyle. I used to buy more expensive clothes. We spent a lot on travel, but now we've cut back. We've been forced to look at our life and say, 'What do we *really* care about?' We've realized that we are happy to have enough money to live a comfortable life—buy healthy, organic foods, go to the gym and practice yoga—but that we don't need any of the trappings. If I made one-third of what I used to, I'd be ecstatic. It's a very different measure. The seeds of my new career are germinating, but they're still young in their life cycle."

• • • •

LIKE SUSAN, Renee Harcourt, 53, and Monica Pasqual, 48, shifted their careers midlife. But they didn't take on just any new profession—they decided to become rock stars.

Renee started playing guitar when she was 12 and wrote her first song when she was in her 20s. But she didn't do music, except as a hobby, until she was in her 40s. Her reluctance stemmed in part from watching her father struggle throughout her childhood to make ends meet as a professional musician.

In her early 20s, Renee worked at an ad agency in Los Angeles. By the time she'd reached her mid-20s, she had already struck out on her own, working as a freelance graphic designer. For the next two decades, her design business was not only a passion but also a reliable source of income.

At age 37, Renee moved from L.A. to the Bay Area. She entered a singer-songwriter contest and won. It made her think that perhaps she should start pursuing a music career seriously. At the same time, however, she felt panicked by the idea. "I thought, At age 39, no one will take me seriously!" Renee said. "Truly, if you're over 20 in the music business, the record labels just aren't interested—you're done, you're all washed up." That's when she met Monica.

Monica had studied classical piano since she was a kid, but health issues interfered with her ability to perform professionally until much later in life. When she was in her 30s, a friend started pushing her to get onstage. They signed up for an open-mike competition in Mill Valley together. Only the friend got sick and didn't show, so Monica had to sing onstage for the first time ever alone. "After that night, I started to take voice lessons, and I found that I loved singing!" she said. "Suddenly, I was like, *This* is what I want to do with my life."

Monica and Renee were at about the same point in their musical careers when they met that fateful night. They hit it off immediately. Since they both lived in Marin, they started playing together at times. "But mostly, we were in competition, vying for the same gigs," Monica said and laughed. "It wasn't until we formed Blame Sally that things really took off." Renee was 44 at the time, Monica 39. Monica brought Pamela Delgado, a guitarist and percussionist, and Jeri Jones, a guitarist and bass player, into the mix. The band has now been together for nine years.

Blame Sally had a ridiculous amount of fun from the start. All the women were in their late 30s and early 40s. During their rehearsals, they would have dinner, drink wine, and work on the vocal parts. Each member wrote and sang songs. Renee explained, "Our attitude was, Let's just do this. Screw the music business. We'll get together once a week and learn songs. It'll be like a book club for musicians." They had no expectations of success, not even getting a gig. "I don't know if it's *because* we had zero expectations, or if there is simply a magic that is Blame Sally because we love each other so much, but the band took on a life of its own and has been unstoppable ever since."

At first, mostly just the members' friends and families came to their shows. But then Blame Sally got a monthly gig at a tiny coffeehouse in

San Francisco, and they started to build an audience. Soon they were playing at music festivals. A year later, a local radio station began airing Blame Sally songs, and eventually the band was picked up on XM radio. Six years later, the women were playing over fifty shows a year, including opening for Joan Baez in San Francisco.

Then, in early 2009, the band hit big-time success. They signed on with a record label for a six-figure, five-year, three-album deal. Although Blame Sally had released three self-produced CDs over the years, *Night of 1000 Stars* is their first commercially produced album. As a result, the band members are now financially able to pursue their musical careers full-time. Take note, ladies: this happened when the band members' ages ranged from 44 to 53.

Renee offered this advice to younger women: "If I've learned anything, it's that it is never too late. Age is all in our minds. When you're very clear about what you want, you can get it." Monica added, "It's funny that we think there are these benchmark ages for when we *should* or *have to* do something, when real life clearly demonstrates that such is not the case."

Inviting Adventure into Your Life

You might feel bored with your life. And you may have lost the courage to do some of the things that you dared to do when you were younger. That makes sense, especially if you have many more responsibilities these days. However, part of the struggle we women face is our tendency to become so encumbered by our daily tasks and obligations that we forget to really *live*.

Here is an exercise to help you figure out what sort of adventure to take, if you are at a loss as to how to step forward into uncharted territory. Imagine that you're going into a bookstore and you have an hour or two to browse and read at your leisure. Which three sections would you go to? Travel? Cooking? Philosophy? Children's literature? Politics? Religion? Business? Pick the first three that come to mind without thinking too much about it. Write them down. Now your challenge is to figure out how to create an exciting job, trip, hobby, or creative pursuit out of these three elements.

Let's consider the case of one of my clients, Chris. Chris had a job at a bank but felt stifled in her creative life. I advised her to try this exercise. When she envisioned herself at a bookstore, Chris found herself drawn to the travel, business, and architecture sections. Next I asked, "What kind of pursuit would allow you to incorporate these three disparate interests?"

Chris struggled at first to come up with an answer. And so I asked her, "What specifically do you like about travel? Is it the escapism? Being immersed in a different culture? Learning another language? Is it because you're interested in the history?" My goal was to encourage Chris to think about the ways in which she might marry her separate passions to meet her needs. She explained that part of what she loved about travel was exploring the different architectural styles of the places she visited, bringing her interests in travel and architecture together.

Chris and I brainstormed. Since she couldn't travel all the time because of work, might she start traveling regularly through the architecture in her own neighborhood? In Manhattan alone, Chris could take herself on new architectural walking tours every weekend. If a historical society already offered such tours, Chris could participate in these, first attending the walks and then perhaps becoming a guide herself. Or if such a service did not already exist, she might offer free walking tours, in which she pointed out sites of architectural interest. Chris thought this would be a great way for her to give back to her community and stay in shape, all while doing something she found tremendously interesting.

Something that starts out as volunteer work might develop into a paying job. Given that Chris had also expressed an interest in business, we talked about how, if her walking tours became popular enough, she might decide to make a full-time career out of the concept. She could hire other people to lead the tours as well. Or she might end up creating similar tours in different cities, which would also give her an opportunity to travel. It might have seemed like a long shot when we were sitting in the therapy room that day, but Chris had the drive, ambition, and business interest to make it possible.

Some women might say, "But I have everything I need! I know who I am, and I'm totally content with what I'm doing in my life. Not only do I not need a career change but I'm not interested in pursuing any new activities or hobbies." It is possible, if this is the case for you, that you are stuck in a rut of routine and familiarity without even knowing it. I suggest you seek out adventure in your life anyway. Do the bookstore exercise and see where it takes you. At a minimum, try preparing a new recipe or listening to a different radio station. There are ways—both small and large—to allow a bit of the unfamiliar into even the most comfortable lives.

Twelve

MAINTAINING
SEXUAL VITALITY

. . . .

SEXUALITY IS JUST as important to our health and well-being as any other aspect of our lives. Sex offers a way of expressing our creativity. It also enables powerful bonding with other people. It allows us to derive pleasure from our bodies, rooting us in our physical presence here on earth. And it helps us to feel more alive, more relaxed, happier, and healthier. Every one of us deserves to look forward to a vital sexual connection with others and with ourselves throughout our lives. We ought to be allowed to find fulfillment in the sexual realm just as we do in the emotional, physical, intellectual, professional, spiritual, and psychological realms of our existence.

When a woman approaches life with a sense of adventure, she is able to harness her sexual power and fully revel in sensual pleasure. Yet the majority of women I've encountered over the years have struggled with issues surrounding sexuality, particularly concerns about losing their sexual attractiveness with age. The dominant question at the 40-something juncture is simply: Can I still harness my sexual power? But the moment they ask this question, some women feel guilty about having such concerns. They express embarrassment at their longing to have men continue seeing them as sexually attractive beings. I emphasize that there is nothing wrong with this; it is a perfectly human desire.

We are animals, after all. Our sexuality is a part of who we are and what makes us tick. There is no reason to feel ashamed of our longing to express ourselves sexually and to enjoy feeling attractive to the opposite sex.

Closely linked to our fear of no longer being perceived as physically appealing is our fear of losing our sexual vitality. I've talked with many women in their late 30s and early 40s who express great concern over the possibility that they'll cease to desire sex as they grow older. Unfortunately, the scientific community helps to perpetuate this belief, and the media often add fuel to the flames. They expose us to an endless deluge of information about the less than desirable symptoms of perimenopause (which generally starts in our late 40s to early 50s) and of menopause itself (which begins one year after a woman's last menstrual cycle). They tell us that, as our hormone levels decline with age, we face a loss of sexual appetite as well as vaginal dryness and thinning of vaginal tissues; decay of vaginal muscles, leading to incontinence; sagging of breasts caused by loss of connective tissue; not to mention hot flashes and night sweats.

But it's a myth that a woman's sexual vitality comes to a screeching halt the moment she turns 40, or even in the decades that follow. In reality, many women who express concerns about losing their sexual vitality at midlife haven't experienced any negative symptoms yet—and they probably won't for years. Not only that, but even when they do hit menopause, most women find that they still have sex drive (even if it is, at times, diminished) and that they can treat other symptoms with lubricating gels and naturopathic remedies.

As a therapist, I've also learned that a lot of clients have a hard time talking about sex. Along with money, sex is the topic clients feel most fragile about and reluctant to address in sessions. My female clients often feel inhibited about openly discussing such an intensely personal and "embarrassing" subject. When a couple come in together, both people tend to feel vulnerable talking about their sex lives because doing so involves a frightening degree of intimacy and self-exposure. That's why I work hard to foster a safe environment, where people can be totally honest, both with me and with one another. My feeling is that it's essential to discuss sex openly, because so many times clients' sex lives are remarkably symptomatic of what's happening at a deeper level in their relationships.

Even as we move into our 50s, 60s, and 70s, our sexual prowess can continue to expand. I know of one woman in her late 70s who still dresses in sexy lingerie once a week and performs a striptease for her husband of fifty years, who is also still sexually vital at age 92! In fact, one of the benefits of aging is that we often become more adventuresome in our attitudes toward sex, as well as more comfortable with our bodies, more appreciative of their ability to give us pleasure, and more tolerant of our flaws. As a result, most women I know point out that they are able to attain orgasm *more* easily the older they get. There's no reason for your sex life to die out at the exact moment when it could be getting more satisfying than ever.

Couples Intimacy Exercises

As I work with couples, I strive to help them understand that, in many cases, neither one of them is to blame for the sexual difficulties that have arisen between them. It often comes down to an issue of *time*—something they generally haven't realized. These days, most of us are cramming forty-eight hours' worth of activity into twenty-four-hour days. We want to incorporate sexual activity into our lives, but it just seems impossible given hectic daily schedules dictated by the demands of children, spouses, parents, friends, bosses, and colleagues.

Viewing a lack of sexual intimacy in this context depersonalizes the subject and lightens some of the emotional strain, making it easier to discuss sex openly. Together, we explore the couple's individual perceptions of time (perhaps one is chronically late and the other is a stickler for punctuality), their daily schedules, and their preferences for time spent together. This conversation allows us to find ways for the couple to connect more powerfully and regularly in the midst of their busy lives.

To help couples understand how time affects their sex lives, and how they can take small but meaningful steps to enhance their intimacy, I invite them to complete these three exercises for the following one or two weeks:

1. Pay attention to and write down the different tasks you perform related to home and family. Note the amount of time you spend on each of these tasks.
2. Track how much time you spend engaging with media and technology, whether it be watching TV, surfing the Internet, talking on the phone, answering e-mails, playing video games, posting to Facebook, or fooling around in any way with your mobile phone, BlackBerry, or other electronic device. Be honest!
3. Observe your feelings during mini-transitions throughout the day. (I define mini-transitions as moments when you are moving between routines, places, people, or events. For example, a mini-transition occurs when one or both spouses leave the house in the morning. Another happens when one or both of them come home from work and they reunite for the evening. And another occurs when the kids have been put to bed or are tucked away in their rooms finishing their homework or playing on the computer and the couples are alone for the first time all day.)

The first exercise—observing time spent on home- and family-related tasks—seems to reveal a consistent theme: women generally carry more of the burden of the household, whether or not they work outside the home. The pattern is particularly evident among mothers.

Statistical research reveals that this is the case in society at large. In spite of the relative equality women have attained in the working world, we still have the bulk of caregiving responsibilities, regardless of job status.

Why is this the case? When I ask that question in therapy sessions, the response I usually get from the men is that their work requires them to spend more hours in the office, or that they have longer commutes, or that they must devote more time to socializing with colleagues outside the office. I wonder if any of these excuses are valid, or if women aren't simply better at multitasking and more committed to keeping the family in smooth working order.

But it doesn't really matter. The point of the exercise isn't to shift societal norms so that men start playing a fifty-fifty role in the household (although that would be great). Rather, the goal is to make both people in the couple more aware of the differences in their schedules. This awareness brings couples one step closer to identifying the underlying tensions that can arise and undermine their sexual vitality. Perhaps, if the men truly grasp how much of an improvement they could see in their sex lives if only they contributed more to household tasks, they will start to do so willingly—without their wives having to engage in "sexual economics" tactics. If nothing else, many men confronted with numerical records of time they have invested in the family compared to their wives feel more empathetic about their partners' exhaustion and lack of sexual appetite at the end of the day.

The second exercise—observing the time spent on some type of media or technological device—is also revealing. I am always amazed at the extent to which these distractions affect modern-day relationships, whether or not women work outside the home. It is almost always the case that both members of the couple find themselves on the computer or watching TV at the end of the day as a means of "getting away from it all." When I ask my female clients what they are doing on the computer at night, most sheepishly answer that they're checking their Facebook pages or seeing what's on sale at Zappos.com.

As we all know, getting on the computer or watching TV can offer a welcome distraction from the burdens of home. But, unfortunately, these activities also can prove detrimental to people's very real relationships with their partners on the other side of the room. I often find that once I've had people track their time spent on media and technology, I don't need to do much else to encourage them to cut back. They can see for themselves how shifting their priorities away from computers, televisions, and handheld devices, and toward each other, will help them rebuild their intimate relationships. They need to make time for sex in their schedules the way they do for exercise, grocery shopping, and paying bills—and playing around with technology is one of the easiest activities to sacrifice.

For the third exercise, I encourage couples to identify the mini-transitions in their day-to-day lives and the feelings that accompany them. In my work, I've found that these mini-transitions generally are *not* comparable to *Brady Bunch* moments. Mike Brady may have returned home from his office to find Carol waiting excitedly to talk to him. But these days, the economic downturn has soured the moods of many and affected the pocketbooks of everyone except those rare people with bulletproof net worths. Not only that but traffic seems to have doubled. Many people have to dive into monitoring the kids, feeding the dogs, or preparing the dinner the minute they walk in the door. Whatever the circumstances, it's unlikely that both people in the couple will be in stellar moods and feel that they have ample time for a courteous "hello," much less an amorous greeting.

As a way of rebuilding intimacy, I recommend that couples give each other just one minute to reconnect during a mini-transition every day. Unfortunately, I find that many couples feel they don't have a minute to spare. Even if they do commit to the practice, they discover after a week or two that it has fallen by the wayside. Most people *want* to make these mini-transitions into meaningful moments between themselves and their partners. Their question is, "How?"

My answer is: "It just takes work." But that work doesn't have to be trying or arduous—it can be very pleasant. The key is to try something different during the transitional moments in order to free yourself from the usual routine. Look at it as an adventure!

One idea is to greet each other without saying anything other than "Hello, it's wonderful to see you." This brevity prevents you from falling into old habits and immediately making demands, such as "John, I need your help right now!" or "Judy, I am really too tired to talk." Another is to stand close to each other, look each other in the eye, and breathe, without speaking or touching at all. Simply allow the nonverbal communication to flow and see what arises. Or you might spend that precious minute hugging and kissing, as a way to fuel the flame for later sexual activity. Whatever method you choose, the point is to give yourselves an opportunity to unwind from stressful events and reconnect with each other for the full minute each day.

The impact of this simple exercise can be profound. I've witnessed couples go from quite frustrated and annoyed with one another to caring and tender. Most people note that spending just a minute together in this peaceful and loving way can set the tone for the entire evening. What's more, many women have told me that they experience decreased fatigue and increased interest in intimacy with their husbands after completing this short daily practice.

When clients take seriously these three exercises—checking in with each other regarding their time commitments to home and family, cutting back on media distractions, and using one mini-transition per day as an opportunity to reconnect—they not only seem less overwhelmed by the idea of temporal constraints on intimacy but also feel more relaxed and in control. They are better able to understand and appreciate their responsibilities and different approaches to their challenging schedules. They appreciate how much of a difference just five minutes of real connection can make in their relationships. As a result, they find themselves relating to one another in a more compassionate, meaningful way.

• • • •

LET'S TAKE A LOOK at one married couple that I worked with as an example of how employing the three exercises we've described might unfold. Sally and Tom were in their early 40s and had two kids, ages 4 and 6. Tom was a stay-at-home writer, and Sally ran a small financial consulting business. They claimed to be a progressive, modern couple and were eager to prove that they didn't play traditional roles. Yet they were struggling in their relationship, complaining that they had no intimacy—sexual or otherwise.

After we'd talked for a while, the major relationship issue became clear. Tom and Sally would get into the same conflict over and over again. It started every night at dinnertime. It was Tom's responsibility to clear the dishes from the table and place them in the dishwasher, give the kids a bath, and tuck them into bed by 9:00 P.M. Instead, Tom would leave the dishes in the sink, go into the den, turn on the computer, and wait until 9:00 before he even started to get the kids ready for bed. They usually didn't go to sleep until 10:00. Sally, night after night, would get frustrated about Tom's lackadaisical attitude toward the nightly routine. She would pester, cajole, and criticize him in an attempt to get him to take his responsibilities more seriously.

In our session, Sally said, "I'm the one who has to pull these sleepy kids out of bed in the morning because Tom didn't get them to bed on time. And I'm the one who has to drag two cranky kids to school every day!"

Tom retorted, "What's the big deal? The kids still get to bed at a decent hour. And they don't need one and a half hours to get ready for school, anyway. They ought to be allowed to sleep in later than the ungodly hour when you wake them up."

At that point, I pulled out the whiteboard and encouraged both Sally and Tom to participate in the following exercise. On one side of the board, I drew Tom's family tree, and on the other side, I drew Sally's. Sally was the youngest of four girls. Tom was the middle child of three, and the only son.

Then I asked them both these questions. When you were little

1. Who did the dishes after dinner?
2. Who gave you a bath, and how often?
3. What time did you go to bed?
4. Who would tuck you into bed?
5. What time did you get up in the morning?
6. How long would it take you to get ready for school?
7. Who took you to school?

Next I asked Sally, "How do you think your role as the youngest child affected your perception of time, as well as your familial roles and responsibilities?" I asked Tom, "How did your role as the only boy affect your perception of time, as well as your familial roles and responsibilities?"

These issues obviously took some time to discuss. But after a while, with the help of further questions from me, Sally and Tom were able to see that their different approaches to handling the bedtime routine didn't need to be viewed as attacks on the other parent. They were reflections of how their families of origin had handled their daily schedules. What their parents did and didn't do, and what had and hadn't worked for them as children, affected their approaches to parenting as adults.

We discussed ways in which Sally and Tom could reach a compromise in this daily conflict. Sally might take over the bedtime routine so that she could follow her idea of what that routine should look like. Tom could get the kids out of bed and off to school in the morning. Or perhaps Tom, when he put the kids to bed, could do so a bit later than Sally would like, and she would agree to wake them up a little later in the morning so they could get enough sleep. In return, Tom would start doing his chores without needing Sally to nag him.

Next, I suggested that Tom and Sally try all three of the exercises outlined earlier. Tom was surprised to discover that Sally spent on average about twice as much time performing family- and household-related tasks as he did. He said he always believed that he was a liberated, modern man—he saw Sally as his equal in every way—and so he had assumed that he was acting like one. He couldn't believe how much of the burden he was allowing to fall on Sally's shoulders. With opened eyes, Tom made an enthusiastic vow to chip in more with chores.

Sally was more surprised by the results of the second exercise—time spent with media and technology. She admitted a few weeks into the experiment that she couldn't believe how many minutes she whiled away each day on YouTube videos and Facebook. She defended some of this behavior as an important way of connecting with friends and family but expressed a desire to contain it. She thought that she might limit her time on the computer to thirty minutes each evening.

Both Tom and Sally felt they benefited from taking the time to connect for a minute or two each day during mini-transitions. They chose the time after the kids had been put to bed to reconnect in a meaningful way. They created a ritual in which each of them lit a candle and told the other person something they appreciated about her or his actions that day. Not only did Tom and Sally revel in the intimacy this ritual created but they also felt it helped to reignite the flames of their passion—and frequently led to sexual activity.

Once Tom and Sally modified their bedtime routine with the kids and began practicing the three time-related exercises, their dynamic steadily shifted. They disengaged from their habitual power struggles, rediscovered the value of time spent together, and brought sex back into their lives. Of course, if Tom and Sally want to continue to see the benefits of these practices, they must do them on a regular basis—daily, or at a minimum several times a week. As with everything in life, it is easy to fall back into our former ineffective routines if we do not mindfully work to change our ways. Practicing these three exercises consistently is what helps couples truly appreciate their reasons for being together.

Committed Gay Couples

Committed gay couples struggle with many of the same issues that straight couples do concerning sex in relationships, including finding time for sexual intimacy. And they can benefit from the same exercises that I recommend to my straight clients. But my lesbian friends and clients have made me aware of a specific sexual challenge many gay women face known as "lesbian bed death." This refers to a couple breaking up because they simply stop having sex.

This phenomenon is likely more common among female homosexual couples than among heterosexual or gay male couples because men, in general, have higher levels of testosterone than do women. Men, therefore, experience a greater sex drive. When both partners are female, and neither feels strongly motivated to initiate physical activity, sex can simply fade out of the picture.

Christie and Lucy, both in their early 40s, live in San Diego. They have been dating for eleven years and living together for eight. Lucy came out at age 18, though she started dating girls when she was 14. Although she slept with two guys in college, she never was aroused by men. Christie came out at age 19, when she was in college.

Having sex regularly is important to Christie and Lucy. They both feel more connected when they are being intimate. However, they also emphasized that their sexual relationship has changed over time. During the first few years, they had sex all the time—morning, afternoon, evening, and middle of the night. Now they have sex about once a week, on average, and it tends to be less spontaneous. Christie said, "We both had to let go of the idea that sex would always be like it was in the beginning of the relationship. Now one of us will say, 'Let's go make out,' which usually, but not always, leads to sex. I guess we used to fit our life in around the sex, and now we fit sex in around the rest of our life."

Christie and Lucy have seen a lot of female couples break up because of lack of sexual intimacy, so they are determined to avoid this phenomenon in their own relationship. They feel lucky that they're still very attracted to one another, but they also work at keeping things interesting and the connection alive. For instance, they believe good communication is critical. Christie said, "We stay in touch with our feelings so that we don't end up carrying around unspoken resentment or anger. When our relationship is strong, it is easier to keep the sex alive. When we are angry at each other, or just emotionally disconnected, we are less likely to want to have sex—unless we are full-on fighting and get to have hot make-up sex." She laughed, and Lucy joined in.

What I admire most about Christie and Lucy's approach to sex is that they have taken specific, committed steps to keep their intimate connection alive. At one point when things naturally began to "ebb and flow," they decided to confront the issue directly by scheduling sex. "We were determined not to be sisters," said Lucy. The couple agreed not to let more than one week pass without having sex.

"I know it sounds lame, but the truth is, if sex is left up to 'the moment,' it just doesn't happen," Lucy explained. "Anyway, sex is like exercise. Some days you really don't feel like doing it, but you push yourself, and then it feels great in the process. You're always happy you did it."

Then one day, about a year ago, Lucy heard about a heterosexual couple who had decided that, in order to enhance their sex life, they would have sex every day for a year. She told Christie about it, and they thought they ought to give it a try. "We were like, 'If the straights can do it, so can we,'" Lucy said. She and Christie committed to having sex every day for forty days in a row.

They were proud to make it to Day 22. While that might have been no great accomplishment within the first two years of their relationship, ten years in, it felt pretty fantastic. Christie and Lucy urged other couples—gay or straight—to try this approach. Lucy said, "We had such a fun time with the challenge. We set a goal and gave it our best. We really felt closer during the process. It was amazing."

Coupled Women, Single Women, and Self-Pleasure

When a powerful, self-confident, graceful woman walks by me on the street, I am always curious about what she has going on. Is she doing a lot of yoga or Pilates? Therapy? Antidepressants? Is she deeply engaged in a spiritual practice? Does she feel proud of her accomplishments? Is she well-connected to a strong support network? Or is she having great sex?

In most instances, it's a combination of several factors—the people who catch our attention often exemplify the Core Values of women with fortytude: grace, connectedness, accomplishment, adventure, and spirituality. But while the exact answer varies, there does seem to be one common thread: almost all these women have strong, positive connections with their bodies and feel comfortable in their own skin. This confidence translates into a lack of shame around masturbation. Adventuresome women are unafraid of being in touch with themselves—literally.

Self-pleasure offers a wonderful way for us to connect with our bodies, give ourselves pleasure, learn more about what turns us on, and build confidence in our sexuality at any age. And while it is an obvious option for people without partners, masturbation is by no means for single women alone. In fact, I find that self-pleasure can be just as important for women in marriages and long-term relationships. Sometimes, coupled women spend so much effort on satisfying their partners' needs that they lose track of their own sexual fulfillment. I encourage all women to experiment with masturbation in order to free their fantasies and open their bodies to even greater pleasure.

Fortunately, over the past two decades, female self-pleasure has been demystified. Movies and television shows have glamorized masturbation, portraying it as a healthy, socially acceptable, and fun thing to do. Sex toys are even being marketed differently. They used to be relegated to seedy shops in the sketchiest parts of town. But these days, you can purchase anything anonymously online, and even the trendy Los Angeles retail store Fred Segal sells hip, environmentally conscious vibrators. In fact, the female-friendly sex toy retailer Babeland collected data revealing that 44 percent of women have used a sex toy, and the majority of these women were in serious relationships. But single women use sex toys, too. According to a recent AARP study of sexuality, 15 percent of single women over 45 have watched adult films and 14 percent have used a sex toy.

In my therapy practice, the topic of self-pleasure has moved from the category of "never to be discussed" to "acceptable topic of conversation." While there are certainly women in parts of the country and within certain subcultures who would turn purple or even be offended by the mention of masturbation, a lot of women have started to feel more comfortable chatting about it with their girlfriends. Talking about sexual self-pleasure is no longer considered taboo or viewed as a kind of perversion; it's become more of the norm. Masturbation is just something that many of us enjoy.

Women who masturbate score higher on self-esteem measures than do women who report not masturbating. Also, women who are comfortable touching themselves have a more positive body image and less sexual anxiety than those who don't. So when it comes to self-pleasure, ladies, embrace that spirit of adventure and enjoy!

Replacing Fear with Curiosity

When it comes to having sex with other people, additional factors enter the mix. Whether we are straight or gay, in committed relationships or dating casually, we all have to deal with our partners' ideas and expectations, hang-ups, turn-ons, and judgments (perceived or real) about our bodies and ourselves.

But why is it that many mature, empowered women still seem to be lacking in a subtle and advanced knowledge of sex? For example, I have clients who have never experienced an orgasm. Yet most women are capable of reaching orgasm—they just have to be willing to experiment a little. It doesn't happen for all women through intercourse alone; some require direct clitoral stimulation.

I think that many of us have felt, and still feel, some shame or embarrassment around our sexuality. Perhaps in our early 20s we didn't know if our partners would perceive us as "easy" or "frigid" and had concerns about our performance in bed. In our late 30s and early 40s, we might become highly attuned to and perhaps a bit obsessed by our sagging breasts, increasing belly pouches, widening hips, or, if the light is on, lessened elasticity in our facial muscles.

But what would happen if we were able to replace our fear with curiosity? What might we experience? What would we hope for going forward? The bottom line is, as human beings, we are supposed to be enjoying sex. If we're not regularly having fun with it, then we need to do some exploration and figure out what's going on.

When women over 35 come to me with questions about their sexuality, I generally guide them through a discussion of these three topics:

1. Past experiences with men.
2. Upbringing, in particular how sexuality was addressed in their families.
3. Dialogue with themselves, their partners, and their female friends about sex.

For topic one, I invite my clients to consider how their past experiences might be influencing their present relationships. We all bring a certain amount of baggage into our current interactions, but this is especially true when it comes to sex. I ask, "What are some sexual experiences you've had that you've been afraid to talk about with others?" I encourage my clients to share those experiences. Being able to talk about them is the first step in releasing any negative energy and clearing the slate for the present relationship.

I also encourage my clients to look for patterns. Identifying a consistent set of behaviors when it comes to sex and intimate partners doesn't necessarily mean that something is wrong with you. It simply provides an opportunity for you to observe what is and isn't working for you right now, so that you can make changes if doing so feels appropriate.

For topic two, I ask my clients these five questions:

1. Who in your family taught you about sex? What do you remember about that conversation? How old were you?
2. What was sex ed like at your school? Was it positive or negative? Who taught the class?
3. What did your friends and classmates teach you about sex when you were young?
4. What do you know now that you wish you'd known when you were younger?
5. How do you feel about sex now?

Obviously, our upbringing has tremendous influence over how we view sex, as well as our connection to our bodies and our partners today. If there are gaps in their knowledge, I suggest to my clients that it might be time to educate themselves—through both books and hands-on experimentation (pun intended).

For topic three, I suggest that women engage in frequent and honest conversations with their trusted girlfriends about sex. In fact, I recommend creating a sex conversation club, which might resemble a book or knitting club. The more adventuresome and experienced women in the group might encourage the other members to try new things. The goal isn't necessarily to be raunchy or racy but rather to create a platform for safe, matter-of-fact discussion with other open-minded women in their 40s and beyond. Such conversations can prove extremely liberating, not to mention a lot of fun.

Sexuality and Power

We modern women have been encouraged from a young age to seek liberation from our traditional roles, and to prove our equality with men. And so women with fortytude forge their way through life with strength, valor, assertiveness, self-confidence, and passion. And many of us also rely on one other quality that equates to power—*sexuality*.

This is where a conflict can arise for women in today's world. How can we truly enjoy sex and our sexuality while still feeling as though we are liberating ourselves from the bonds of conventional thinking about women as sex objects? How can we continue to validate ourselves as a separate yet equal gender when we continue to receive the message that our physical attractiveness matters in terms of our perceived value to society and worthiness as human beings? How can we rely on our sexual allure and female charms to connect to—and, yes, even influence—men without feeling as though we're using our sexuality as a weapon?

I would venture to say that power equates with awareness of self and of the intentions behind the choices in our lives. I constantly ask my clients, "Are you doing this out of fear of losing control?" Fear, as we know, does not create power. When we operate strictly from love and curiosity, by contrast, we can recognize our true power.

Thirteen

DATING AFTER 40

. . . .

WHEN I REACHED my mid-30s and found myself still single, I began to have a recurring dream. I was dressed in a wedding gown, wearing an engagement ring, and standing at the altar of a church. But there was no man. My mom would show up and start presenting me with all the guys I had ever dated, even my seventh-grade boyfriend. "Is this the groom?" she would ask, and I would shake my head. "No, that's not him . . ."

At 40, I am still not married, though I have been in and out of long-term relationships. And I take comfort in knowing that I am not alone. In fact, I'm far from it. According to a *New York Times* analysis, this is the first time in history when more American women—just over 50 percent—are living without a husband than with one. Of course, a small fraction of these women are cohabiting with their committed partners in arrangements that resemble marriage in all but the formal paperwork or religious ceremonies. But most are single—never married, divorced, or widowed.

Many single women in my private practice and group sessions have a true sense of freedom that married or coupled women don't have. Some of them are totally content with their lack of an intimate relationship, or happily dating one or several men. Yet I find that, in general, a lot of negativity surrounds being single after 40. As they get closer to this threshold age, a majority of my single clients start to fear that they

- Will no longer be viable on the dating scene because of a perceived lack of attractiveness and sex appeal. They worry that they are becoming "invisible" to potential mates.
- Won't be desirable to men who want to have children, because they are no longer as fertile as women in their 20s and 30s.
- Made mistakes in breaking up with previous boyfriends. They start to second-guess their choices.
- Will never find wonderful partners because they have failed at many, or even just one, long-term relationship.

When women allow their fear to take over, they usually end up ignoring their own voices, values, and needs. As a result, they may shut themselves off from all sorts of positive options for moving forward with their lives and instead make choices that are detrimental.

Some women fall prey to the negative message we still get from society that says, "If you're single after 35, there must be something wrong with you." They may feel so bad about themselves, and their self-esteem become so diminished, that they lower their standards and embrace men who ignore their strengths. This makes me wonder, Is having this guy (who treats you poorly, cheats on you, doesn't contribute to the household) in your life *really* better than having no guy at all?

Fortunately, more and more single women are coming to feel empowered, fulfilled, and comfortable with themselves and their lives at any age. The stereotype of the older, single woman as sad, lonely, and desperate for a partner no longer holds true. According to a large-scale survey by the AARP, about a third of single women ages 40 to 69 are dating exclusively, another third are dating nonexclusively, and the majority of the remaining third aren't really interested in dating. Only 13 percent of those women surveyed were single and looking for a mate. And while the single women in the study reported feeling lonely more often than the married women, 93 percent said they felt that their independence was important to their quality of life. As for winding up alone in old age, that's unfortunately just as likely for married or coupled women as for singles—men nearly always die younger, leaving their partners alone.

It is critical for single women to continue to feel positive about themselves, their attractiveness to potential mates, and their ability to meet and settle down with a great love (if that's what they desire), even after the age of 40. If we allow ourselves to be undermined by societal misconceptions that our chances at love and coupledom are over once we enter our fifth decades, we harm only ourselves. And if we constantly bombard ourselves with negative messages, such as "I'm an old maid" or "I'll never find anyone at this point in my life" or "There must be something wrong with me," then we'll make those thoughts a reality. We will be all the more likely to feel bad, act unwisely, and dig ourselves deeper into a negative, depressive, self-doubting, self-limiting hole. If we're going to go forth with fortytude, then we must change our attitude about being single and dating after 40.

The Dating Game

The simple truth is that the best way to embark on dating at this point in our lives is to look at it as an adventure. It can be a challenge, to be sure. But if we see it as a way to have fun, try different activities, meet new people, go to new places, and otherwise push ourselves out of our comfort zones, then we can get a lot more enjoyment from the dating game.

One extremely popular option these days is online dating, which has become increasingly socially acceptable since it was introduced in the mid-1990s. Online dating can prove efficient and inexpensive. A lot of people believe it is worth the effort required to post a profile, sort through candidates, and strike up e-mail-based conversations before meeting because they can safely prescreen potential partners. Online dating also enables you to meet people far outside your usual social circle and even geographic area. Furthermore, many single women feel that online dating saves them from having to shove themselves into crowded bars where they can hardly hear other people speak, go on awkward blind dates with their mothers' best friends' sons' roommates from college, or spend money on tickets to events only to discover they don't like their dates, much less the bands.

Still, some women who have tried online dating have not experienced relief, much less enjoyment. Maybe they met people who were much older or heavier than they appeared in their online profile pictures (this goes both ways: women are often afraid to post their real ages for fear that others will not respond to their ads). Maybe they questioned their ability to strike up a relationship through virtual communication. Or maybe they simply felt uncomfortable meeting up with strangers from the Internet. But for all those who find online dating a disappointment, a slightly greater number (52 percent, according to a Pew Internet & American Life Project survey) report having a positive experience.

I generally suggest that single women *not* date online, go to bars, get set up on blind dates, or buy tickets to expensive events if they sincerely feel that they won't enjoy themselves. However, I also encourage them to enter the dating world with levity and a sense of adventure. When they proceed with this attitude, they usually have a lot more fun. And isn't that the point?

• • • •

FOR ANDREA CARLOS, being single at 40 did not come easily. But while she struggled at first, Andrea has made reasonable compromises and found her way to a place of contentment.

Andrea lives in Portland, Oregon, where she works as a freelance writer. She met her husband at age 29, and they got married not long after. They thought about having kids but kept putting it off. Then, when she hit her late 30s, Andrea realized that she wasn't happy in her marriage.

At age 39, Andrea got divorced, which turned her life upside down. She went through a period of depression, feeling very down on herself for having failed at marriage. She also didn't know how to be single, because she had been in a serious relationship since she was 23. She felt lost. The weekend would come, and she had no idea what to do with herself, or any clue how to find another relationship. "I didn't know who I was," she said. "I kind of felt like my life was over."

Andrea had to spend several years after her divorce rebuilding her self-esteem and rediscovering herself. She started to see a therapist for the first time. She said, "All I could talk about in therapy was wanting another relationship. The therapist said, 'What's growing in *your* garden?' What he meant was 'You need to focus on who you are as a person.' It really made me think. When something ends and you have this big void, you are responsible for doing something about it."

So Andrea started meeting other single women her age and forming deep bonds with them. She learned from her friends about dating and discovered the world of online dating. Her friends pointed out that, whatever age you are, there are always single men your age around— you just have to find them. She also took up a variety of new activities. With time and concerted effort, Andrea managed to change her attitude about being single at 40. She said, "I realized that age is just this thing that we tell ourselves. You're never too old to do anything."

As soon as she'd regained her sense of self and begun taking control of her life, Andrea started having fun. At 41, she looked around and realized that she was having the time of her life and feeling great. She said, "I was getting a lot of positive feedback from men, and I was having some of the best sex of my life. I also realized that I'd just given myself over to my relationships in the past. I was doing what I wanted to do for the first time in my life."

But it wasn't only her attitude toward dating that changed after the divorce. Andrea began approaching her entire life with a greater sense of adventure. For example, while she always was athletic, she wouldn't have taken on truly challenging activities before. Soon after the divorce, she bought a road bike and joined a seven-day, five-hundred-mile bike trip across Oregon.

A friend who was going through a divorce at the same time helped Andrea tremendously. He encouraged her to try a weekend-long self-improvement course in which she had to write down her life goals in the spiritual, intellectual, physical, and emotional areas of her life. It got Andrea thinking, "Why am I putting things off? I should be enjoying my life *now*." Among the other changes she was making, Andrea quit her job and started her own writing business, which she feels were great decisions.

One year Andrea and a single girlfriend decided that, rather than spend their holidays at home feeling sorry for themselves, they would go to Nepal and work at an orphanage. Andrea had been to Nepal before, so she found an organization that put together volunteer trips, and she and her friend took off. Andrea had a life-changing experience. She said, "There was a woman who worked there as a caretaker of eleven boys. She didn't seem to have any family. And yet all you had to say was that you enjoyed the meal she'd cooked, and she'd start dancing around the kitchen! It made me realize that my expectations of life were so big. I thought, Here is a person with barely enough food, no husband, no kids, and she's happy. So why can't I be happy?"

Soon after she returned from Nepal, Andrea began to seriously date a man named Bob. Today, Andrea, who is 47, lives with Bob. The two of them recently bought an organic farm together and are growing their own vegetables and fruits. They hope to have chickens someday, too. Though neither of them has ever done anything like this before, they love it.

One of the hardest things for Andrea has been giving up the dream of having her own children. The friend with whom she traveled to Nepal adopted a baby girl from China, but Andrea decided not to go that route. Bob, who is six years older than Andrea, felt that he was too old to have children. Andrea was faced with a very difficult decision: stay in this relationship and not have kids, or break up and adopt on her own. She felt that it was more important for her to have the happy relationship, although she still experienced pangs of disappointment.

At first, Andrea felt resentful toward Bob for not agreeing to have kids. Then she realized that both people have to want to have children in order for parenting to work. And in the end, she couldn't resent Bob, because she could have left him if she had wanted to. "It was my decision," she said, "so I take responsibility for it. Everything is a trade-off."

Andrea feels that it is critical to take the time to discover what you want from life separate from anyone else being in it. "What do you love? Art? Exercise? Do you have a goal you've never had time to achieve? Carve out the time to do those things and you'll be happy," she said emphatically.

Cougars

Women with fortytude know how to capitalize on their strengths. These days, many single women who are fully confident that they're still sexually desirable well into their 40s, 50s, 60s, and even 70s are finding an outlet for their passion, energy, confidence, and vitality: younger men. Over the past few years, these women have come to be known as "cougars."

Initially, the term "cougar" was used in a pejorative fashion. Instead of characterizing older women as strong, fearless, and desirable, it stereotyped them as sexual predators obsessed with launching themselves at unsuspecting younger men. But that's changing—and fast. Forty-plus-year-old women are reclaiming "cougar" not as an insult but rather as a signifier that they dare to be bold and live life to the fullest. Many are even proud to declare that they have joined the cougar camp. And why shouldn't they be? Men have been happily dating, marrying, and having children with women who are ten, twenty, and even thirty years younger than they are for millennia. It's about time society allowed women to do the same, without ostracizing them.

Raz, a 41-year-old Iranian woman, is in a serious relationship with a man ten years younger than she is. She pointed out that, while it is possible for older women to date younger men in Iran, the men, in particular, are strongly censured for such behavior. In many cases, family members cut ties with them. Raz feels grateful to be living in America, where she and her soon-to-be husband will not suffer negative repercussions because of their age difference.

These days, women are acknowledging—passionately, proudly, and publicly—that there is absolutely nothing wrong with seeking out (or even just fantasizing about) younger men. As a result, we are becoming more empowered to celebrate our sexuality however and form relationships with whomever we please, without worrying about being labeled, judged, or outcast by society.

• • • •

LISA SUNDSTEDT IS a successful comedian in Los Angeles—and a proud, happy, and confident woman. At age 42, Lisa has chestnut brown hair, bright brown eyes, and a boyfriend who is thirteen years her junior. She makes it clear that neither she nor he, or pretty much anyone in their lives, has a problem with that.

Since her mid-20s, Lisa has been a successful writer, voice-over actress, and stand-up comedian. She created and produces the now longest-running all-female comedy show in the country, "Pretty, Funny Women." And yet, until quite recently, she was miserable and lonely. One relationship after another failed. "The funny thing is," she said, "I'd achieved everything I thought I wanted in life. On the outside, people would think, She's got it all. But I felt like I wanted to die." Eventually, Lisa became so depressed that she was suicidal.

That was when she realized that she was an alcoholic, and had been since she was 15 years old. When she turned 40, she got sober.

About a year and a half later, Lisa was invited to perform stand-up at a private party in a town south of Los Angeles. She hadn't wanted to go. It was raining, and she didn't know the people, and she wasn't getting paid much. But Lisa's mother said, "Go. You never know when you might meet someone."

Lisa responded, "That's ridiculous. I never meet people at parties like this. They're all with someone. And anyway, I'm working." But she went.

At dinner, Lisa sat with the DJ—a cute guy named Nicholas, and the only other person working the party. He told her later that he was immediately attracted to her. But Lisa didn't pay him much attention. She was nervous, focused on getting onstage. After her act, Nicholas asked Lisa if she was single, and she said yes. He told her that he was single, too, because some time ago his fiancée had been killed in a car accident. He also said he was 30, which she thought was too young. But she was taken aback by his willingness to bare his soul, as well as his gentle yet straightforward manner in approaching her. So when he asked her out, she said yes.

On their first date, Lisa found out that Nicholas actually was only 28, but they had fun and enjoyed each other in an easy, comfortable way. Lisa found Nicholas earnest and kind—the opposite of the "show business type" she usually dated. So she continued to see him. Lisa and Nicholas enjoyed great sex and open communication. Soon enough, they found themselves in a serious relationship.

Lisa admitted she'd thought for a long time that Nicholas was too young. She had never dated anyone more than two to three years younger than she was. "I was ready to break up about it many times," she said. "I know, it's just age. It's just a number. But it's a big gap between us."

Lisa worried at first about not feeling attractive or sexy enough with Nicholas because of their age difference, but that turned out not to be an issue. She told a story about how, two years before meeting Nicholas, she'd copied down an affirmation from a book: "I'm divinely irresistible to my perfect mate." She had stuck a Post-it with this slogan on her mirror, but after some time it had fallen off. One day Nicholas found the Post-it on her bedroom floor and said, "You are divinely irresistible to me!" Lisa smiled hugely. "It's true. He can't keep his hands off me. And that's when I realized that I'd manifested what I had asked for."

Age does affect their relationship, however, since Lisa is confronting the pressing issue of her fertility. She and Nicholas are trying to get pregnant, and her doctor has told her that at age 42, nearly 43, the chances aren't great that it will happen naturally. Fortunately, Nicholas is willing to adopt or use an egg donor. Lisa said that Nicholas has completely restored her faith in men.

Lisa has embraced being with a younger man with enthusiasm, courage, and confidence. She is on the forefront, serving as a positive role model for what a "cougar" can and should be—a powerful, loving woman who has met a fantastic match and doesn't allow the thirteen-year age difference between them to bother her.

• • • •

IXTLA VAUGHAN IS an attractive, fit 43-year-old woman who lives in Bozeman, Montana, with her two children and her boyfriend, Jon. Ixtla and Jon, who is twelve years younger than she is, have been together for five years and have lived together for four.

Ixtla had married and divorced twice before meeting Jon. She had two children in her second marriage and divorced when she was 36. At the time, she worried about how her dating would affect her boys. But it never occurred to her to be concerned about being attractive to or having too much baggage to interest potential partners as a result of being over 35 or a mother. She said, "I always was very up front, and told men right away my age and that I was a mother. My boys are dynamic and easy, so I figured anyone that didn't want to know them probably wouldn't interest me, anyway."

After the divorce, Ixtla continued to have an active and stimulating life. She worked as a graphic designer and also completed a major remodeling of her house. She spent all her time with her boys during the weeks when they stayed with her, and enjoyed socializing and participating in various sporting activities during the weeks they stayed with their father. She also had plenty of friends and a half brother around to help out. She dated but wasn't obsessed with finding a new partner. Her circle of friends, all healthy outdoors types, included quite a few people in their 20s and 30s. One of them happened to be a young man named Jon.

"When we met, I didn't really consider Jon a candidate for a long-term relationship," Ixtla explained. "I was nearly 40. He was newly 28, gorgeous, and had no steady anything. Neither of us was in the place where commitment made any sense." But they were extremely attracted to one another and enjoyed spending time together when Ixtla didn't have the boys. She found Jon quiet, clean, easy to be with, and emotionally reserved. At the same time, she enjoyed his boylike ability to "totally goof off."

For the first few months, Ixtla felt that it was important to keep her time with the boys uncomplicated by not introducing Jon to them, and Jon respected that choice. Ixtla said, "I gave my kids as much unadulterated time as possible, and Jon never communicated anything other than 'It's all good. Call me when I can see you.' My mantra was Keep it simple, and his was, too."

Fortunately, when Ixtla was ready to introduce Jon to the boys, they really liked each other. The boys thought Jon was "cool." Even after five years, they call him their "very, very good friend." Jon is careful to give Ixtla's children plenty of space and the freedom to approach him when they so desire.

I wondered if Ixtla ever worried about being sexually attractive or appealing to Jon because of their age difference. She said that she'd already had two C-sections, as well as stitches and, after she met Jon, had had a brain hemorrhage. So she hardly felt like "the same carefree beauty" that she had been in her 20s and 30s. "I feel conventionally middle-aged," she said. Yet she wasn't concerned about her "jiggly bits, wrinkles, and lines." She viewed them simply as signs of her life experience.

Although Ixtla and Jon's age and experience disparity is obvious, the relationship is working out well for both of them. Initially, Jon felt that getting married and having his own children were important to him. But since moving in with Ixtla, he proclaims that his desires have morphed and he's never been happier. "I don't know if we're destined to grow old together, but that's okay," Ixtla commented. "My wish list is to have a great family, do what I love with the people I love, and be happy and healthy. So far, so good."

The Dating Toolbox

Here is a series of exercises that I enjoy introducing to my single clients. I refer to them as the metaphorical Dating Toolbox.

1. A Mantra

Every woman should have a mantra that will help her lighten up and remind her to enjoy the dating game. Before I go on a date, I always say my mantra—"For shits and giggles"—out loud. This reminds me to take it all in as life experience, and to have a good laugh about it with my friends later. After each date—whether it was great or horrible—I am able to have a smile on my face because I accomplished my goal. I did it "for shits and giggles." When I suggest using a mantra (mine or one of their own choosing), many of my clients initially look at me quizzically. "Really?" they say. But most soon realize the value of this tool. It brings levity to a topic that can be daunting, depressing, and frustrating. It also gives you perspective, reminding you that this is, after all, just a date.

2. Your Needs List

In addition to focusing on the five Core Values, women with fortytude should go into the dating game with mental checklists of their five most critical needs. One might assume that women entering middle age have a clear idea what their needs are. But I cannot tell you how often, when I ask my clients to describe their needs, I am met with blank stares.

Here is an example. If you are a single woman who craves rigorous exercise, then you most likely need the freedom to move. A man who seemed not to understand this need—perhaps he expressed his passion for lazing around the house during his downtime, or showed his lack of interest in physical activity through his out-of-shape physique and made negative comments about your "obsession"—most likely would not be the best match for you. Other women have a similar need for solitude, or for intellectual stimulation.

Another, subtler need that many women seem to ignore or neglect is the need to be heard. Somehow, in spite of the progress society has made in giving women the floor, many women's voices still are not being heard. I often watch this happen during direct interactions in couples therapy sessions, but I've also observed it informally during conversations at restaurants. The man speaks, and perhaps he even pretends he's paying attention, but he doesn't fully take in, acknowledge, or validate the woman's point of view. If you feel the need to be heard (and almost all of us do), then you should look for that deep listening quality right away in the men you date.

Unfortunately, many women mistakenly ignore their needs, fearing that there are very few available men interested in dating a woman in her 40s or above. They feel that they have no right to be picky or insist on having their needs met. Furthermore, many women assume that they can modify their partners' behaviors once they're in stable relationships.

But I invite you not to fall into either of these traps. You must be willing to make compromises. But you ought to go out into the dating world with a set of standards, knowing which of your needs you are *not* willing to sacrifice. And I suggest you not make the mistake I've watched many people make of imagining that you can change your partner later. Most of the time, you can't. What you see is what you get.

3. Toned and Flexible Flirting Muscles

Going on a date and flirting are sports that must be practiced, just like running, biking, and yoga. You have to keep the muscles toned and stretched. Practice makes perfect! If you've been out of the dating game for a while, have a longtime single friend give you a refresher course. Then go to a bar, or the gym, or the local dog park to hone your skills. If you don't develop your flirting muscles, you'll be out of touch with your amazing 40-something-year-old self. You won't fully appreciate just how fabulous and desirable you are to those potential mates on the other side of the room or cyberspace or cubicle wall.

Then again, as with exercise, if you need a rest from working out those flirting muscles, take a break. Don't overextend yourself. Take a night or two off to stretch and relax, enjoying a girls' night in with wine and lots of laughter, or simply curl up in your own bed watching your favorite movie.

4. Your Gut

How many times have you ignored your instincts when you met someone? You go on the first, then second, then third date, all the while aware of the red flags, yet somehow ignoring that gut feeling that says, "This isn't right." We all can fall prey to using our heads, basing our decisions on how the person looks on paper or what we think we should be feeling. But doing so is nearly always a mistake.

For example, have you ever dated a man who had one too many drinks every time you went out? I have. I found myself rationalizing his behavior, saying, "Perhaps he's just feeling a little nervous with me" and "It's okay, he's probably stressed from work" and "He's a big man, so he can handle drinking an entire bottle of red wine." I ignored my belly, which was saying, "This guy is not safe." Later, it turned out that he was an alcoholic. So when you go on your next date, bring your gut and your head. Trust yourself to know what's good for you.

Whether you're gay or straight, never been married, divorced, or widowed, just turned 35 or about to turn 50, you have the potential to meet a terrific, suitable partner. Dating honestly can prove one of the most effective ways to push ourselves out of our comfort zones and find adventure in our everyday lives. It introduces us to new people, places, and situations all the time.

While we may be inclined to tell ourselves a story about dating after 40 being bleak and terrifying, it doesn't have to be that way. As women with fortytude, we have more options than ever before, from dating online to checking out much younger men. The fundamental truth is, the more you make an effort to enjoy your single status and see dating as fun, the more content you will be. And the more content you are, the more positive energy you will radiate to friends and strangers, and the more you will attract people to you.

PART V

SPIRITUALITY

· · · ·

In this day and age, people have distinct views about the meaning of the word "spirituality." The past few decades in America have seen a huge rise in yoga, spiritual retreat centers, Kabbalah, astrology, New Age practices, and Buddhism. In fact, a December 2009 Pew Forum on Religion & Public Life survey revealed that many Americans blend faiths and practices, and don't feel a need to place themselves in any one religious category. For example, they might attend a Christian church some Sundays but also practice meditation to calm their minds and visit psychics for guidance in life decisions. One-third of those surveyed said that they regularly attend religious services at more than one place, and one-quarter reported sometimes attending services of a different faith.

Yet this mix-and-match approach to spirituality does not seem to correspond with a weakening in faith as a whole. On the contrary, spiritual experiences and beliefs appear to be on the rise. Many of us feel a strong pull to reach out to others in a meaningful way, and to connect regularly with a life force larger than our own.

I must admit that, before September 11, 2001, I didn't pay much attention to spirituality. I occasionally read books by spiritual authors such as Deepak Chopra, but I never sought to affiliate myself with a specific religion, doctrine, or movement. But then, on that clear blue, sunny day when I awoke to my mother's frantic phone call around 9:30 A.M., everything changed.

I had flown from San Francisco to New York's JFK Airport on the red-eye the night before, so I was half-asleep when I finally picked up the phone. "Mom?" I mumbled.

"Sarah! Turn on the television! New York City is under attack," my mother said with genuine urgency.

I simply could not make sense of what she was saying until I followed her orders and saw images of the Twin Towers in flames on every news station. I couldn't move, yet all I wanted to do was run down to the buildings and help those poor people who were frantically waving their shirts out the windows, trying to attract the attention of anyone who could save them from their doom.

It was then I noticed that the streets were eerily quiet, as if we were in the midst of a huge snowstorm. I paced the apartment for the remainder of the morning. Then I received a call from the administrator at St. Vincent's Hospital in Greenwich Village. She told me that the hospital was in serious need of mental health practitioners to greet the families and friends of missing loved ones and help them locate their people—dead or alive.

I immediately rushed down to the hospital. Out front, hordes of people wandered aimlessly with blank looks on their faces. Many had posted MISSING signs printed with photos of their loved ones' faces on the hospital walls and nearby lampposts. Billows of smoke still emanated from downtown.

The administrator guided me to a windowless room with a number of small tables and chairs. She then handed me a directory of names of individuals who had been saved from the buildings. The line of people waiting anxiously to talk to someone who could impart reliable information wound far down the corridor.

The experience was surreal. Never in a million years would I have imagined that I would be looking into the eyes of hundreds of people from all walks of life, all of whom had been affected by one horrible murderous act. I tried to help them find their loved ones by searching the directory, calling one hospital after another in the tristate area, and then contacting the morgues.

I met with over 175 people during the fourteen hours I spent in that dingy basement. But out of all those people, one stood out for me. He was a 24-year-old blond-haired, blue-eyed kid from New Jersey whose brother was an employee at Cantor Fitzgerald, an investment bank with offices in the World Trade Center. Judging from his build, he easily could have been a lacrosse player or wrestler.

As I began the normal procedure, asking his brother's name and background information, I looked up and saw, really saw, the young man with bloodshot eyes sitting across from me. I didn't know what to do, so I asked if he was hungry. He nodded his head. I gave him a granola bar supplied by the hospital. But the young man couldn't even open the wrapping because his hands were trembling so terribly. He looked me in the eye and said, "I know he is dead. I just know it. Weird. I just talked to him this morning on his way to work."

Out of the blue, I thought to ask him, "Do you believe in God?" He said, "Yes, I do. I'm Catholic."

I said, "Your brother will need your prayers. Go to church and pray." I was at a loss as to how to comfort this man. Yet I felt that, at that moment, the only option was to pray. I couldn't convince him that his brother was alive. In fact, I was almost 100 percent sure he wasn't, since Cantor Fitzgerald's offices were on the 101st floor of the North Tower. I just obeyed a powerful instinct that told me it would help this man to seek comfort in his connection to God.

For the first time in my life, I realized how necessary spirituality is. During those times when we are confronted by atrocities like the *events of 9/11, we need a source of comfort and a way to give our lives meaning. I have no idea what happened to that young man, but I keep him, and all the other families I assisted on that dreadful day, close to my heart.*

Spirituality—when it comes to women with fortytude, at least—is not about achieving enlightenment or mindlessly obeying a set of rules but rather about looking for inner peace. It helps you understand your life experiences and give them meaning. It provides a way to take yourself out of your own head, so that you can delight in the smallest things. It suggests that you have faith and trust in something bigger than yourself, and are able to hold on to a sense that there is more to life than the items in your daily planner. It reflects the crafting of your own approach to religion and purpose, love and loss, eternity and the soul.

Fourteen

ABANDONED ADULTS

. . . .

AS WE MAKE our way through our 40s, many of the people we care most about—our parents, siblings, and close friends—also will be moving into a more advanced stage of life. As we all know, yet so frequently choose to ignore, with age, unfortunately, come illness and death. In all likelihood, there will come a time during our passage into midlife when we will find ourselves abandoned by people upon whom we used to rely heavily for support, wisdom, courage, and loving acceptance. They will pass away or they will fall ill, and we will transition into caretaking for them. This is yet another reason why we must summon up our strength as we enter our fifth decades, root ourselves deeply in our spirituality, and move forward with fortytude.

To do this, I believe that it is important to understand grief and its purpose. Grieving is like learning how to swim: you don't know what to expect; you just feel for a long time as if you're drowning and will never be able to surface from the sadness or overwhelming sense of loss.

Jessica serves as an example of someone who had to "learn how to swim." Jessica initially came to therapy with her husband because their youngest son was having difficulty in school. During the course of her treatment, Jessica's parents fell ill and died within two months of one another.

Jessica, who was in her mid-40s, was tame in her lifestyle, well-mannered, and smartly dressed. She had grown up in a conservative Jewish family in Connecticut, with parents who fulfilled her every wish. In return, she obeyed their commands, working in Manhattan as a lawyer, dating only highly educated Jewish men, and eventually marrying a very successful accountant.

However, after the deaths of her parents, Jessica seemed to undergo a personality transplant. Suddenly she started arriving to her sessions late and wearing tight jeans and sweaters better suited for a teenager. She would tell me that she had been driving on the freeway at eighty-five miles an hour. Also, Jessica admitted to drinking more frequently, which greatly upset her husband. Perhaps Jessica had developed a death wish in response to the loss of both her parents, but I believe that this was just her way of grieving. Although she wasn't conscious of it, she was acting out all the behaviors her parents had forbidden when they were alive. The only way Jessica felt that she could "learn how to swim," or overcome the grief, was to act out.

Eventually, Jessica began processing her grief in a productive manner during our sessions. She acknowledged her feelings of betrayal at having been abandoned by both her parents in such a short time, and admitted that she was angry with them. She also confessed to the guilty pleasure of doing everything her parents had not allowed her to do. As we continued to work together, Jessica was able to understand the grieving process better. She didn't know which emotion was about to show up, just as when, the first time she swam, she didn't know how to take a breath with every stroke. Once Jessica was able to come to that realization, the grieving process became more tolerable for her.

While there are plenty of other Jessicas trying their best to learn these lessons, our society seems to want to expedite grief. Often we have little sympathy for people suffering from the serious illness or death of a loved one. If you are in a caretaker role for an elderly person, you are expected simply to add that to your already heavy burden of managing a career and a partner, and providing for your children, and consider yourself lucky if you get much assistance—unless you pay an exorbitant amount of money for a nursing home. Or, if a loved one dies, you get a day off to go to the funeral, and then you're expected to be back on your feet, sucking it up and coping just fine. If someone had invented a pill for mourning, I bet at least half of us would be taking it.

It's unfortunate that we don't even like to talk about aging and death in our culture, much less confront these grim realities head-on. Nor do most of us know what to do for other people when their closest friends and relatives fall ill or pass away. But I will say this: there can be a silver lining to our pain at the loss of loved ones. I often remind my patients who are grieving that when you're feeling most uncomfortable and unsettled in your life, you're usually going through an intense period of growth. Grieving is a part of the healing process, and part of coming to terms with what life is all about. When you force yourself to sit with difficult emotions, it makes you dig that much deeper into your spirituality—recognizing and acknowledging the core of who you are, and grounding yourself in your divine purpose here on earth.

Death of a Friend

Whether because of breast cancer, a car accident, old age, or something far less common, we all will lose friends, and with increasing frequency the older we get. If we're lucky, we will know that the death is coming, and we'll have time to prepare—to say our farewells, make our amends, and treasure our last moments together. At other times, death arrives unexpectedly, leaving the living with a sense of unfinished business. It is our duty, as those left carrying the torch, to make peace with the loss of dear friends. Even if we feel as though we can't let someone go, when she or he passes away, we must eventually acknowledge what has happened and heal our psychological wounds.

Brenda, 41, from Park City, Utah, recently shared her thoughts on a close friend's passing. "Jim was 38, a father, a doctor, a husband, a son, and a friend. He was the one who introduced my husband and me. When Jim died from cancer, he left behind a wife and 3-year-old son. His life was cut short, and his son will never know his dad. That's so sad. But the really poignant thing for me was his funeral. Over 350 people came to his service that day—350-plus people who were somehow impacted or changed by him. What an amazing testament to Jim's life. It got me to thinking, and wondering about the purpose of *my* life.

"To me, success now equates with the extent to which I've developed and nurtured relationships with my husband, my family, and my friends (and not just my Facebook friends). It means being sure that my kids can sleep safely at night, comfortable in their world, in their own skins, knowing that they are loved and free to chart their own courses and make choices that will impact their own lives. Success is being a substantial part of my community and giving back to my little piece of the world.

"It's really easy to forget these things and to get caught up in the insignificant stuff, like the guy who got the job I was hoping for, or a career that I might be missing out on by being a stay-at-home mom, or even my expanding midsection. But it comes back to you really quickly when something happens to someone you love or when you hear about a tragedy like Jim's death."

As I read Brenda's words, it reminded me that, when it comes to death, so often we just want to be heard. We all want an opportunity to share our stories of mourning and loss, as well as our favorite recollections of joy and celebration with our loved ones. This simple act of telling others about the people in our lives who have passed away can be an important way to heal and move on. And we all can look for ways in which to honor our friends who have died by bringing their values and finest qualities into play in our everyday lives.

Unexpected Widows

Many women will face widowhood as they age, since men generally marry younger women, and women live on average seven years longer than men. Today, about 11 percent of American women are widows. At age 65, 36 percent of women have had their husbands pass away, and there are four widowed women for every one widowed man. Over the age of 65, more than half of the women in the United States have lost their partners.

Yet while many of us are—at least intellectually, if not emotionally—prepared to lose our husbands when we reach old age, few of us anticipate losing a partner when we are still in middle age. For women who must confront the tragedy of becoming widows when they are in their 40s and 50s, the loss can prove especially difficult. Many of these women struggle to resume their lives after the deaths of their husbands, particularly if they have young children. Yet while it is true that some women never fully recuperate from the profound grief of losing their partners, other women manage to go on and even flourish.

• • • •

KIM RUOCCO, 46, lives in Massachusetts with her two sons. She grew up in Reading, Pennsylvania, and met her husband, John, during her sophomore year in college. Kim described John as "the life of the party. He was really dedicated and loyal, fun and handsome and in shape, a lot of fun to be with, and everybody's best friend. He was protective of me and of his family." It wasn't until many years later that Kim discovered John suffered from depression.

When they got married, John joined the Marines as a fighter pilot. Shortly after they had their first child, he was deployed twice: first to Bosnia, then to Somalia. This was the first time Kim could recall seeing

John depressed. She was 32 at the time, and he was 31. "He was holding on to me tight, like a lifesaver," Kim said. "I felt really frustrated, because I had this baby and I wanted him to be strong, but then again, it was nice to be needed by him."

As he sank deeper into a depressive slump, Kim spoke with John about seeking help, but he said that the culture of the military wouldn't allow for that. He felt certain there would be negative ramifications for his career. So Kim secretly called psychiatrists at other bases. The experts said that they probably *would* force John to take a leave of absence. "This was the mid-nineties," Kim explained. "A lot has changed, but back then, they would've taken away his wings for nothing—just for being on cold medications. There's no way he could have gone on anti-depressants."

Fortunately, John pulled himself together without outside help. As soon as he was back to his usual self, he was deployed again. The whole episode had lasted about three months. Kim later learned that John's mother had suffered from depression, so he had a genetic predisposition to it.

Eventually, John and Kim had a second child and moved to Virginia, so that John could take an important job at the Pentagon. It proved to be a stressful position. In addition, he was in constant physical pain from old sports and Marine injuries. Kim therefore decided to take John up on a deal they had made when he joined the military: he'd promised her that, if she ever wanted him to get out, he would. She told him she was ready to go home to Massachusetts and have him take a regular job, perhaps as an airline pilot. "I thought he'd given 100 percent to the Marine Corps, and it had exhausted him," she said.

John agreed, and he began accumulating flying hours so that he could apply for a job at a commercial airline. Then September 11 happened. John said, "This will change everything for us." And he was right: the airline industry tanked. Furthermore, John felt there was no way he could leave his comrades-in-arms during such a critical time. He did, however, agree to join the reserves.

Kim moved back to Massachusetts. Meanwhile, John applied for an airline job. But shortly thereafter, he got called off reserves to fight in Iraq, and a perfect storm started to brew. He already had the baseline inclination toward depression. Soon he also was suffering from post-traumatic stress disorder. And, on top of everything else, John found out that the airline hadn't given him a job.

When John returned from Iraq for Thanksgiving and Christmas, he was deeply depressed. He told Kim that he'd "seen the face of evil," which he had never said about his experiences in Bosnia or Somalia. He was impatient with the kids, had low energy, and wouldn't communicate openly with Kim. She again encouraged him to get help, but he refused. He was still convinced that admitting to problems would ruin his military career. Kim said, "If someone, a mentor, had said to John, 'This happened to me, and I got help. You can, too. You'll be able to get back out there,' then maybe John would've done it. But no one did."

John's colleagues didn't know anything was wrong with him. "In fairness to them, they had a lot to deal with themselves," Kim explained. "Also, they were protecting him because they thought so highly of him." Her voice cracked, and tears came to her eyes. "A lot of Marines have said since, 'I knew your husband, and you wouldn't believe what he did for me—he saved my life, he covered for me. He went all out while he was there in Iraq.'"

On January 5, 2005, John had to go to California to join his squadron before being redeployed to Iraq in March. That was the last time Kim and the kids saw him. He started to cry at the airport. As they parted, John said to Kim, "How did you get so strong, and I'm so weak?"

For the next few weeks, John continued to struggle, and Kim spoke to him every day. Then, on Super Bowl Sunday in February, when the New England Patriots (Kim and John's favorite team) were playing, she tried many times to call John, but he didn't pick up the phone.

When he finally answered, he said that he hadn't watched the game. At that moment, Kim knew something was terribly wrong. She finally asked the dreaded question: "Are you suicidal?" John assured her that he could never leave her and the boys. Still, after talking for some time, John agreed to check himself in to the hospital.

As soon as she hung up the phone, Kim knew that she had to take action. After having seen John endure the roller-coaster ride of debilitating depressive episodes, she recognized that this time was different. She booked a seat to California on the red-eye that very night. "In retrospect, I should've called 911," Kim said.

She landed first thing in the morning and immediately called the hospital. John hadn't shown up. She called his work, but he hadn't shown up there, either. So she rented a car, and drove to the hotel where John had been staying. "When I arrived," she said, "I could see these haphazardly parked cars with Marine stickers on them, so I knew that it was an emergency situation. I raced up the stairs and saw a few Marines coming around the corner with tears in their eyes. I collapsed: I knew that was it."

Kim tries not to plague herself with what-ifs. What if she had called 911. What if she had forced John to get help months, or even years, before. What if she had called someone in the military that night before getting on the plane . . . She imagines that perhaps John's soul had just been too damaged, and there was no way to repair it. But she can't help but fault herself at times for not having insisted that he seek help sooner.

Unfortunately, in the coming days, the cops, the church, and the civilian trauma team didn't prove very helpful. Kim's life passed by in a blur of chaos, tears, and pain. Eventually, she found a wise liberal female minister with a sense of humor who became her grief counselor.

Then one day Kim spotted a brochure the casualty officers had left for TAPS—the Tragedy Assistance Program for Survivors. She assumed it was only for the families of soldiers who had been killed in action. But six months after John's death, she contacted them to see if they could offer her any assistance. Bonnie Carroll, the chairman and founder of TAPS, got back to Kim directly, saying, "We're here for you. How can we help?"

When Kim attended the first TAPS conference, on Memorial Day 2006, there was only one other suicide survivor present. Kim felt inspired to take action, gathering more military suicide survivors and encouraging them to speak out about their experiences. In 2009, largely thanks to Kim's efforts, there were hundreds of suicide survivors at the TAPS conference. "We're getting rid of some of the stigma of suicide," she said.

Kim values the opportunity she has had since John's death to reach out to other suicide survivors, connect deeply with them, and help them move on. She feels that all of us are responsible for what we make of our life stories. "It's not what happens to you; it's what you do with it that counts," Kim told me. "Once you accept that there's a plan for you, then you see every day as a gift. If you dwell on the bad things that happen, you will be stuck. You have an opportunity to take what's happened to you and use it to your benefit. When you hit rock bottom and burn up like a phoenix, you can rebuild yourself in a stronger, more powerful way, in a way that is better for yourself and those around you."

Orphaned over 40

Isn't it funny how, no matter how old we are, the clock always seems to stop when we interact with our families? Take a moment and think about your behavior when you are in the workplace or with your friends, versus your behavior when you visit your parents. Somehow, we cannot help but regress into our childhood roles when in the presence of our progenitors. The memories and habits of when we were young act as body snatchers, and we become children again, dressed up in adult body suits. I shudder to think about the times when, as fully grown and supposedly mature adults, my sisters and I have fought like little girls about things that clearly had *nothing* to do with the present.

According to *The New York Times*, adults over 80 are the fastest-growing age-group in the United States. Caretaking for our aging parents can prove a tremendous strain on our emotional health, our relationships with our family members, and our finances. It also raises all sorts of questions. Do we attempt to care for our aging parents our-selves, or do we move them into nursing homes or assisted living fa-cilities? How do we handle their nurses and doctors, their medications and insurance? How do we and our siblings or other relatives divide up the assets or debts and manage the estate? How do we balance our own needs with the needs of those who rely upon us? It's a conundrum that few people are able to find their way out of easily.

How we cope with our parents' aging can be a huge issue as we move into our 40s and beyond. But certainly among the most traumatic events of all, no matter what our relationship with them was like through-out our lives, are our parents' deaths. Of course, we all know that it is inevitable. The time will come when, in the natural order of things, we will watch our parents pass away. But their deaths can throw us com-pletely off-course when they happen. For the lucky ones, our parents represented home, safety, familiarity, love, and acceptance; and when they are gone, we feel unmoored.

• • • •

CARRIE IS LUCKY. She had a strong, positive relationship with her mother all her life, as did her siblings and her father. They didn't have any unfinished business when her mother died. Also, her mother didn't suffer too long before passing away. Nevertheless, Carrie, who was just 30 years old at the time, describes her mother's death as one of the most traumatic events in her life.

Now 40, Carrie is the mother of three. She and her husband live and work in New York City. Carrie described her mother, Abigail, as "a force of nature," with curly red hair, outrageously bright nail polish, and a loud, raspy laugh. She never had a career until her 40s. At that age, she started a successful company, even though people told her she couldn't do it. Her attitude was that life is what you make of it.

Carrie was 27 and in graduate school when her mother was diagnosed with cancer. Abigail went in for surgery to have a tumor removed, thinking it was "no big deal." But the doctors discovered that the cancer had spread, and that Abigail would have to undergo chemotherapy.

Abigail treated the cancer as something to be beaten, not given in to. "She never talked about the fact that she could die—not once," Carrie said, eyes glistening with tears. "She wasn't in denial, but she simply wouldn't listen to anything negative, from the doctors or anyone. She refused to be a burden to anyone. She made it fun to be around her, even when it was hard on her and she felt very ill. She treated her illness as a continuation of her life." Unfortunately, Abigail eventually passed away.

Abigail had insisted that her funeral be a celebration rather than a somber affair, so the family requested that everyone wear bright colors to the service. Abigail even asked to be buried in her fur coat. Over a thousand people, including her manicurist, came to bid her farewell.

Carrie felt fortunate to be so close to her family; she had a lot of people around her to talk with and share in the burden of her mother's death. They frequently used humor to cope with the pain. Every year on the anniversary of Abigail's death, Carrie, her father, and her siblings go out for dinner. They share funny stories about their mom.

After her mother's death, Carrie, who had been working as a television producer, decided that she had to do something to make the world a better place. So she and her brother started a business that raises money online for nonprofit organizations. She feels that this the best way to honor her mother's life.

Recently, Carrie realized how busy she had become with three kids and her nonprofit work. She couldn't imagine how her mother had managed with four kids and a business of her own. "We never once felt that she wasn't there for us," Carrie commented, dabbing at her eyes.

These days, Carrie most misses her mother not being there to see her grandchildren grow up. She said, "This year, on the anniversary of my mom's death, I took my 2-year-old upstairs to bed. I often read him *The Little Engine That Could*, which was my mother's favorite book, but I hadn't in a pretty long time. That night, when I asked him what book he wanted to read, out of nowhere he said, 'The I think I can book.' I have to imagine that my mother had a hand in his choice that day."

Erik Erikson described old age as the eighth stage of life. During this stage, he argued, people must come to terms with their mortality. Some will gaze back with satisfaction on what they have accomplished, achieving ego integration. Others will sink into a state of despair, feeling bitter and unhappy with their lives. Whether our parents take a positive or negative outlook on their own lives can have a tremendous impact on how we view ourselves and our well-being.

But whether our parents adopt an attitude of celebration, as Abigail did, or one of mourning and regret as they approach their own graves, we must reach a final stage of differentiation from them. If we are truly to grow up, then we need to separate out our egos and life stories from those of our families of origin. We need to take responsibility for who we are and the choices we have made, and step fully into our adult skin.

Good Grief

Many people are familiar with Elisabeth Kübler-Ross, a psychologist who highlighted the five stages of grief. Kübler-Ross argued that, when confronted with a traumatic loss or illness, we move from denial to anger to bargaining to depression, and then finally to acceptance.

She herself pointed out that people don't necessarily move through the stages in a prescribed order, and I concur. In my experience, the grief process can be circular. We might move through our anger to acceptance, only to find ourselves weeks later back in denial, and then angry again when something powerfully reminds us of our loss. The one fact that we can take comfort in is that, even if our state of mourning feels permanent, it never is. Time really does heal our wounds, and eventually almost all of us will recover from the loss.

Culturally, we place a strict time line on grieving. But in reality, you can't rush the mourning process. As a psychotherapist, I have found that the more you allow yourself to feel, the less time it is likely to take for you to move on. "Good grief" means allowing yourself to be sad, to cry, to feel homesick, to get angry and rage against God, to feel overwhelmed by loss, and to reach out to others. "Bad grief" means denying your emotions, or even getting angry or frustrated with yourself for feeling them. We are better served by giving ourselves time to sit with and deeply feel our emotions than by attempting to drown them in alcohol or suppress them altogether. Our bodies respond physiologically to the trauma of loss, and we need to respect that. We heal by embracing our grief with compassion and tenderness.

In practical terms, I do recommend a support system—a therapist, spiritual leader, or grieving group. Definitely seek help if you begin isolating yourself from others or discover that you can't get out of bed in the morning. If you need to go on antidepressants for a short while to help you get through the trauma, that's okay, too. We ought not to feel any shame or face any stigma for making such a choice to care for ourselves.

As Carrie and Kim did when their loved ones died, it can be very helpful to think about how you'd like to channel your grief into making the world a better place. I find that clients benefit most when they think about what gifts their loved ones shared most often with others and figure out how they can continue to re-give that energy to the rest of the world.

This exercise also proves helpful to some people. I suggest that my clients who are grieving set aside a certain time each day—say, from 4:00 to 4:15 P.M.—to think about nothing but the people they've lost. It may seem counterintuitive, because others always are telling us *not* to think about those who have passed. But whether you take fifteen or even just five minutes to really be with this person, you can create a beautiful and meaningful ritual for yourself. Light a candle, play her favorite song, write him a letter or an e-mail, or, like Carrie, read her most adored book aloud to your child. Take the time to do something that will help you be in touch with your emotions.

We can't stop time, and we certainly can't cheat death. At some point in our adult lives, all of us will be abandoned by those we loved. And while the passing away of those near and dear is almost always traumatic, it does not have to be a tragedy. We can choose to share their spirit with others through our own efforts. We can carry the light and love and laughter of the people who have left this earth with us for the rest of our lives.

Fifteen

CHANGE YOUR NARRATIVE

. . . .

"YOU CAN'T CHANGE what's happened in your life, but you can change your narrative." This is something I say frequently to my clients—and now I'm sharing it with you. It's a powerful spiritual lesson that you can apply to your life regardless of your religious orientation. What it means is this: while facts remain facts, and sometimes the reality is indeed cold and hard, you can choose to interpret events in many ways. You can tell a sob story about your failures—things that have gone wrong, opportunities missed, and people who have given you short shrift—or you can turn things around and talk (to yourself and others) about all that you have: the blessings big and small, your gratitude and your gifts, how you've overcome adversity and learned from your mistakes, and what you look forward to. You may not be able to change the actual events of your life, but you certainly can rewrite the script of the movie about it that plays in your head.

Existentialist philosophers spoke of the "anguish of freedom." This refers to the fact that we have many options in life but no guarantee of a particular outcome. In our society, we tend to forget that with freedom often comes anxiety. Our choices are not always easy to make.

Sometimes, we forget altogether that we have a choice. But we always have the option to change our narrative. We get to determine the stories that we tell ourselves about who we are, where we've come from, and where we're going. We can frame our life histories in a positive light, or we can turn them into something negative. For example, you can use the word "horrific" in telling a story about something unwelcome that happened to you—like losing a job—or you can use the word "absurd." How does choosing different language help you feel more at ease?

Once you recognize that part of your "anguish of freedom" is coming from the fact that you are developing yourself and pushing yourself to be your best self, you can feel more confident in making a risky choice. Think about not having the freedom to choose at all. What would become of you then?

• • • •

I WORKED WITH a 39-year-old client named Juliet who needed to change her narrative. Fifteen years ago, Juliet was a straight-A student at a university in the Midwest, possessed of a mind for numbers and an eye for wealth. After getting her B.A. in just three years, she earned herself a spot at a top-notch business school and paid her own tuition. She then moved to New York and joined one of the nation's leading financial institutions, where she committed to working seventy-five to one hundred hours a week under the unforgiving fluorescent office lights.

Because Juliet was determined to succeed, she gave everything she had to her career. She encountered many a glass ceiling—and they generally were a lot thicker than she expected—but she didn't let that dampen her enthusiasm. She realized early on that, if she really wanted to climb to the top, it was going to demand sacrifices. So she made those sacrifices—taking on extra projects and frequently giving up weekends to get things done.

After ten years of exhausting devotion to her job, Juliet was rewarded with a senior position and promised more shares in the company, higher bonuses, and greater employment security. All of Juliet's plans for the future, including her investments and 401(k), were tied directly to her stock options.

It isn't surprising that Juliet's intense focus on her career affected her personal life. At 37, she wasn't married, nor did she have a serious partner, although she would have liked one or the other. Every once in a while she would go out on a blind date that a friend had set up, but she found there just wasn't time to pursue a serious relationship. She justified her choice to forgo a relationship by telling herself, "I'm here in New York to forge my way in my career and to be financially independent. No matter what happens, I'll thrive."

But when she came into therapy, Juliet admitted that sometimes she wasn't entirely convinced her sacrifices were worthwhile. When she was up at the crack of dawn, BlackBerry in one hand and coffee in the other, running to catch the subway to work, or slumped in the back of a town car after a fourteen-hour day, staring numbly at her reflection in the window, she would think, "I hardly recognize that pale, beleaguered woman." Juliet had started to wonder, "Is this all there is? Have I missed out on the opportunity to have a family of my own, travel, and pursue hobbies because I've been so driven to succeed in my career?"

Amid these doubts and fears, Juliet's one consolation was her nest egg. She kept her spirits up by reminding herself that, someday, the money would grant her the freedom to do what she wanted to do and be who she wanted to be—a freedom that she willingly had sacrificed to embark on her career. Someday, she would be able to have the things she truly desired, including some hard-earned time off and a partner with whom to share it.

Then, boom. The latest economic crisis hit, and everything changed. Juliet's stock in her company, which had been valued at $70.00 a share, plunged to just $1.50. That's no typo. Because of her loyalty to her firm, Juliet chose to stick with it even as things got worse. Consequently, the nest egg she had worked so hard to build up was completely wiped out. Her lifelong dream—of being financially independent—was gone and, with it, all the time she had invested.

Shortly thereafter, Juliet witnessed several of her co-workers, with whom she had been colleagues from the beginning, get laid off. Nothing could have been more upsetting than to see people who had logged nearly as many hours as she had being escorted out the front door by security with everyone watching the humiliating departure.

The despair that Juliet felt was almost unbearable. But the amazing thing about life is that this very end-of-the-world-as-we-know-it moment, this destruction of everything that Juliet had worked so hard to achieve, provided her with a brilliant opportunity. The question Juliet had been asking herself for years—"Is this all there is?"—suddenly shifted. Now, Juliet chose to take a long, hard look at herself and ask "Who am I, really?"

As soon as she started to ask this question, Juliet realized that she was going to need the help of a therapist. She'd always had suspicions about therapy, viewing people who saw therapists as either "really sick" or simply not having the strength or willpower to get their lives in order. But when she thought about the choices she had made, such as forgoing Sunday brunches with her friends and forgetting to call her parents on special occasions, she decided that she had to make a change. For years she'd had no personal life other than working out regularly. What was her identity outside of being a fit, attractive, successful career woman?

When Juliet first came into my office, she looked exhausted and downtrodden, yet she was willing to roll up her sleeves and dive right in. She immediately started to share her feelings of the past six months. The more Juliet spoke, the more I realized the root of the problem: she was providing a distorted view of her narrative. Not only was she telling herself that therapy was "a crutch for the weak" but she also felt as if she was "an idiot" for not cashing in her nest egg when the stocks were still viable, and for letting everything in her life other than her career fall by the wayside for so long.

I recognized in Juliet a scenario I had encountered before—the overachieving woman who feels she has failed for the first time. Juliet simply had no framework for dealing with her change in circumstances. I pointed out that her fifteen years of top-of-the-line banking experience hadn't been a waste simply because she had seen her savings dry up overnight. She had gained invaluable expertise in a tough, highly regarded field. She had made her way in a man's world, breaking down barriers for future generations of women. She had learned many skills not only in finance and banking but also in organizing a chaotic schedule, connecting to people of many cultures, and inspiring a team.

I told Juliet, "The hardest task for you is to practice patience. Figure out what you will choose to have happen next in your life, and be mindful of the possibility that it may not all fall into place overnight the way it has in the past. In the meantime, what you can do right away, because you have absolute control over it, is start telling yourself a different story—one in which you cast yourself as the pioneer, not the victim or the loser."

For the following year, Juliet and I worked collaboratively on rewriting the script of her life. She made a conscious effort not to see her current situation as disastrous or her past choices as mistakes but rather to see herself as a brave woman on a harrowing yet rewarding journey. She realized that she did appreciate how much she had learned and accomplished during her career. She had pursued her dream of forging her way in a man's world. She had knowingly made sacrifices, and perhaps now was a time to shift her priorities, but her sacrifices were in part responsible for getting her the power, prestige, and knowledge that she had accumulated thus far.

Making that mental shift opened Juliet to a whole new level of life experience. For the first time, she found herself connecting with her spiritual side. She examined her values and realized that what mattered most was her desire to strengthen her relationships with her brother and her two nephews. She wanted to spend more time with them. While she enjoyed her line of work and didn't want to get out of banking altogether, she also knew that she would never go back to the insane hours that she had spent in the office during her 20s and early 30s. Instead, she would balance work with play, making a concerted effort to reconnect with friends and go on dates at least once a week. In other words, Juliet's fifteen years of hard work hadn't been a waste. Even though her bank seemed to be on the brink of collapse, she could continue to be a successful banker and build on her valuable experience. She would simply do so with a more even-keeled, less self-sacrificing approach.

I moved from New York to Los Angeles and had to stop seeing Juliet as a client. Six months later, I got this e-mail from her, which made me smile:

Dear Sarah, I wanted to share my news with you. I am relocating to Hong Kong, where I accepted a job at a top-notch bank. As you always said, "My narrative is under my control," so I thought you would appreciate this postscript. I surprised my friends and family, but most of all, I surprised myself. It will be a huge change. The hardest part will be my separation from my family, and no doubt our dynamics will change. But leaving my old job after 15 years is a relief, as is moving to an exciting new part of the world. Rather than parting armed with a list of complaints about my former employer, I have opted for a positive, more graceful exit, which I am happy about. I want to take this opportunity to thank you again for everything. I hope that our paths will cross again.

All of us have the same opportunity right now that Juliet had with the economic crisis. For all the bad news the crisis brought, it also has provided a priceless opportunity for some of us to ask ourselves, Who am I, really? and What do I choose to do about my life? None of us has to make the story a sad one. It is our choice to focus on the positive elements of our experience. Furthermore, we can create out of our lives powerful tales that will inspire other women to change their narratives.

• • • •

"I COME FROM an abuse story," Reverend Sara said. "When you come from that, you believe you'll never be beautiful again, you'll never be loved again. When you're in the high of the abuse cycle, you feel like the most important person in the world. When you hit low and finally get away, you feel so low."

Reverend Sara, 52, has short brown hair and a petite frame. She grew up outside Charleston, South Carolina. After majoring in art in college, she went on to seminary. There she got involved in teaching art to inmates at a local prison. Later she began working exclusively with women in prison, developing a program to help them build skills and enhance self-esteem.

At age 23, Sara met the man who ended up becoming her husband. Rob was a professor, quiet and reserved but seemingly kind. Yet as soon as they had moved in together, it became clear to Sara that Rob wasn't healthy for her. At the same time, she was still an innocent girl who "didn't know that abuse was possible for me—for women in prison, sure, but not in my world," she recalled.

After about a year and a half, Sara decided to leave Rob. But just then, she discovered that she was pregnant. She thought, "I have to marry Rob now." And so she did. They had four children in rapid succession. Meanwhile, Sara finished seminary and continued her work in prisons.

Rob became more verbally and emotionally abusive. He would yell at Sara, criticize her, and tear her down. But since she was working with women who had been kicked, stabbed, and raped, she didn't think her situation was that bad. After all, she had no visible scars.

Things grew worse. Rob isolated Sara from her family, refusing to allow her to speak with her parents. He cornered her and threatened to hurt her with a knife, sometimes in front of the kids. They would run and hide when he got home from work. She and her children started to have nightmares about Rob killing them. A neighbor overheard Rob screaming at Sara and told her to get out, but she still wasn't ready to take action.

Then one day when she was in her mid-30s, after feeling despair and hopelessness, Sara looked at her life and realized that she, like many of the prisoners she had worked with, was in an abusive relationship. "It was very, very scary," she said. "I was like, What the fuck, God? What happened to me? How did I end up here?" She had been this innocent girl, and suddenly she was in a miserable, dangerous marriage. She didn't understand how her narrative could have changed so radically in such a short time.

"I'm smart enough to be able to talk and pray my way out of despair," Sara explained. "So I did that until I just couldn't anymore, until I thought I was going to die if I didn't make a change. Then I told the kids, 'Okay, we're going for a ride. It's going to be really hard, but we're going to do it.'"

Sara had heard the stories of women she had been working with, so she knew what to do. One afternoon while Rob was at work, she packed up her kids and three suitcases and walked away from the house, leaving everything in it behind. Unfortunately, for legal reasons she still had to take her kids to visit with their father once a week. Sara felt traumatized by her anxiety during these times, fearful of what Rob might do to their children.

Sara continued working as a minister in a church and in prisons, but nobody knew what was going on in her life. She thought that if she spoke about Rob's abusive behavior, he would find out—and start treating her and the kids even worse. "To this day, I still worry that he'll come after me," she admitted. In addition, she worried that her congregation would judge her unworthy of her leadership position.

It wasn't until two years ago, as she neared her fiftieth birthday, that Sara decided to disclose her life story from the pulpit—and change her narrative once more. She said that the scripture passage about Jesus and the woman at the well had inspired her. "Jesus had been walking all day. He was tired and hot. And then this Samaritan woman, who was from a different tribe, offered him water. They had an amazing conversation, and he truly saw her. He listened to her story." Sara was preparing a sermon on this passage when it hit her: "It's time for me to tell my story." And so she did. "I looked everyone in the eye and told it from my heart."

Although it made her nervous, sharing the truth about her history of abuse and ongoing fear of her husband proved to be a tremendously valuable experience for Sara. It deepened her relationship with her congregation. "Part of my not talking about the abuse was because I was a minister!" she exclaimed. "I was supposed to be enlightened. But telling my story has helped me connect with people in a more powerful way. There's no judgment; they understand that I'm just like them. It's enabled me to finally let go of that old story and start telling a new story."

Sara said that most of us put up barriers to protect ourselves from others, but as a result, we end up putting ourselves in prison. "We have to open those bars to experience meaningful relationships. We have to be real to connect. That was the lesson I learned that day in the pulpit, opening my heart to all the world."

Sara had this advice for other women in traumatic situations or abusive relationships: "All you have to do is step into the light. Sometimes you can only put one foot in. But you see that light beam and you say, 'I'm stepping in.'"

Sara paused for a moment, then continued. "We have to be able to say, 'This is where I am.' Then we let the spiritual energy carry us. When we turn to spirit, there's healing and hope and other women doing the exact same thing. I guess the message is that the spiritual realm is the realm of joy on the other side of hope. We are not alone, ever, whether it's God or Mary Magdalene or Jesus or a sister who sees us. We're moving together."

• • • •

JENNIFER LOWE-ANKER, 54, lives in Bozeman, Montana, where she works as an artist and enjoys mountain climbing. She turned what could have been a tragic time for herself and her family into a sparkling moment, an opportunity to explore new directions in her life and move on with even greater fortytude.

When Jennifer was in her 20s, she met and married a fellow mountain climber, Alex Lowe. They traveled and climbed together for eight years before having three boys. Then, when Jennifer was 42, Alex and his best friend, Conrad Anker, went on a climbing trip. Conrad returned, but Alex died in an avalanche.

Needless to say, Jennifer was devastated, as were her children. Then, within the next five years, Jennifer also lost her mother and her sister. But rather than be overwhelmed by her grief, Jennifer chose to continue celebrating life, appreciating small joys such as her garden, taking on exciting new projects, and even finding a surprising new love.

Jennifer and Conrad mourned the loss of their close friend Alex together, offering each other comfort and solace. Over time they realized that they were attracted to one another and had fallen in love. They got married and have been together ever since. Jennifer said, "Conrad has been a wonderful father to the boys. He is very sweet and understanding. He officially adopted them when we got married. He's been a huge blessing for all of us."

Two years ago, Jennifer published a book about her life entitled *Forget Me Not*. "Alex's death was horrible," she said. "But had it not happened, lots of things would've been different in my life. I wanted to write about that."

For example, Jennifer wouldn't have established a foundation in Nepal. Many of the climbers who scale Mount Everest and the other high mountains of the Himalayas are sherpas. These locals—though marvelously acclimatized to the altitude—do not necessarily receive adequate technical training. Conrad and Jennifer founded the Khumbu Climbing School to provide locals with vocational training in order to keep them safe on their climbs.

"Alex loved getting to know the indigenous people wherever he traveled," Jennifer said. "He especially loved the sherpas in Nepal, where he had been on seven or eight expeditions." She had never had the opportunity to join him there, however, since they had young children. The pilgrimage to Nepal after his death was a particularly meaningful journey for her, and she knew that the climbing school would have meant a lot to Alex.

I asked Jennifer where she had found the inspiration to take on so many exciting, creative, outward-focused projects in response to so much loss. She replied, "I think whenever people are faced with loss and grief, for whatever reason—whether it's a loss of place or the loss of a loved one or a war—those kinds of things bring to the surface something deep within us that we don't always know we have: an ability to cope, an ability to turn around and see that you can find hope somewhere or another. That's what gives us the ability to be such a primary force on this planet."

How to Change Your Narrative

In attempting to change their narratives, many people get stumped by their belief systems. Our belief systems have a great deal to do with the roles we played in our families of origin. In every family, people tend to adopt certain archetypal positions. Someone is the Hero, someone is the Mascot, someone is the Villain, et cetera. Here are some examples of roles people play in their families:

- The Star. This person is considered the special one, the superperformer of the family. He or she usually does achieve a great deal. But his or her mistakes are ignored or easily forgiven.
- The Problem. Therapists refer to this person as the "identified patient." He or she generally struggles with some issue, such as alcoholism, an eating disorder, or disciplinary problems at school. But the family blames him or her for all their problems.
- The Skeptic. This person calls into question all the family's decisions. He or she avoids taking risks.
- The Cheerleader. This person stands on the sidelines, cheering other family members on but avoiding stepping into the limelight for fear of failing.

I had a client, Laura, who was the Star of her family of origin. She had achieved a great deal of success—straight As and athletic prowess in school, graduation from a top university, winning major cases as an attorney. In addition, she'd gotten married in her mid-20s to a wonderful man and had two kids in her 30s.

Although Laura very much wanted to start her own business as a jewelry designer, she came to see me because she found herself stuck. She had dropped down to part-time hours at her law firm so that she'd have time to explore her entrepreneurial ideas. But as a result of playing the Star role throughout her life, she found herself reluctant to actually open her jewelry business. She had never fallen and so couldn't bear the thought of failure.

After we'd worked together for some time, Laura got up the courage to start her business. Even then, however, she struggled. She was frustrated when sales didn't take off right away. And she couldn't bear the fact that, in this new job, she received no daily accolades. "I don't know if I'm wasting my time, on the right track, or just making a mess of things!" she moaned.

In exploring her narrative with her, I pointed out that Laura had to let go of her attachment to being forever the Star. It was time for her to recast herself in a new role. For example, she might be the Adventurer, fearlessly seeking out new life experiences. Sure, the business might not succeed. But that wouldn't mean Laura had failed. On the contrary, she would have taken a risk and pursued her dream. She would be best served by viewing that step alone, regardless of outcome, as a huge triumph.

I also have met many women who played the role of Cheerleader in their families. Their siblings were highly accomplished, as were their parents, so they chose to cheer them on. These Cheerleaders downplayed their own successes, staying on the metaphorical bleachers and probably limiting themselves in what they attempted to achieve. These women, whether they took on that role as children themselves or saw their mothers playing it, rooted for their parents, friends, husbands, children—anyone but themselves. Then, when the Cheerleaders reach 40, many of them have an awakening. They realize that they don't want to be on the sidelines anymore. They want to take an active role, and they finally have the confidence to do so. They want to be the Heroes, the Adventurers, only they don't know how.

Changing your narrative means saying, "I'm not reacting to anything around me. I'm listening to my true self." But you can't do that until you have gained awareness of the role you played in your family and how that's been to your advantage and disadvantage. Putting a label on it will help you objectively evaluate how remaining loyal to your childhood role has helped and hindered you in moving forward as an adult.

Next, consider the metaphors that come to mind when you ponder the role you used to play and the role you want to play in the future.

Don't spend too much time analyzing this step. Just go with what first comes to mind, your gut instinct. A client once told me that when she imagined trying to shift her role from the Cheerleader to the Star, it made her feel like she was in a naked dream, the kind where you show up at school with no clothes on. She felt overexposed.

Finally, engage in a deep, honest dialogue with yourself to ensure that you're coming to your own conclusions and not relying on someone else's opinion. You may want to draw on the support of a therapist or coach and will certainly want the help of your trusted friends.

I turned to my friends for assistance as I considered moving from Manhattan to Venice Beach in California for a change of pace. I almost never relied on my friends in these situations because I was a therapist and thought I was supposed to know what to do. But during that time, I realized how important it was to show my friends my vulnerability. I said, "I don't know how to make this decision. I love New York and have so many friends here. But at the same time, I feel as if I need to try living somewhere else, somewhere less frantic and with better weather. What should I do?" They said, unanimously, "You need to move to Venice." That slight push was what I needed to make my plans a reality.

Let's go back to Laura, the attorney who was starting her own jewelry business. Once we'd talked through her childhood role as the Star, I asked Laura if she was prepared to change her narrative. She responded, "Yes, I'm really going to do this." So I asked her to tell me what skills from the Star role she'd been able to apply as a lawyer. She said that she was able to do things rapidly and well. I pointed out that starting your own business does not necessarily require rapid assessment; it requires patience.

Then I had her describe the feelings that came up when she thought about not being a Star but rather being an Adventurer—letting go of her need to be perfect, in control, and successful at all times. She told me that she felt stuck, and that made her anxious. The metaphor she came up with was that she was trapped in an elevator and couldn't open the doors. She was starting to panic.

We can have great difficulty in changing our narratives as adults because we are so stuck in the roles we took on as kids. It makes sense, because this is the only way we have known of being in the world. In order to modify our roles—whether at work, in our families, or with our friends—we must find our authentic voices.

It also helps to maintain our sense of humor. We can only benefit from appreciating the absurdity and uncertainty of life. Sometimes things aren't going to work out for the best. You might have a terrible month, or year, or decade in your business or in your relationship. It's critical in these times to take a step back and say, "Oh well! Life is absurd; I'm just doing the best I can. Maybe I'm making a fool of myself, but does any of it even matter in the end?" Embrace the irony and let go of some of that serious, judgmental edge.

My friend Amy, whom I have known since we were both 6, has an uncanny ability to lessen my anxiety and make me laugh uncontrollably by adopting metaphors that are both kooky and profound. After we had discussed the concept of changing your narrative, and how we can't do that all at once, she shared this thought with me: "It's kind of like we all are on the subway platform waiting for the express train to take us to our destination as quickly as possible. We let the local trains pass by us even though they, too, would get us where we want to go. One local train passes, and then another, and then another, until, what do you know? We have, idiotically, just waited for forty-five minutes to get on the darn express train, when we already would've arrived had we taken the local train. Perhaps we were not meant to skip stops en route to our destination that day. Perhaps we were meant to notice things in between, and not be so obsessed with 'getting there' that we sacrifice the journey. So basically, we all ought to consider taking the local train. What's the rush, anyway?"

Changing your narrative takes work. And it almost always involves some major risks. But it is a critical component of tapping into your spirituality because it allows you to let go of old patterns and make psychological space for new views and attitudes. When you make bold choices, speak with your authentic voice, frame your story in a positive light, and move courageously into the unknown future, then you truly embody fortytude.

Sixteen

FINDING YOUR OWN PATH

. . . .

THE MOST POWERFUL recent contribution to spiritual thought may be the idea that you get to choose your concept of God. Never in human history have individuals in so many parts of the world enjoyed so much freedom to create their own definitions of spirituality, religious practice, and the divine as they do today. With this freedom can come tension, if our God is not the same God that our parents accept, or if our spiritual paths differ from those of our partners; or if we haven't yet managed to find a set of religious principles and ideals that we feel comfortable with and want to embrace. But it also opens us to wonderful opportunities to develop belief systems that truly work for us and to forge our own paths in the world.

It may sound strange to some, but I found deep spiritual satisfaction in surfing. At 38, having just moved from New York to Venice Beach, California, I was looking for something to bring peace to my life. When I started surfing, I found it frustrating. It was difficult not to allow my ego to get in the way. I'm used to being a fairly competent athlete, but those first few times in the water I couldn't even stand up on my board for more than a couple of seconds. I felt embarrassed and impatient to improve.

The first step in my spiritual journey with surfing, therefore, was letting go of my harsh judgments about myself. My instructor pointed out that naturally I wouldn't become an expert overnight. I would enjoy myself a lot more if I consciously embraced being a beginner and with it the wonder, thrill, and anticipation of trying something new. It was an excellent lesson, and one that can apply to all of life. Often, our fear of looking like fools keeps us from taking risks, especially after the age of 35. But when we shy away from fresh and challenging experiences, we only limit ourselves.

Once I got into the flow, I fell in love with surfing. While I'm out on the water, nothing else matters. The waves change every moment, so I have no choice but to pay attention to what I'm doing at all times. I am totally present in a way that I've never been before. My usually racing thoughts settle down, and I enter a meditative state. What's more, I find that surfing offers a powerful metaphor for life: there are good days and there are bad days. But whether I wipe out or have the ride of my life, one thing is certain: another wave is always on the way.

I've discovered that, even if you take your spiritual pursuits seriously, you won't necessarily get the answers to your questions right away. You're unlikely to attain enlightenment after two surf sessions or ten yoga classes, or a month's worth of visits to the church or temple. Sometimes we can burden ourselves with unrealistic expectations, and when we do, we risk giving up if we don't attain instantaneous results. It's critical to remind ourselves that there is a reason why these endeavors are called "practices" and not "instant fixes"—they take time to master and make a lasting impact on our habits of mind and overall sense of well-being.

• • • •

MALLIKA CHOPRA, the 38-year-old daughter of the international bestselling author and self-help expert Deepak Chopra, has been meditating every day since she was 9 years old. She is a warm, kindhearted, down-to-earth woman with bright, large brown eyes and a slender figure. An accomplished author in her own right (*100 Promises to My Baby, 100 Questions from My Child,* regular Huffington Post blogger), Mallika is the perfect combination of geek and glamour.

People who don't know her well might imagine that Mallika would or should have attained enlightenment or somehow ascended from the earthly plane after so many years of a dedicated spiritual practice. But she is a real person—a wife and working mother of two who has a rich, complex life and struggles at times just like the rest of us. And, like so many other women out there, she loves her chocolate and Coca-Cola.

Mallika feels blessed to have benefited from Transcendental Meditation (TM) since she was a girl. Meditating helps her to create silence in her mind and reduce stress. But she emphasizes that, as with all good things in life, it requires discipline. In her early 30s, she went through something of an identity crisis. She loved being a wife and mother but found herself wanting more professionally and longing to individuate herself from her famous father. After some personal exploration through TM, she founded Intent.com, a wellness website that she continues to operate.

Continuing the spiritual tradition her father began when he was 36 years old, Mallika has asked her daughters to meditate. She sets the time of their sits according to their age—so they meditated five minutes when they were 5 years old, nine minutes at 9 years old, and so on. Now that they are getting older, it is their choice, but they enjoy meditating and freely choose to practice. Mallika feels that this spiritual pursuit has brought her entire family closer together.

I find this story fascinating because so many women at midlife—myself included—tend to think, "Oh, if only I had started meditating (or going to church/temple or doing yoga or whatever practice we enjoy) when I was younger, then I'd really have life figured out by now. Yet, as Mallika's experience clearly demonstrates, while having an active spiritual life can help people handle stress and challenging life moments, it doesn't solve all our problems or grant us magical powers to transcend life's pain. At the same time, if it can create within us a sense of calm, a bit of faith that everything will be okay, and an ounce more compassion for others—even for just two minutes—then we might begin to notice the bigger difference that spirituality can make in our everyday lives.

A Bright Light

As I reflect upon moments when I have felt discouraged with the state of the country, the environment, or my own life, I realize that I have found it immensely valuable to look to other women for inspiration. In truth, I didn't fully access my spirituality until, at age 36, I met Zainab Salbi, the short-haired, wide-eyed, exotic beauty who founded Women for Women International when she was in her early 20s. This nonprofit organization sends money and letters of support to women in war-torn regions around the world—such as the Democratic Republic of Congo, Afghanistan, and Sudan—so that these victims of violence can rebuild their lives and become self-sustaining.

I already was impressed by Zainab's achievements and her dedication to women worldwide, but I was truly astounded when I learned the details of her life story, recounted in her memoir *Between Two Worlds*. In the book, Zainab tells of how she grew up during a tremendously dark and confusing time in what used to be a magnificent country—Iraq. The daughter of Saddam Hussein's personal pilot, she was raised in Baghdad under the dictator's ever-threatening watch. While her parents did not approve of his violent leadership tactics, they felt obligated to act like friends of Hussein in order to preserve the lives of their family members.

Zainab was raised Muslim and always felt a connection to the divine. In fact, she started praying daily as a teenager, imagining herself as an ant, totally insignificant before God. She felt grateful to her mother for giving her a valuable lesson in spirituality that transcended religious lines. Zainab said, "My mother used to tell me that all I needed for prayer is to smile every day. She told me to find God everywhere: in the smell of a flower, in the touch of the sun on my neck, and in the beauty of a caterpillar."

When she was 19, Zainab moved to America for an arranged marriage to an Iraqi man. But shortly after she arrived, she discovered that her new husband was abusive, so she left the marriage with no money and no job. Then Zainab had a spiritual crisis. She found herself struggling to make ends meet in Washington, D.C., cut off from her parents and devastated by the war in her home country. "I lost my faith," she said. "I thought, Why has God done this to me?"

Fortunately, Zainab met Amjad, a generous, tender, and profoundly spiritual Palestinian American, only a year or so later. He helped her recover from the trauma of her first marriage and the increasing problems in Iraq. He said, "You're only angry at God because you love Him." And Zainab realized he had a point.

Zainab and Amjad got married when she was 23. In lieu of going on a honeymoon, they founded Women for Women International because they felt that they had to respond to the plight of Bosnian women being placed in rape camps. Through the dedicated efforts of Zainab, Amjad, and a handful of volunteers working on a shoestring budget, Women for Women slowly but steadily grew into an organization that today has assisted nearly one-quarter of a million women and raised over $80 million in aid and microfinance loans. Even though Zainab and Amjad have since split as a couple, they remain close friends.

Zainab elucidated two critical experiences that brought her in touch with her spirituality as an adult, deepening her faith in God and strengthening her resolve to make the world a better place. The first was witnessing her mother's gracious and peaceful approach to her own death. Zainab was in her 20s at the time. Her mother died of ALS, more commonly known as Lou Gehrig's disease. As her body deteriorated, she made a blanket out of knots, asking for forgiveness each time she tied a knot. She also wrote letters to all the people in her life telling them how much she loved them. "It was profound," Zainab said. "She handled her death so well. It made me appreciate my life even more."

The second experience was when Zainab was in her early 30s and attended a leadership retreat on a Native American reservation. It was her first time camping with no electricity or running water, and Zainab developed a rich connection with nature. She also had a breakthrough. The participants went into a sweat lodge one night, and "something transformed" for Zainab. "I remember leaving the sweat lodge and crying for hours, releasing so much," she said.

Afterward, Zainab felt inspired to tell her friends the true story of her life in Iraq. Previously, she'd kept it a secret from everyone except Amjad. "Not one of them judged me, as I had feared for so many years," Zainab said. "On the contrary, they all had wonderful responses. They all saw me for myself, not as 'the pilot's daughter,'" she said.

Many people have asked Zainab how she can handle working in the midst of wars and tragedy, and keep smiling. "They wonder," she told me, "how can I meet women whose legs have been chopped off and whose children were forced to eat their mothers' flesh? How can I meet women who were raped so much that their internal organs ruptured and got out of their bodies? How can I meet women who have been pinned on a cross as men raped them while others danced and drummed around them?" The truth is, for the longest time, Zainab didn't know how to deal with the horror. She would work herself into a state of absolute fatigue. She would sob and scream for the world to hear the women's cries of suffering.

But then Zainab adopted her spiritual practices: meditating, reading the poetry of the Sufi mystic Rumi, practicing yoga, regularly connecting with nature, and serving others. "My silence is able to take me to perhaps a nanosecond of awareness, of seeing our oneness and interconnection," she explained. "And these nanoseconds are enough to put perspective on many things—how it is so not worth being upset by the mundane things in life, by the harsh word of someone in our life or a passing stranger, or by the judgment of our own ego. These practices help me to see the beauty and the magnificence of God, of this world, and of the universe even in the midst of the darkness, so that I can smile and keep on going."

Zainab has found her practices to be an effective way of bringing peace, comfort, and joy to herself and others. "While I still struggle with my inability to deal with the pain," she said, "I have learned to see the light inside of me and outside of me. I do slip sometimes and not meditate, not read my Rumi, not practice my yoga, or not go to nature and just be. But over the years, I have learned to regret these slips."

Zainab said something that touched me deeply. "You know, I thought I was helping the women through my work with Women for Women International, only to realize that they are the best teachers I could have. These are women who have survived wars, seen loved ones killed, tortured, and mutilated in front of them, been raped themselves, witnessed the burning of their homes, been displaced, and lost everything they once had. They have seen darkness at its core, they have faced it, and they have triumphed over it every time they manage to dance and sing. And they dance and sing quite often."

She continued, "It's humbling, seeing them dance. They leave me to wonder, Who am I not to dance? Who am I to take my life so seriously? Who am I not to celebrate life and see its beauty? If they can dance, who am I not to? From the women, I learned to look darkness in its eyes and not fear it anymore, but rather know that I can be stronger than it and that I can walk through it. Through the eyes of the women to whom I have dedicated my life, I learned to see light in the middle of the darkness, for it is always there, always. I learned that humanity may have its cruelty, but it also has its beauty and light—and for that, I will continue my work."

Changing Faiths

Faith in America is in a state of flux. According to a 2009 survey by the Pew Forum on Religion & Public Life, about half of Americans have changed their religious affiliation at least once in their lives. Most people who left the faiths of their childhood say that they did so because they stopped believing in those spiritual teachings. Many who remain unaffiliated with any religion report feeling that religious people are hypocritical and judgmental, religious organizations have too many rules, and religious leaders are too interested in money and power. Others choose to follow a different religion and find satisfaction there.

Gabriella is a 39-year-old mother of two who converted from Catholicism to Judaism when she was in her 20s. Gabriella grew up in Guadalajara, Mexico, the youngest of twelve children in a very traditional Catholic home. She had a First Communion ceremony, attended church every week with her mother, went to confession, and did "everything that you were supposed to do." But as soon as she moved out of her parents' house, when she was in her early 20s, she lost interest in the religion.

When she was 25, Gabriella met a Jewish man named Ron at a bar, and they fell in love. In order for her to marry him, Ron insisted that Gabriella convert to Judaism. But she didn't feel resistant to the idea, since she already had decided that Catholicism was not for her. Furthermore, it made sense to her that she convert so that they could raise their children in the Jewish culture.

Gabriella and Ron moved to the United States, and she discovered a warm, welcoming temple with a wonderful rabbi not far from her new home. She learned about not only Judaism but also history and how to look at religion in a cultural context. She also became fluent in English. She said, "Judaism resonates with me more than Catholicism because it's more practical. It never felt right telling some priest my deepest secrets, which were supposed to be sins. I'd think, You priests don't look so almighty to me. But a rabbi is not supposed to be better than you; he's just a normal human being. Also, you don't go to hell or heaven; you're supposed to be a good person just to be a good person. That makes a lot of sense to me."

Since separating from her husband a year before we spoke, Gabriella had continued to practice her adopted Jewish faith. She observed the high holidays, although she didn't go to temple on a regular basis. And she was still raising her two children to be Jewish. She told me, "I think what happened was that my beliefs were already kind of Jewish. For my own comfort and well-being, it makes sense for me to be Jewish in every single way. I take my children to Mexican ceremonies because, for me, they are cultural, not religious. But being Jewish makes my life easier, and it also fits my morals. For example, when I mess up with someone, I'm not supposed to say ten thousand Hail Marys to make it better; I have to make amends."

Gabriella always will be grateful to her ex-husband for introducing her to Judaism and opening her eyes to another spiritual path. Her story, like Mallika Chopra's, demonstrates that faith does not necessarily provide a Band-Aid solution for all of our pain and suffering. It doesn't make us holier than thou, or allow us to rise above the day-to-day trials and tribulations of life. What it does, in the best circumstances, is give us an opportunity to seek further clarification about who we are and what we want out of this short life.

A Spiritual Community

One of the most potent benefits of spirituality can be joining a community—whether that takes the form of a church, mosque, temple, or synagogue, yoga studio, parenting network, or book club. When you make the effort to integrate yourself into a group of like-minded people who all are oriented to a higher purpose, creating substantive connections with others, and making the world a better place, then you have an amazing support network to tap into during times of need.

Natalie Jones, 45, and a Latter-day Saint, feels that the close-knit Mormon community has been a great source of love and strength in her life. Natalie in particular appreciates the visiting teaching program. She explained that you don't get to choose to whom you pay visits. Rather, the Relief Society president of the congregation assigns you "to people whom you may or may not normally choose as friends." Also, your assignments change every few years, so that you're always meeting new people.

Natalie said, "Sometimes it can be uncomfortable at first, but I have always eventually developed a close friendship with these sisters. And I have had the opportunity to get to know some remarkable women whom I otherwise would never have known. I truly feel like I have thirty to forty friends in my ward [congregation] who are my 'cheering section' in life. They always are there for me because either I have had the opportunity to teach them or they have visit-taught me."

Through visiting teaching, Natalie met her dear friend Pearl, who passed away recently at the age of 102. During their many visits, Pearl told Natalie incredible stories about her life journey, filled as it had been with both sorrow and joy. Pearl had been widowed in her early 30s with five young children and another on the way. While she was in the hospital delivering her sixth child, one of her other children became ill and passed away. She remarried and had five more children, also raising her husband's three children. Then she was widowed again in her 70s. On her hundredth birthday, Pearl had 51 grandchildren, 147 great-grandchildren, and 32 great-great-grandchildren. "Pearl had a great sense of humor and a wisdom about her that helped me put my own life in perspective," Natalie said. "It was always a mood lifter for me to visit with her."

A few months after Pearl died, her daughter brought Natalie something that Pearl had made. At the time, Natalie was going through one of the greatest challenges she had ever faced. "I knew when I saw that gift from Pearl that she loved me, and wanted me to know that I could conquer these challenges. I knew that she was cheering me on from the other side," said Natalie, with tears in her eyes. And so Natalie's gift of visit-teaching Pearl had found its way back around; even after passing away, Pearl was able to visit-teach Natalie.

There's no need to be Mormon to create such a system among your girlfriends or within your community. Even if you don't belong to a particular religion, you can create a buddy system with other people who share your values. Establish a regular time to meet in person at least once a month. Sign up to visit and bring each other food when any one of you is going through a challenge, whether it's the birth of a child, an illness, or the death of a loved one.

To foster the spiritual connection among the group members, be sure to focus on meaningful conversations about what is really going on in your lives. Often, we unconsciously revert to chitchat about the weather or the latest happenings on *American Idol*. Be courageous and dive deeper into the difficulties and rewards of your career, relationships, and your own spiritual journey so that you can meet others on a heart level. Consider ending your time with your community with a gratitude practice, in which each person states explicitly what she appreciates about her life.

Spiritual Struggles

Not everyone finds her spiritual path as easily as did Mallika, Zainab, Gabriella, and Natalie. We can encounter stumbling blocks on our spiritual journeys for a number of reasons. Perhaps we experience conflict with a parent, partner, or friend over our decisions to pursue certain paths, which they feel are inappropriate or flat-out wrong. Perhaps we fall out with a priest, rabbi, minister, lama, or other spiritual teacher, discovering that he or she is corrupt or not living in accordance with our community's prescribed values. Or perhaps we simply have crises within ourselves, realizing that we no longer believe what we used to believe or no longer feel aligned with our former religions. In these moments, we must reach deeper than ever before into our core beings and discover what resonates with our spirits.

Fortunately, there are several ways to access this self-knowledge. We might read books, magazine articles, speeches, or blog postings by known experts whom we respect. We might have conversations with people we admire for the way they have chosen to live their lives. We could meet with a therapist, life coach, or spiritual leader. Or we might choose simply to turn silently inward and consult ourselves.

It can prove an all-consuming and even heart-wrenching process to discover what makes spiritual sense to us in this mad world. Fortunately, many options are available. Yet the downside is that few filters exist to help us distinguish the charlatans from the true masters, the worthwhile practices from the fads of the moment. Sometimes finding our spiritual paths simply takes time and experimentation.

• • • •

BARBARA VERROCHI, 48, is one of the most spiritual people I have ever met. A yoga teacher in New York City, Barbara speaks in her classes about common challenges to our connection with the divine, including loneliness even in the midst of a crowd; cities filled with fast-moving, stressed-out people, honking horns, and ringing cell phones; and the common belief that loss of youth somehow equals loss of spirit.

"Now is a difficult time for people," Barbara said. "They're breaking down because the world is breaking down. Energetically, people are having anxiety attacks, bipolar disorder is on the rise, and so are

ADD and autism . . . People are seeking to connect back to themselves and connect to everyone else."

Barbara herself has been able to defy these challenges by practicing yoga for two-plus hours daily for nearly twenty years. She said, "I'm always trying to be conscious. There's a lot of speed in our culture, and we keep getting speedier and more disconnected from ourselves. I'm very speedy by nature, so I do a lot of work to stay grounded."

In her classes Barbara emphasizes the power of the breath to connect us with our bodies and calm the mind. She also makes frequent use of laughter to remind people that they don't have to be as intense about their spiritual practices as they are about everything else in their lives. Yoga class is one place where they have permission to let go of their drive for perfection.

Yoga, in Barbara's view, is about attaining a deep happiness that isn't fleeting. This process comes from freeing ourselves from attachments. "All spiritual practices are about surrendering our addictions to sex, drugs, power, money, and other things we think we need in order to be happy," she explained. In addition, yoga helps us open our hearts and minds, learn to rely on the breath for focus, release negative energy, and let go of identifications with things outside ourselves, such as ideas about what we "should" be. The magic of yoga is that, when we practice, we feel lighter and at the same time more grounded.

Barbara advised women who are seeking a spiritual practice to find a teacher or tradition that resonates with them, and to stay with that practice for a long while to see what it has to teach them. It's best not to jump among teachers or disciplines, because doing so only creates more fluctuations in the mind. She said, "We are living in an exceptional time when the United States is full of amazing teachers in Buddhism, yoga, and many other disciplines. Even if you live in the wilderness, you can listen to their teachings online. These traditions can coincide with your existing religious practices or be complete practices in themselves."

Discovering Your Own Sense of Spirituality

A critical part of fortytude involves coming to terms with the life that may exist beyond this life, the meaning that we want our existence here on earth to have, and the faith that will help us make it through good times and bad. Yet when I mention the idea of discovering their spiritual sides to my clients, some of them struggle to figure out what that even means. I suggest this exercise to clarify what holds the most value in their lives, and how they might tap into a soulful connection with themselves.

Pretend that you have one week alone on a tropical island, or in a room with blank walls, or on a boat—it doesn't matter where precisely. The important factor is that the place does not contain anything from your life back home. You've got all the food and water you need for the week, but otherwise you are limited in what you can take. No computers, BlackBerrys, or iPhones, no Internet connection for Twitter or Facebook, no e-mailing, text messaging, or even making old-fashioned phone calls. Put aside the constant buzz of technology and desire to check in with others. You are permitted to bring just three items with you. What would you choose?

The three things you would bring to your designated location say a lot about who you are and what truly matters to you. Maybe you bring a certain novel or book of poetry, a needle and thread, a beautiful painting, or a musical instrument. In this case, you might want to seek out creative pursuits, going on a weekend writing workshop, taking an art or sewing class, or picking up that dusty guitar and vowing to practice once a week. Perhaps you bring a language kit for learning French or Mandarin Chinese, which suggests that you like adventure. In this case, it might be time to plan an overseas trip or, at a minimum, find someone to meet you for a weekly language exchange. Or maybe you bring a boogie board, a mountain bike, or running shoes. For many people, working out is the surest way to tap into the innermost sense of self. If you haven't been making your favorite sport a priority, take a look at your schedule and figure out how you can fit it in. If you haven't found enjoyment in your body at all, consider trying out a variety of physical activities to see if one resonates with you.

This exercise is highly practical, in that it suggests how you might reprioritize your time in the present moment. But it also provides clues to a much bigger question: How can you be more in touch with your spirit? Take away your roles, your job, and your relationships. What is your life about without these defining elements? When you're not "the teacher" or "the sales representative" or "the soccer star" or "Mom"; when you're not "the organizer" or "the wallflower" or whatever other notions you may have about yourself; when you're simply *you*, alone and alive, what is it that you're all about?

Reflecting on this topic is sure to provide you with an opening to understanding your individual conception of spirituality. And what pursuit could be more worth our precious resources than setting ourselves on the spiritual path, which ultimately has the power to lead us to peace and fulfillment?

Conclusion

GO FORTH WITH FORTYTUDE

. . . .

PERSONALLY, I DON'T like the word "happiness."

To be clear, I'm a big fan of happiness itself. It's just the present-day understanding and use of the term that I object to. "Happiness," at least in our modern society, is too often equated with fame, power, financial success, and the accumulation of possessions. Or it is defined as having a traditional (although increasingly rare) family structure—2 (happily married, heterosexual) parents and 2.5 (perfect) children.

But how much control do we really have over attaining massive wealth or finding the ideal partner? We might waste our lives searching for fortune or Mr. Right and miss every exotic destination, every moving moment and glorious mountain peak, every inspirational person, pleasant distraction, or fascinating side trip that we could have been reveling in along the way.

Furthermore, even the term "the pursuit of happiness" strikes me as odd. It implies that happiness is running away from us and we're desperately chasing after it, trying to catch it in our butterfly nets. It suggests that happiness is something we have to strive for rather than something we already have a right to experience simply by being alive.

What we might enjoy seeking is a life lived in accordance with our Core Values rather than one based on our achievements or roles that have been defined for us by society. Achievements and roles change constantly through our lives, anyway. You lose weight by doing the latest trendy "cleanse," then gain the weight right back, then figure out what your body really needs and stabilize at a size that's best for you. You win an Employee of the Month award but get laid off the next year in the recession. You're single, then married, then divorced, then re-married, and then widowed. You're childless; then you're a mother of one, then two, then three; then your kids are grown, and you're experiencing an empty nest. You're a daughter; then both your parents pass away.

Sometimes, the accomplishments and roles you thought you'd attain—you wanted to have children but never did; your husband left you, or you left him; you never got around to the career you'd imagined having because you chose to be a stay-at-home mom—never materialize. Sometimes, your priorities shift: what was important at age 18 might seem petty by the time you're 38, only you may or may not have taken the time to notice.

But while these external factors inevitably evolve, our values, which are internal, tend to be more stable. With grace, you rise above your difficulties with a calm wisdom, judging neither yourself nor others. Through connectedness, you form and maintain mutually supportive relationships with other people. When you are accomplished, you have mastery over one or more areas of your life, deriving a well-deserved sense of pride from these activities. Adventure leads you to take on new challenges regardless of your age, making the most of the opportunities that surround you. And spirituality brings you in touch with your innermost essence, offering you access to strength and joy through hard times as well as brilliant ones.

Ironically, our values can, at the same time that they ground us, provide a more freeing way to define ourselves. Instead of saying, "This is what I do," we say, "This is what I am about." Nothing is more attractive than a 40-plus woman who has focused on what matters most to her, as opposed to blindly following a prescribed path, and who therefore exudes confidence in herself and enthusiasm for her life. Among women ranging in age from early 30s to late 90s, those who adhere to their Core Values and treat these as their guiding principles most consistently find their way to self-acceptance, personal power, and peace, as well as a generous attitude toward other people.

Fortytude in Action

I hope that the women profiled in this book, combined with the exercises provided throughout, have served as inspiration for incorporating the Core Values into your everyday life. Overall, there are steps you can take to help stay committed to these values. The first is to write the values down somewhere obvious, where you will glance at them every day. I have all five words spelled out on a whiteboard that I keep in my office. Each day, I place a check mark next to the value once I've made at least a moment of time for it. You could do the same thing with a paper fastened to your refrigerator, or a note in your iPhone or Black-Berry.

You might also consider writing down specific goals, particularly related to the values you're having the most difficulty pursuing. Ample psychological research has pointed to the effectiveness of goal setting in helping us turn our wishes and hopes into reality. Let's say you feel you are lacking adventure in your life. You might set a small goal, such as trying one new vegetable every month, or a stretch goal, like traveling someplace unusual over your kids' summer break. If you are feeling a desire to connect more deeply with friends, you might resolve to establish a weekly women's group or book club.

In addition, it helps when we women hold each other accountable for sticking to our values. We can become frustrated with the social forces that may influence us to veer off course. Our families might demand more time, more energy, and more sacrifice from us. Members of our community might judge us if we choose to follow an unconventional path. Or we undermine ourselves with questions such as What will *they* think of me if I drop my corporate career just when I'm hitting the peak of my success? or How will *they* react if I choose to adopt a child as a single mother? or What would my pastor/rabbi say if I wanted to explore another religion? But if we make our decisions based on such outside factors, we risk finding ourselves later in life feeling unsatisfied and untrue to ourselves. By taking responsibility for helping one another stay committed to our values, we do our part to ensure that more of us find our way home.

Yet we don't want to take ourselves *too* seriously. Although we may set out with the goal of "mastering" the five Core Values of women with fortytude—grace, connectedness, accomplishment, adventure, and spirituality—none of us ever can accomplish this task fully. As with most things in life, no matter how much we focus on self-actualization, we always will find opportunities to develop ourselves further. A spiritual teacher of mine once said, "You're perfect just the way you are. . . . *And* you've got room for improvement."

Rather than turning fortytude into another source of stress in our already busy lives or another measure of how we're falling short, we would benefit most from thinking of it as a lifelong journey. As we travel down this road together, with both hands removed from our eyes, we will grow daily our authenticity, courage, depth, commitment to contributing to the world, relatedness to others, and delight in the sacred as well as the mundane.

The Fortytude Movement

As we move into our fifth decades and beyond, our bodies are going to go through changes: wrinkling; perimenopause, and then menopause; as well as loss of bone density; infertility; and even a diminished sex drive. In addition, we are likely to face significant difficulties, such as losing friends or family members, battling cancer, switching careers or partners, and watching our children become teenagers and then adults. We need to acknowledge these changes and accept the challenges they present.

Unfortunately, we also must acknowledge that society traditionally has defined certain areas—such as sexuality, sensuality, desirability, and attractiveness—in terms that exclude women over 40. But that tide is turning. We are slowly but surely seeing more and more women 40 and older being lauded as sex symbols, powerful contributors to the planet, and vibrant individuals.

Fortytude strives to offer us the courage, guidance, and psychological insights necessary to define our lives for ourselves, regardless of the mixed messages that might have confused our thinking until now. The women we've met in this book serve as leaders of this movement, demonstrating how it is entirely possible not only to remain relevant but also to move into our fifth decades stronger than ever. Just take this recent example: a 76-year-old nun from Spokane, Washington, completed an Ironman triathlon—swimming 2.4 miles, biking 113, and running 26.2—a seemingly impossible feat for most of us at any age.

We are grown women, responsible for our own lives and blessed to have a great deal of freedom. So let's open our minds and explore who we are and what we might become. Let's recognize the sources of any outdated self-concepts. Let's use this time in our lives to listen to the most self-assured voices we hear inside ourselves, and to observe the actions of the most inspirational women around us. Let's allow these positive forces to serve as our guides for moving forward.

As we grow older, aging itself is not the challenge. The challenge is how we approach the process. Many factors come into play, including society's perception of who we should be at a certain life phase, our families' expectations for the paths we should travel, our peers' beliefs, and so many other influences swirling around us. At some point—and for many women, this happens around that critical juncture of turning 40—we start defining ourselves by our goals and using our Core Values to help us navigate toward our destinies.

Having fortytude means realizing that while you can't control what happens to you, you *can* control your reactions to life's events. Either you can allow current and future challenges to knock you down, making you fearful, morose, and bitter; or you can embrace your future with curiosity, knowing that your life is yours for the making. You can crawl under your blanket, turn on the TV, and let the good times pass you by. Or you can take your nephew to the park and joyously observe his 3-year-old wonder at ants crawling into their homes. You can go online, date, and meet a wonderful, loving partner. You can even set your sights on crossing the finish line of a marathon. Age cannot be an excuse for abandoning your hopes and dreams. The bottom line is, the choice is yours.

NOTES

. . . .

Cancer Institute Fact Sheet, October 2006, http://www.cancer.gov/cancertopics/factsheet/Detection/probability-breast-cancer.

44 *About 2.5 million breast cancer survivors in the United States*: American Cancer Society, "How Many Women Get Breast Cancer," *Medical Review*, September 16, 2008.

PART II. CONNECTEDNESS

57 *Connectedness is critical to every aspect of our health and well-being*: Fox News, "Research: Loneliness Tied to Poor Health in Old Age," March 26, 2009, http://www.foxnews.com/story/0,2933,510748,00.html; BBC News, "Friends Help People Live Longer," June 15, 2005, http://news.bbc.co.uk/2/hi/health/4094632.stm; Tara Parker-Pope, "What Are Friends For? A Longer Life," *The New York Times*, April 20, 2009, http://www.nytimes.com/2009/04/21/health/21well.html.

Chapter 4. Female Friendships

59 *Study of nurses with breast cancer*: Tara Parker-Pope, "What Are Friends For? A Longer Life," *The New York Times*, April 20, 2009, http://www.nytimes.com/2009/04/21/health/21well.html.

Chapter 5. Mentoring

75 *Evidence of discrimination against female leaders*: Alice Eagly and Linda Carli, "Women and the Labyrinth of Leadership," *Harvard Business Review*, September 2007.

76 *The female leadership style may flourish in the twenty-first century*: "Women Leaders Study: The Qualities That Distinguish Women Leaders," Caliper, 2005, http://www.caliper.com.au/womenstudy/.

79 *Women make up 15 percent of the U.S. armed forces*: Department of Defense, "Report to the White House Council on Women and Girls," September 1, 2009.

79 *230,000 American women have served in the wars in Iraq and Afghanistan*: Kimberly Hefling, "Back from Combat, Women Struggle for Acceptance," Associated Press, December 14, 2009, http://abcnews.go.com/politics/wirestory?id=9328019.

82   *About one-quarter of Americans volunteered in 2009*: U.S. Bureau of Labor
     Statistics, "Volunteering in the United States, 2009," January 27, 2010,
     http://www.bls.gov/news.release/volun.nr0.htm.

Chapter 6. Intimate Partnerships

87   *The work of Dr. John Gottman*: "John Gottman," http://en.wikipedia.org/
     wiki/John_Gottman; John M. Gottman, *The Marriage Clinic* (New York:
     W. W. Norton, 1999).

90   *A five-to-one ratio of positive to negative interactions makes a relationship last*:
     Gottman, *The Marriage Clinic*, p. 35.

93   *National Opinion Research Center research on infidelity*: Tom Smith, "Ameri-
     can Sexual Behavior Trends, Socio-Demographic Differences, and Risk
     Behavior," NORC, March 2006, http://www.norc.org/news/how+many
     +spouses+really+cheat.htm.

94   *Quotation from* Passages: Gail Sheehy, *Passages: Predictable Crises of Adult
     Life* (New York: E.P. Dutton, 1976).

PART III. ACCOMPLISHMENT

103 *Women develop mastery with age*: Thea Singer, "The Midlife Confidence
     Surge," *More*, February 2008, http://www.more.com/2024/3490-the-
     midlife-confidence-surge.

Chapter 7. Will I Ever Be Good Enough?

112 *Impostor syndrome; women internalize failure*: Satoshi Kanazawa, "The
     Impostor Syndrome," *Psychology Today*, July 26, 2009, http://www
     .psychologytoday.com/em/31314.

115 *Six percent of women in the United States will struggle with an eating disorder*: The
     National Institutes of Mental Health, "The Numbers Count: Mental Disorders
     in America," 2010, http://www.nimh.nih.gov/health/publications/the-
     numbers-count-mental-disorders-in-america/index.shtml#eating.

115 *48 percent increase in eating-disorder hospitalizations among patients aged 45 to
     65*: Yafu Zhao and William Encinosa, "Hospitalizations for Eating Disorders
     from 1999 to 2006," Health Care Cost and Utilization Project Statistical
     Brief #70, http://www.hcup-us.ahrq.gov/reports/statbriefs/sb70.pdf.

Chapter 8. The Accomplished Partner

122 *Husbands with wives who make more money*: Sam Roberts, "More Men Marrying Wealthier Women," *The New York Times*, January 18, 2010, http://www.nytimes.com/2010/01/19/us/19marriage.html.

123 *Men are seeking accomplished partners*: Deborah Siegel, "The New Trophy Wife," *Psychology Today*, June 1, 2004, http://www.psychologytoday.com/articles/200401/the-new-trophy-wife.

126 *Howard Gardner's theory of multiple intelligences*: "Howard Gardner," http://en.wikipedia.org/wiki/Howard_Gardner.

Chapter 9. The Accomplished Mother

132 *Women at elite colleges shifting attitudes about being stay-at-home moms*: Louise Story, "Many Women at Elite Colleges Set Career Path to Mother-hood," *The New York Times*, September 20, 2005, http://www.nytimes.com/2005/09/20/national/20women.html.

133 *Over 70 percent of women with children under 18 are in the labor force*: Nancy Gibbs, "What Women Want Now," *Time*, October 26, 2009, http://www.time.com/time/specials/packages/article/0,28804,1930277_1930145,00.html.

135 *Only 67 percent of U.S. children grow up with two married parents*: The National Marriage Project, "The State of Our Unions 2009," December 2009, http://www.stateofourunions.org.

Chapter 10. The Accomplished Career Woman

146 *Aspirational treadmill*: David Leonhardt, "Maybe Money Does Buy Happiness After All," *The New York Times*, April 16, 2008, http://www.nytimes.com/2008/04/16/business/16leonhardt.html.

147 *Over half of all mothers with children under age 3 are employed full-time*: U.S. Bureau of Labor Statistics, "Employment Characteristics of Families—2009," News Release, May 27, 2010, http://www.bls.gov/news.release/famee.nr0.htm.

147 *40 percent of women say they are primary breadwinners*: Nancy Gibbs, "What Women Want Now," *Time*, October 26, 2009, http://www.time.com/time/specials/packages/article/0,28804,1930277_1930145,00.html.

PART IV. ADVENTURE

Chapter 12. Maintaining Sexual Vitality

174 *Symptoms of menopause*: Robert S. Porter, ed., "Women's Health Issues," The Merck Manuals Online Medical Library, 2004–2008, http://www.merck.com/mmhe/sec22/ch241/ch241f.html.

176 *Women carry more of the burden of the household*: Karla Henderson and Katherine Allen, "The Ethic of Care: Leisure Possibilities and Constraints for Women," *Society and Leisure* 14: 97–113.

186 *44 percent of women have used a sex toy*: "Babeland Statistics," online document, http://www.babeland.com/about/presskit/about/stats.

186 *AARP study of sexuality*: Sarah Mahoney, "The Secret Lives of Single Women," *AARP the Magazine*, May–June 2006.

186 *Women who masturbate score higher on self-esteem, more positive body image*: "The Health Benefits of Sexual Expression," Katharine Dexter McCormick Library, Planned Parenthood Federation of America, April 2003.

Chapter 13. Dating after 40

191 *Just over 50 percent of American women live without a husband*: Sam Roberts, "51% of Women Are Now Living Without Spouse," *The New York Times*, January 16, 2007, http://www.nytimes.com/2007/01/16/us/16census.html.

192 *Single women aren't sad, lonely, and desperate*: Sarah Mahoney, "The Secret Lives of Single Women," *AARP the Magazine*, May–June 2006.

194 *52 percent report positive experience with online dating*: Mary Madden and Amanda Lenhart, "Online Dating," Pew Internet & American Life Project, March 5, 2006, http://www.pewinternet.org/reports/2006/online-dating.aspx.

PART V. SPIRITUALITY

207 *Many Americans blend faiths and practices*: Charles M. Blow, "Paranormal Flexibility," *The New York Times*, December 11, 2009, http://www.nytimes.com/2009/12/12/opinion/12blow.html.

Chapter 14. Abandoned Adults

215 *Statistics about widows*: Wilma Mankiller et al., *The Reader's Companion to U.S. Women's History* (Boston: Houghton Mifflin, 1998).

220 *Adults over 80 are the fastest-growing age-group*: "The New Old Age" blog, *The New York Times*, http://newoldage.blogs.nytimes.com.

222 *Erik Erikson described old age as the eighth stage of life*: Erik Erikson, *Identity and the Life Cycle* (New York: International Universities Press, Inc., 1959).

222 *Five stages of grieving*: Elisabeth Kübler-Ross, *On Death and Dying* (New York: Macmillan, 1969).

Chapter 15. Change Your Narrative

225 *Existentialist philosophers spoke of the "anguish of freedom"*: Steven Crowell, "Existentialism," Stanford Encyclopedia of Philosophy, http://plato.stanford.edu/entries/existentialism/.

Chapter 16. Finding Your Own Path

248 *About half of Americans have changed religious affiliation at least once*: "Faith in Flux," Pew Forum on Religion & Public Life, April 27, 2009, http://www.pewforum.org/faith-in-flux.aspx.

ACKNOWLEDGMENTS

. . . .

Thank you to MeiMei Fox, my writing partner. Without you, *Forty-tude* would not have blossomed the way that it has. You were able to synthesize my thoughts and truly understand the message that I wanted to convey to the reader. This book exemplifies your gift as a listener, friend, writer, and woman of fortytude.

Thank you to Mom, Dad, Andie, Charles, Jen, and Allen, for enduring this process of discovery and renewal, for allowing me to include so many details of your lives, for always supporting me, cheering me on, and providing me such valuable advice even when you felt I wasn't listening.

Thank you to Candace Bushnell, Binky Urban, Andy Barzvi, Barbara Jones, and Leslie Wells for recognizing and appreciating the importance of shedding light on what it means to journey into our 40s with fortytude, for your outstanding editorial assistance, and for believing in me.

Thank you to the faculty and staff at Ackerman Institute, NYU School of Social Work, and Four Winds Hospital. Without your expertise, wisdom, and encouragement, I would never have arrived at the place where I am now.

Thank you to all the courageous women who agreed to be profiled in this book, for participating in lengthy and often challenging discussions with open hearts and generous spirits. Also, to all those who helped me connect with these women, especially the ones who organized the initial focus groups across the country: Katie Stein, Nancy Rubin, Betsy Fischer, Leighton McCool, Courtney Nichols, Mandy Ginsberg, Fae Beck, Meredith Lavitt, Julie Blackwell Stamstead, Nicky Striefler, Elana Finestone, Hilary Armstrong, Rachel Brokaw, Sabrina Lee, and Jacque Fait.

Thank you to the friends who have left indelible marks in my life and who continue to do so: Carrie Wolf-Bragoner, Christa Robinson, Jennifer Karetsky-Andres, Amy Redford, Nina Bauer-Shapiro, JJ Ramberg, Alexandra Bailliere-Treadwell, Anne Wilson-Payne, Melissa "Missy" Davis, Laura Keeton, Kristi Jacobson, Caren Ezratty-O'Connor, Kristin Lemkau, AK Kennedy, Catherine Levene, and Sascha Rice. And to the posse in Venice, California. You know who you are. Thank you for making my transition from the East Coast to the West Coast that much easier. Here's to more book club meetings, Sunday Fundays, Family Nights, and surf sessions at Sano, Sunset, and Mondo.

Thank you to the women who took me under their wings during the times when I felt I could not fly: Nora Ephron, Cheryl Gould, Kiko Itasaka, Millie Myers, Susan Lasalla, Goldine Nicholas, Mary Slawson, and Malinda Chouinard. I can honestly say that each and every one of you have provided me unconditional love, nurturance, wisdom, and most important, your humor.

To *all* of the women in Rwanda, Bosnia, and Haiti: Your ability to celebrate life through loving, laughing, singing, and dancing with steadfast determination is truly amazing. You are our teachers.

Thank you to the men whom I've dated: all of you have questioned if you've helped me to build my fortytude. The answer is yes!

© Gillian Zoe Segal

SARAH BROKAW is a licensed therapist with a practice in Beverly Hills, California. She holds a Master's degree in social work from New York University, is also a professional certified coach, and is active in philanthropy. The daughter of legendary newsman Tom Brokaw, she lives in California.